Start Your Own

PET BUSINESS AND MORE

Additional titles in *Entrepreneur's* **Startup Series**

Start Your Own

Arts and Crafts Business
Bar and Club
Bed & Breakfast
Business on eBay
Business Support Service
Car Wash
Child Care Service
Cleaning Service
Clothing Store
Coin-Operated Laundry
Consulting
e-Business
e-Learning Business
Event Planning Business
Executive Recruiting Service
Freight Brokerage Business
Gift Basket Service
Grant-Writing Business
Home Inspection Service
Import/Export Business
Information Consultant Business
Law Practice
Lawn Care Business
Mail Order Business
Medical Claims Billing Service
Personal Concierge Service
Personal Training Business
Pet-Sitting Business
Restaurant and Five Other Food Businesses
Self-Publishing Business
Seminar Production Business
Specialty Travel & Tour Business
Staffing Service
Successful Retail Business
Vending Business
Wedding Consultant Business
Wholesale Distribution Business

Entrepreneur MAGAZINE'S

startup

Start Your Own

PET BUSINESS AND MORE

Pet Sitting • Dog Walking
Training • Grooming • Food/Treats
Upscale Pet Products

Entrepreneur Press, Eileen Figure Sandlin and Cheryl Kimball

EP
Entrepreneur. Press

Jere L. Calmes, Publisher
Managing Editor: Marla Markman
Cover Design: Beth Hansen-Winter
Production and Composition: Eliot House Productions

Library of Congress Cataloging-in-Publication Data

Sandlin, Eileen Figure.

Start your own pet business and more/by Entrepreneur Press and Eileen Figure Sandlin.

p. cm. —(Start your own series)

Includes index.

ISBN-13: 978-1-59918-186-8 (alk. paper)

ISBN-10: 1-59918-186-X

1. Pet industry—Management. 2. New business enterprises—Management. I. Entrepreneur Press. II. Title.

SF414.7.S28 2008

636.088'7—dc22 2008004943

Printed in Canada

13 12 11 10 09 10 9 8 7 6 5 4 3 2 1

Contents

Preface

Imagine creating the perfect business that allows you to work with someone you love, set your own hours and start making money with a minimal financial investment.

You've just found it. The book you're holding is a blueprint for launching one of five hot businesses—businesses that are in demand because people universally put a high value on their pets and treat them as treasured members of their family. There are three pet service businesses discussed in this book, including pet sitting/walking, dog training and pet grooming; as well as two retail businesses, which include pet food/treats, and upscale pet products. All of them appeal to the fundamental human need to take good care of their pets as well as the desire to shower them with lasting tokens of affection. At the same time, these ventures probably also appeal to a prospective pet-business owner like yourself because of your own love of animals. What better way to make a living?

There definitely is money to be made. According to a recent national pet owner survey, 69.1 million American households have at least one pet. So chances are excellent that people right in your own city or even your own neighborhood will be prospects for the services or products you offer. Take your business further afield by advertising, either through word-of-mouth, or in print or virtually, and you'll expand your entrepreneurial horizons even further. Case in point: Cesar Millan, the world-renowned dog behavior specialist (aka "dog whisperer") found his calling as a child in the streets of Mexico, when he could always be found surrounded by packs of adoring dogs. After coming to the United States, his reputation grew thanks to some coveted media coverage, and he spun his unique "communion" with canines into a rewarding career. And you could, too!

OK, so maybe you won't get your own cable TV show or national acclaim like Millan has, but entrepreneurial success definitely is possible, even when there's a downturn in the economy. It does take commitment and patience, though, as well as enough start-up cash to work your way through the early phase of your new business, which is when income tends to be low. It also takes shrewd planning. So toward those ends, this book covers all of the steps necessary to establish a viable pet-focused small business, including:

- Determining the demand for your service or product, and crafting a dynamic marketing plan to reach prospective customers
- Establishing an effective business structure and naming your business
- Setting up an efficient home office
- Creating a viable business plan to serve as a roadmap to success
- Identifying business professionals who can help you reach your financial and business goals
- Purchasing the equipment and tools needed to ply your new trade
- Buying or leasing a building for a retail pet business
- Purchasing, storing, and tracking the merchandise you sell
- Harnessing the power of the internet so you can sell your products and services *without* the expense of a bricks-and-mortar location
- Manufacturing pet products and food
- Recognizing when it's time to hire employees and how to do it
- Advertising your business to attract customers

- Generating positive press for free
- Managing your finances and understanding the relationship between income and expenses

Another important part of this how-to book is the advice you'll find from successful, experienced pet industry professionals. Their comments and stories appear throughout this book, and will give you special insight into the issues that can impact your fledgling business. But what you won't find here is a discussion of industry-specifics like how to train dogs or how to give a pet a to-die-for clip job. We're assuming you already have those skills, or you plan to get some hands-on training from a qualified practitioner. What you will find is an affordable, fast-track route to establishing a pet business that can reap big "kennel rations." So dig in. You're in for a *pawsitively* exciting journey!

1

Barking Up the Right Tree

When you think back to your childhood, is there a warm and fuzzy memory of a four-footed or winged companion in whom you confided your deepest secrets? Do you gaze into pet-store windows and vicariously tickle the puppies under the chin? Or have you ever considered buying a sweater for your horse, some galoshes for your cat, or some Armor All for your armadillo? If so, then you understand what it means to be a pet lover—and that's probably why you're interested in starting a career in the pet-care industry.

As you no doubt know, we Americans are in love with our pets. In 2004, we spent $34.5 billion on our cats, dogs, birds, fish, horses, and other pets, according to the American Pet Products Association (APPA). In 2005, that figure was expected to jump by another $1.4 billion, continuing a decade-long trend of pet-spending increases.

This is good news for aspiring pet-business owners like you. No matter whether you're interested in providing hands-on pet care or selling pet products like toys, food, and treats, the prospects for success in a pet-care business are excellent. It's easy to see why when you take a look at the APPMA's breakdown of the estimated $35.9 billion in 2005 sales across pet product and service categories:

Category	Estimated 2005 Spending
Food	$14.5 billion
Supplies/medicine	$8.8 billion
Veterinary care	$8.6 billion
Live-animal sales	$1.6 billion
Pet services (grooming and boarding)	$2.4 billion

"The strong growth in the [pet-care] industry demonstrates what an important role pets are playing in the lives of Americans," says Bob Vetere, APPA COO and managing director. "They have become a part of the family. Spending across all sectors, from pet food and veterinarian care to toys and treats, reflects what lengths we are willing to go to for our pets."

As a result of this desire to pamper and spoil those pets, pet-care businesses are playing an increasingly important role in the lives of pet owners. Busy people rely on these professionals to look after their pets while they're away at work or on vacation. They turn to pet-care services for care they may not feel qualified to provide themselves, such as grooming and training. They also buy pet food and toys at specialty shops or online and turn to the internet to search for retailers far and wide that carry the things that will appeal to their little darlings' palate or sense of fun.

Fun Fact

Presidential pets have their own museum in Washington, DC. More than 1,500 artifacts and photos of famous pets, ranging from George Washington's horse, Nelson, to President and Mrs. Bush's Scottish terrier, Barney, are on display in this charming museum. The Presidential Pet Museum is located 19 miles from the White House on Route 4.

It's a Zoo Out There

A lot of people think of dogs and cats when the subject of pet care comes up. But Americans keep any number of pets in their homes, and unless you're a dog trainer or pet groomer, you're likely to encounter some of these animals at one time or another. To illustrate, the American Pet Products Association (APPA) breaks down pet ownership in the United States as follows:

Animal	Total in U.S.
Cat	90.5 million
Dog	73.9 million
Other small animal	18.2 million
Bird	16.6 million
Reptile	11.0 million

In addition, the APPMA estimates there are 139 million freshwater fish and 9.6 million saltwater fish swimming around in tanks or ponds in or around U.S. homes.

It's not hard to figure out why pets are so pampered and integral to people's lives. They bring us joy, they love us unconditionally, and they even lower our blood pressure and give us a sense of well-being. They also fill the aching void left when children leave the nest or a spouse dies; for childless couples, a pet is "someone" on whom to lavish affection and gifts. Many people consider their pets their "kids," and even relate to them better than they do to people!

This love of pets is also often the reason why people decide to start pet-care businesses. "We started our business with the intent to help animals and to point people in the right direction to help animals," says John Zambelli, owner of NaturesPet.com, an online pet-food business in Elmwood Park, New Jersey, that specializes in all-natural pet food. "By feeding pets properly, you give them a good shot at a healthful life. This type of business was the right thing to do for us, and we knew the money would follow."

In this book, we give you the advice you need to start one of five different types of pet-products and pet-service businesses that are in demand today: pet sitting/dog walking, dog training, pet grooming, pet-food sales, and upscale pet products. Each of these businesses can be started as homebased enterprises with a fairly low financial investment. Two can be started as strictly internet businesses to really keep costs low. And all of them can be launched and run successfully by the owner, without any assistance from employees—at least until the time comes when you want to grow and expand the business beyond what you can personally handle.

The information and advice you'll find in this book relates strictly to the business side of running a pet-care business. In case you do happen to need instruction in the specialized skills necessary to groom cats and dogs or train them to be well-mannered, we've included contact information in the Appendix for a number of professional organizations and schools you can explore.

Read on for a look at the five types of pet-care businesses discussed in this book.

Pet Sitting/Dog Walking

If you are charmed by all things furred, feathered and finned, this is the profession for you. As a professional pet sitter, you will care for people's pets while they're away, either for the day or for longer periods like during vacations or business trips. Pet sitters play with their charges, feed them, brush them, and possibly give them medication or injections. They often offer other services to make life easier for their customers, like cleaning up accidents and changing cat litter boxes, bringing in newspapers and mail, watering plants and taking out trash.

Dog walkers take pooches out for their daily constitutional one or more times a day, either individually or in small groups. In some cities across the United States, like New York, dog walking alone can be a booming business. But it's actually more common for dog walkers to offer additional services, including playing with and feeding pets, bringing in newspapers and mail, and turning lights on and off.

Both pet sitting and dog walking are still in their infancy as recognized professions. According to an industry expert, only 3 percent of households nationally use a pet sitter or dog walker. Even so, that adds up to 50 million to 60 million visits annually, according to the same source—and that number is on the rise. In fact, the outlook for pet sitters and dog walkers has never been better. Some estimates put the number of bonded and insured pet-sitter businesses nationwide at 10,000 (regrettably, there are no stats on the number of dog walkers).

Just a few decades ago, these two professions didn't even exist. Instead, people relied

Bright Idea

When selling services like pet sitting, dog walking, and in-home dog training to new clients, offer to provide a list of references, even if your business is bonded. Giving a key to and allowing a stranger (you) into their homes while they're away will make clients understandably nervous, and being able to check your references will put their minds at ease.

on neighbors to watch and water their pets while they were away on vacation, or they dropped them off at kennels. But all that changed in the '70s with a decrease in stay-at-home moms available to let the dog out or take the cat to the vet. Also, young couples began postponing their plans to have a family in favor of establishing their careers and often adopted pets to fill the void. Finally, an upsurge in business travel that started in the '80s and continues today also contributed to the need for the services of a pet-sitting or dog-walking professional.

The field is wide open, so now is a great time to jump in with both paws...uh, feet!

Dog Training

Part instruction, part psychology, the field of dog training requires great people skills as well as a love of canines. Dog trainers will tell you that you're not just training the pooches—you're also training the folks who live with them. So you have to be able to talk to them kindly, deal with them patiently, and reinforce their behavior—then do the same with their furry friends. While a background in psychology can be helpful, a true love of both people and pets and a desire to help them goes a long way to ensure success in this career.

People have been training dogs professionally for decades, although the training wasn't always done humanely. Prior to World War I, trainers used patience and rewards to school dogs. But with the war came the need for a lot of four-footed "soldiers" who could work in the trenches alongside human handlers. The military often used harsh techniques to train the animals they needed quickly—techniques that included choke chains, punishment, and fear.

But in the '70s, a trainer who would become a legend began to teach people how to use kinder and gentler techniques to train animals. Barbara Woodhouse, an Irish dog trainer, believed there were no bad dogs, only inexperienced owners, and espoused the use of rewards and treats to train pets. Her 1982 book, *No Bad Dogs: The Woodhouse Way*, became a classic.

By the late '80s, there was a resurgence of a type of training that had been invented 30 years before. Largely due to the efforts of animal behaviorists Karen Pryor and Gary Wilkes, clicker training made a comeback. It uses a small mechanical device that serves as both a conditioned reinforcer and a signal that a reward is coming later.

Fun Fact

The American Pet Products Association says the top four pet-industry trends for 2008 will be: new pet products by big name companies (Omaha Steaks, Harley Davidson, and Old Navy), hotels with pet-friendly policies, dental products as well as self-flushing litter boxes, and luxury items to spoil your pet.

Running with the Alpha Dogs

Barbara Woodhouse may have been one of the first to theorize in her seminal 1980s book that there are "no bad dogs," only inexperienced owners. But it took an immigrant from Mexico with an engaging smile and dark hair wing-tipped with silver to make canine behavior modification into an art form.

Dog behavior specialist Cesar Millan—known popularly as *The Dog Whisperer*—has hosted his own shown on the National Geographic cable network since 2004. During each episode, Millan demonstrates various techniques for rehabilitating dogs who are aggressive, phobic, frightened, or just plain insecure.

The show is wildly popular—even among viewers who don't own dogs—because of Millan's unique gift for "connecting" with dogs and teaching their owners how to become the "pack leader" their pet innately needs. But this is a technique that entails much more than teaching a dog basic tricks like how to stay or sit. Rather, it involves being a "dog counselor" who corrects unwanted behavior by setting boundaries the pet's owner may have previously been unable to establish.

The sheer popularity of Millan's show is a good indication that there is a need for dog whisperers, which means there's an opportunity for dog trainers like you to specialize in training animals with behavioral problems. While a cursory review of the internet did not turn up any credentialed or certified "dog whisperer" schools, there are quite a few books in print by experts like veterinarian Dr. Ian Dunbar that discuss canine behavior modification. It also should be noted that many dog behavior specialists do not agree with Millan's methods. Still, if you're interested in creating a niche for your new dog training business, becoming a dog whisperer might be a good way to build your business.

Although clicker training was initially ridiculed by trainers, "click and treat" training is now the standard in modern dog training, or as Wilkes says, "the first major improvement in dog training in about 15,000 years."

While there are no statistics on the number of dog trainers in the country because the profession is not licensed, the Association of Pet Dog Trainers has about 5,000 members. And with an estimated 74 million dogs in America, there's lots of room for good trainers to enter the field.

Pet Grooming

From bathing and clipping to tying bows and cleaning ears, the nation's approximately 50,000 to 70,000 pet groomers do more than just change pets' appearances—they also make them feel better both physically and psychologically. The loving touch of a groomer can calm a skittish pet, reassure a frightened pet, and make a well-adjusted pet wriggle with pleasure. In addition, groomers are often the first to notice that a pet has a skin condition, ear mites, or other medical issues that should be brought to the attention of a veterinarian.

In addition to having a true love of animals and enough physical strength to lift big animals onto grooming tables and into tubs, groomers must be behaviorists who know how to handle biters and scratchers. They also need the same kind of patience and good humor when relating to pet owners, so a general love of humankind is a necessary trait for a groomer.

Of all the businesses discussed in this book, pet grooming is undoubtedly the oldest. While records of dog-grooming parlors date only to 19th-century England, it's pretty apparent from paintings by the masters and others that dogs have been groomed for many centuries (the evidence can be found in 14th-century paintings that depict what might be assumed to be coiffed pets sitting at the feet of their masters and mistresses). But it wasn't until the 1893 publication of the book *Ashmont's Kennel Secrets* that recommendations for washing and grooming were spelled out in detail.

Kennels started the modern trend toward grooming by washing and fluffing pets in their care so they could be returned fresh and sweet-smelling to their owners. When grooming tools like electric clippers and other modern supplies debuted in the late 1940s, the practice began to gain a foothold in mainstream America. But it wasn't until the explosion in pet ownership that occurred in the mid 1950s that grooming services became less of a luxury and more of a necessity. Since the '80s, there has been another boom in pet grooming, largely for the same reasons that pet sitting and dog walking have become so popular.

While many groomers choose to establish their businesses in a building, it's possible to do the work out of a salon set up in your home. (You can either have pet owners drop off their animals or you can pick them up yourself.) A third possibility is to set up a mobile business that brings the salon right to your customer's home. This type of business operates out of a specially outfitted van that has the same equipment and offers the same services as a site-based shop.

There are several companies that offer mobile turnkey franchises that can make it even easier to establish your business. They provide everything from specially equipped mobile vans to sales and marketing support. For the purposes of this book, we will assume you are planning to establish your own grooming business rather than purchasing a franchise. But in case you'd like to explore the possibility, you'll find contact information for some mobile franchises in the Appendix.

Demand for pet groomers is expected to rise 12 percent by 2010, according to the U.S. Bureau of Labor Statistics. Petgroomer.com, the industry's largest internet resource, reports that career opportunities are nearly endless because there are more than 4,000 dogs and cats for every U.S. grooming business—making this a great time to be considering this field.

Bright Idea

The pet industry is such big business that there are ad agencies that specialize in animal product marketing, public relations, and animal welfare promotion. Two to check out are Orca Communications Unlimited of Phoenix (orcacommunications .com) and Animal Voices of Davis, California (animal voices.com).

Pet Food/Treats

Whether it's bricks-and-mortar or virtual, a pet store that specializes solely in pet food and treats can be a great moneymaker. Many pet owners today are willing to spend top dollar to buy the best of everything for their "fur children," including food and treats. Your challenge, then, is to find a niche, such as all-natural food products, and offer a wide assortment so you can position yourself as a leading provider of these items.

And you'll have plenty of products to choose from. There are all-natural (that is, human-grade) foods, specialty foods for diabetic pets or pets with kidney problems, and raw-food diets, as well as food for pet birds, livestock, and exotic animals like snakes. There are even bakeries that specialize in making dog biscuits and other tasty treats. In addition, some pet-food stores choose to stock other pet-related products, like collars and leashes. Whether you should do so, too, depends on how much you can afford to sink into your inventory and how much room you have to stash the products until they're purchased or shipped out.

According to statistics from the U.S. Census Bureau, there were 15,890 pet and supply establishments in 2001 (the latest year for which data is available), with sole proprietorships numbering 7,945. The Census Bureau doesn't capture information about how many of these establishments are internet-based, but you can be sure that no matter how many there were then, the number is growing now because an online store is such a cost-effective way to start a pet-food business. There's virtually no building overhead if you work out of your home, and it's possible to make arrangements with manufacturers to drop-ship product (that is, arrange shipping directly from the manufacturer to your customer) so you don't even have to store and ship the product yourself. All you need is a merchant account to accept credit card payments or a PayPal account, and you can ship products all over the world.

The cost to establish a site-based store obviously is higher, but it may be the right choice for you. By specializing in one type of product, you can keep the store fairly simple (basically, four walls with shelves). The key will be to find a good location and the right product mix, as well as a great staff to assist you when it comes to keeping the business running.

The pet-food industry has come a long way since the first processed food for dogs was invented in 1860 by James Spratt of Cincinnati, who was inspired to make biscuits when he observed canines gobbling up the hardtack discarded by sailors in seaports. His Spratt's Patent Meat Fibrine Dog Cakes were made of wheat, vegetables and other ingredients, and were quickly copied by other enterprising dog-food companies.

Prior to that time, pets in urban areas were fed scraps from their masters' tables, as well as raw meat. (In fact, people of great means and royalty often fed their pets specialty diets that were delicately seasoned to appeal to their finicky palates.) But a shift away from table food occurred during the lean years following the Depression when people needed less expensive ways to feed their animals. As a result, home diets began to contain less meat and more grains and cereal, a trend that was replicated in the canned dog food that debuted in the 1940s. Dry dog-food pellets became available after World War II and consisted of either biscuit or crumbled biscuit (known as kibble). Then the Purina Co. took dry dog food to a new level in the 1950s when it invented a way to process dog-food pellets that were larger in size yet lighter in weight. This saved money for the manufacturer while giving the appearance that consumers were getting more food for their money.

In 1969, the pet-food industry did an about-face on the subject of all-meat diets. A researcher at the University of Pennsylvania School of Veterinary Medicine said too much protein was harmful to dogs and recommended fortifying their diets with nutrients and carbohydrates. This ushered in the age of nutritionally complete diets, and since then, specialty diets for "patients" with kidney, heart, and other diseases, as well as food for pets in various life stages, have become common and give pet-food shoppers a wide range of meal choices for their four-footed friends.

In recent years, there has been a lot of controversy about pet-food ingredients, with accusations that they are not wholesome and nutritious. For this reason, a number of companies now manufacture all-natural products, while others have duplicated the raw-food diets of yesteryear and market them as the ultimate in all-natural diets. In any event, pet food has come a long way, and you'll need to do some basic research to figure out exactly what your business niche should be.

Stat Fact

Thinking about taking your pet-products company online? That could mean big business. Americans spent $66.5 billion online in 2005, according to comScore Networks, a global information provider and consultancy—up 29 percent from the previous year. Nearly $16 billion of that amount was attributable to holiday season sales.

Upscale Pet Products

The urge to splurge on pet clothes, toys, and other goodies has been around for a while now. But ever since Hollywood starlets started carrying their pooches around in designer bags and tucking them in to sleep under silk comforters on custom-made beds (and getting press for doing so), the upscale pet-products industry has exploded. Doting owners can now adorn their pets with rhinestone tiaras, pearl collars, and cashmere coats. They can wheel them around in luxury strollers or tuck them into glove-soft leather totes.

As with a pet-food business, it's possible to sell products entirely through a website. But you could also sell exclusively to retail outlets like pet boutiques or pet stores. Or you can open your own retail location. If you establish a store and your product mix is truly exclusive and expensive, you'll probably be more successful if you open in a resort area, in or near an upscale neighborhood (can you say, "Rodeo Drive?"), or in an exclusive mall. The rent in such locations may be very pricey, but it will be worth it when you reach people with a lot of discretionary income and the desire to lavish it on their best friend(s). Some of these business owners choose to manufacture the products they sell, which you'll find out later isn't as difficult as it might seem. "Manufacturing gives you more control," says Exton, Pennsylvania, pet-product manufacturer Joyce Reavey. "I know I won't run out of inventory, and I always know what the quality is like. That's important to me."

Meet the Experts

In addition to the in-depth business information and statistics contained in this book, you'll find a lot of comments and insight straight from the mouths of pet-care business owners who generously agreed to be interviewed for this project. They have commented on everything from advertising to financing, and plenty in between. They've also agreed to serve as a resource for you in the future if you ever are stumped by a particular situation or if you have specific questions that can only be answered by someone with field experience. You'll find their contact information in the Appendix. These pet-care business experts include:

- *Teoti Anderson*. The owner of Pawsitive Results LLC, a Lexington, South Carolina, dog-training business started in 2001, is also president of the Association of Pet Dog Trainers and an award-winning writer who has published three dog-training books.
- *Susan Benesh*. The owner of VIPoochy, a wholesale/retail distributor of upscale pet products founded in 2002 in Columbia, South Carolina, designs and manufactures the products she sells. In addition to her pet business, she also has an etiquette consulting business.

- *Jennifer Boniface ("Aunt Jeni").* The owner of Aunt Jeni's Home Made in Temple Hills, Maryland, is a nutritionist and manufacturer of natural raw-food products for dogs. This multifaceted entrepreneur has a bachelor's degree in animal science and a master's degree in animal nutrition, which qualify her to do the formulation and design of the products she has manufactured since 1997.
- *Diane Burchard.* The owner of Teca Tu—a Paws-Worthy Emporium & Deli, an upscale pet-products store and wholesaler in Santa Fe, New Mexico—began as a wholesaler in 1989 who manufactured her own branded pet apparel, neckwear, bowls, and treats, then gained retail experience via her previous 400-square-foot import business. Teca Tu was named the Upscale Pet Boutique of the Year by *Pet Products News* in 2002.
- *Jamie Damato.* The founder and training director of AnimalSense—Canine Behavior and Training in Oak Park, Illinois, holds a bachelor's degree with majors in psychology and communications and has extensive experience working with animals. She founded and operated Out-U-Go Pet Care Services, a pet-sitting business, in 1996, then sold the business to David Lipschultz (see bio, below) before establishing her training business. She's a certified dog trainer and behavior consultant who has worked with more than 12,000 dogs and trained about 7,000. She discusses dogs on the airwaves as a frequent guest on *ABC 7 News Chicago*.
- *Leonard Green.* The president of the Green Group—an entrepreneurial consulting firm in Woodbridge, New Jersey—founded the holistic pet-food company The Blue Buffalo Co. in 2002. Annual sales for this subsidiary—one of 14 companies under the Green Group—were a staggering $6 million in 2004, thanks to landing a significant piece of business with PetSmart.
- *David Lipschultz.* The owner of Out-U-Go, an Oak Park, Illinois, pet-sitting business, also owns Urban Tailblazers, a Chicago-based dog-walking and pet-care service provider. Lipschultz bought Out-U-Go from Jamie Damato (see bio, above) in 1996, then bought Urban Tailblazers in 2000 because the first company was running so well he needed a new challenge. He says he's always been a big animal person but did a number of different things, including managing a restaurant, before he fell into pet sitting as a profession. Now he can't imagine doing anything else.

Fun Fact

In the 1940s, Ed Lowe, inventor of Tidy Cat kitty litter, attended cat shows and cleaned hundreds of litter boxes every day in exchange for booth space to display his clay-based product. His first bags of cat litter, which he packaged by hand in 1947, were simple brown bags of clay with the words "Kitty Litter" written on them.

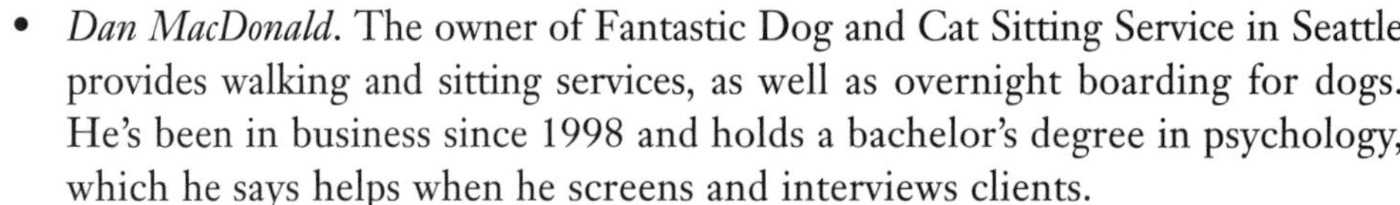

- *Dan MacDonald.* The owner of Fantastic Dog and Cat Sitting Service in Seattle provides walking and sitting services, as well as overnight boarding for dogs. He's been in business since 1998 and holds a bachelor's degree in psychology, which he says helps when he screens and interviews clients.
- *Barbara Menutes.* The owner of Barbara's Cat Grooming in Houston has more than 12 years' experience grooming cats and dogs. She also has a long history of animal care, having started as kennel help in a pet shop bathing puppies at age 16, then working her way up to bather and brusher before learning how to groom. Menutes specializes in grooming hard-to-handle animals.
- *Amanda Miller.* Miller is the co-owner of Poochie of Beverly Hills with her partner and mother, Cathy Jackson. Founded in 2001, the online company is based in Scottsdale, Arizona, and sells high-end pet beds to specialty boutiques, gift stores, and furniture stores. Miller and Jackson design the beds, select fabrics and trims, and oversee production at the furniture manufacturer that makes their products. Miller holds an associate degree in manufacturing, while Jackson has a bachelor's degree in interior design.
- *Joyce Reavey.* The owner of Pawsitively Posh—a designer, manufacturer, and online wholesaler of upscale pet beds and other products in Exton, Pennsylvania—is an award-winning doll and jewelry designer who started her pet business in 2004 after being laid off from a 20-year career in doll designing with Franklin Mint. She has taken courses in fine arts and design over the course of her career and says her business is the perfect place to use both her design and management skills.
- *Jerry Wentz.* The owner of Homesitters of Raleigh, in Raleigh, North Carolina, since 1985 is also president of the board of directors of the National Association of Professional Pet Sitters and an arbitrator with the Eastern North Carolina Better Business Bureau.
- *John Zambelli.* The co-owner with his wife, Diane, of NaturesPet.com—an online pet-food business in Elmwood Park, New Jersey—has more than 30 years of experience in the retail and direct marketing industries. He established NaturesPet.com in 1996 as a part-time business when he discovered there weren't many holistic pet foods he could feed to his dog. After the company he was working with "turned into dust," as he puts it, he made a huge career shift and joined NaturesPet.com on a full-time basis.

So are you ready to make your mark on pet care? Then turn the page and let's get started.

2

Pet Sitting/ Dog Walking

Imagine a job where you get paid to play and romp with God's littlest creatures every day, spend time outside in the park, and set your own work pace depending on your personal goals and needs—and do it all with minimal overhead and expenses. Those are some of the benefits of a career as a pet sitter or dog walker.

According to educational association Pet Sitter International (PSI), professional pet sitting is one of the fastest-growing homebased service businesses in the United States. And it's not hard to figure out why. People are busier than ever. Both single people and partners in two-career marriages or relationships may have jobs that take them away from home on business, or they work long hours that keep them occupied elsewhere for extended periods of time each day. Rather than just leaving beloved pets on their own for many hours at a time, some people engage the services of an in-home pet sitter or walker to care for their pets in their absence.

That's where you come in. Take a love of animals, add a pinch of business skill, and stir in a knack for managing details, and you can be a tailblazer—uh, make that trailblazer—in an exciting new industry. The field is wide open for new entrepreneurs like you to build a business you enjoy that can support you and your family. That is, as long as you don't mind working days, nights, weekends and holidays—in short, any time other people need you so they can take vacations, business trips, and so on.

Despite the fact that you get to play with friendly little animals as part of your job, being a pet sitter or walker isn't just a stroll in the park. Experienced sitters/walkers will tell you that the pace can be frenetic, and a lot of stamina is necessary to keep up with the requirements of the job. Depending on the number of regular clients you have, you could find yourself working a shift that far exceeds eight hours, which is why some pet sitters find themselves hiring part-time help relatively soon after establishing the business. But of course, the more work you have, the more successful your business will be.

Earnings Potential

So how much can you earn? Pet sitter Jerry Wentz of Raleigh, North Carolina, says it really depends on where you're doing business and how many visits you physically can make in a day. "You can make this business whatever you want it to be and earn as much as you want," says Wentz, who in addition to running his pet-sitting company serves as president of the board of directors of the National Association of Professional Pet Sitters (NAPPS). "I know many people who have no other means of support for their family other than a pet-sitting business, but you have to make sure you start your business in a place where there's a good demand. If you do that, it's possible to make a good living."

Someone who provides day dog-walking services in New York City, for example, can easily charge $25 a walk, while in a small town, you may only be able to charge $10 per visit—and some clients may balk at that. Add on some part-time staffers, and your earning potential rises quickly.

So here's an easy way to estimate what you might make. Using a figure of $16 per visit, which Wentz says is the national average for pet sitters, determine how many visits per day you think you can handle. If you're planning to service just one or two communities, you should be able to make more visits in a day because your travel time between homes will be shorter. So let's say you can handle eight 25-minute visits a day. Here's the math:

8 visits x $16/visit = $128 per day

$128 x 5 days/week = $640 per week

$640 x 50 weeks (two weeks off for good behavior!) = $32,000 per year

Bump that up to 10 visits per day at $18 an hour, and you'll earn $45,000 per year. Add two more visits per day at the same rate, and you're up to $54,000. And if you're in New York where the cost of living is higher and people don't blink at $10 cups of hotel joe, those 12 daily walks at $25 each will earn you the princely sum of $75,000.

Incidentally, it's customary to charge an additional $1 to $3 for each extra animal in the same household, which of course would improve your bottom line. For instance, a sitter who charges $18 a visit for one pet would charge $19 to $21 for a two-pet household, $20 to $24 for a three-pet household, and so on. And we're also talking cross-species pet sitting here—one dog and two cats, for instance, would be a three-pet-household visit.

Winding Down

While there's no doubt that starting a business requires a lot of personal sacrifices, one thing you absolutely must not toss away is all your personal downtime. It's easy to get burned out when you're launching any new business, let alone one that requires you to be on the job evenings, weekends, and holidays. Experienced pet sitters and dog walkers recommend building time off right into your schedule, whether it's for activities like a family wedding or your kids' Little League games or simply to unwind at the end of long days spent feeding and exercising man's (and woman's) best friends.

After you set up your schedule, stick to it. Naturally there will be times when you'll want to help out a favorite client who unexpectedly needs a pet sitter, but for the most part, you should guard that downtime with your life because your sanity depends on it. Instead of spreading yourself too thin, try developing a network of trusted local pet sitters or trained helpers who can help you preserve that precious time off.

However much you charge, pet sitters like David Lipschultz in Oak Park, Illinois, strongly recommend taking some of that money back out of the business in the form of a salary. "You are an employee of the business and as such you're a business expense," he says. "I've seen friends with small businesses put every dollar back into the business, and as a result they really don't know how much the business is worth."

Lipschultz said he doesn't take a big salary—only as much as the accountant says he can take and an amount that shows the IRS that his business is sound and legal. Also, having a salary and being able to produce a pay stub is necessary if you ever need financing for anything from a car to a home.

A Day in the Life

As a pet sitter or dog walker, the lion's share of your business workday will, of course, be taken up with animal care you'll provide in your clients' homes. The number of times you'll visit a home in a single day will depend on the type of animal you're servicing. For instance, cats usually require one to two visits a day, while dogs will need two to four visits—each of these visits incurs an additional charge. The average visit is about 20 to 25 minutes.

Although many pet sitters specialize in the care of just one or two types of pets, like cats and dogs, some provide basic care for a wider range of animals, including birds, cats, fish, reptiles, and other small animals like ferrets. Some pet sitters even specialize in the care of farm animals like horses.

Among the things pet sitters typically will do during a home visit are:

- Play with and walk pets
- Feed pets and provide fresh water
- Scoop and/or change cat litter
- Give medication and/or injections (like insulin shots and fluid therapy)
- Lavish love and attention on pets

In addition, pet sitters often provide additional services that have less to do with the pets themselves and more to do with their environment. Some of these services may include collecting mail, packages, and newspapers, checking the exterior of the home to make sure all is secure, setting the alarm system properly, and watering plants. Finally, pet sitters may offer pet taxi services (usually to and from the

Dollar Stretcher

Instead of buying plastic bags for disposing of animal waste, use the small plastic bags you get from the grocery store. Not only is the price right (free), the plastic handles can be tied together to close the bag securely so you don't have to worry about using twist ties.

vet), vacation house sitting (i.e., actually living in the house with the pets while the owners are away overnight), and pet-waste removal.

People who specialize in dog walking usually provide general care like exercising, walking and playing with pets, and checking food and water levels. Dog walkers normally don't administer medication or do any of the specialized jobs a pet sitter may take on because they're usually in and out of clients' homes so quickly. But as a courtesy they make sure all is well in clients' homes. For example, if a pet knocked over a potted plant the dog walker would sweep up the mess so the pooch in his or her care wouldn't get hurt.

Tip...

Smart Tip

The average 25-minute visit for either a pet sitter or a dog walker gives you plenty of time for walking, feeding, playing, and providing lots of affection. It's especially important to talk to the pets—if their owners are away on vacation or business, yours will be the only voice they'll hear during those lonely days on their own.

Pet care aside, you'll also have a fair number of business-related activities you'll need to attend to on a daily basis to keep the business operation running smoothly. On a typical day, you'll take phone calls from prospective clients or answer e-mails with requests for information, then schedule those who are interested in using you. You'll meet with prospective clients and their pets in their homes so you can assess whether the pet (and its owner!) seems friendly enough to work with. Advertising and marketing to attract new business will take up some of your time, as will networking to develop relationships with veterinarians, pet-supply store owners and other pet-related business owners who could be a source of referrals. You'll be in charge of your business's finance department, which means you'll send out monthly invoices and reconcile your accounts as payments are received. Finally, when your business grows to the point where you need the assistance of a staff of part-time sitters or walkers to help service all your clients, you'll have to devote some time every day to personnel administration tasks like scheduling, training and payroll.

Beware!

If you're planning to care for or board pets in your own home rather than your clients', make sure you check the local and state regulations. Many municipalities restrict the number of pets you can have in your home at one time, while in some states, caring for more than three pets in your home means you're running a kennel.

You also may choose to generate a contract for every customer you serve. Seattle pet sitter Dan MacDonald, who has a two-page contract that spells out his services and rates in detail, says, "I wouldn't even go out of the house without a contract. People are too sue-happy." Check out the sample contract on page 18 that you can use in your business or modify to meet you needs.

Sample Pet-Sitter Contract

Owner's name: ______________________________

Address: ______________________________

City, State, Zip: ______________________________

Cross streets: ______________________________

Home phone: ______________ Business phone: ______________

Cell phone: ______________ E-mail address: ______________

Pet-sitter service needed:

From (Date): ______________________ (Time): __________

To (Date): ______________________ (Time): __________

Number of visits per day: ______ Owner can be reached at: ______________

Pets' names/descriptions:

______________________ Cat _____ Dog _____ Other ______________

______________________ Cat _____ Dog _____ Other ______________

______________________ Cat _____ Dog _____ Other ______________

______________________ Cat _____ Dog _____ Other ______________

Special instructions: ______________________________

____

Location of pet food: ______________________________

____

Additional services (no extra charge):

_____ Newspapers/mail (leave on/in: ______________)

_____ Alternate lights _____ Water plants

Vet's name/phone: ______________________________

Emergency contact: ______________________________

Total number of visits: ______________ Rate per visit: ______________

Terms: 50 percent down when key is picked up; 50 percent upon return of key

______________________ Date ______ ______________________ Date ______

Pet Owner

Owner, Buffy's Pet-Sitting and Dog-Walking Service

> **Smart Tip**
>
> A procedures manual is very helpful for training employees. Seattle pet sitter Dan MacDonald's 25-page manual covers protocol (what to do with keys), behavior (no joking with homeowners), what to wear (no T-shirts with words), and how to interact with pets. Says MacDonald, "You need this to protect yourself."

Equipment

One of the beauties of going into business as a pet sitter or dog walker is that your equipment needs will be very modest. Naturally, you'll need basic office furniture and supplies to outfit your office, as well as a reliable vehicle to get to and from your jobs, all of which we'll discuss in greater detail in Chapter 10. Otherwise, all you'll need to do your job will be a "toolkit," such as a backpack, with a few inexpensive basics. These basics include a cat box scooper, a dustpan and short-handled brush, disposable gloves, disposable bags for bagging up animal waste, paper towels and antibacterial hand cleaner, and a flashlight for looking under furniture for elusive pets that disappear when you arrive. A big supply of dog and cat treats, as well as a pet carrier or pillowcase and towels for safely transporting animals to the vet, are also handy to have. Dog walkers will also need a poop scooper and disposable bags for cleaning up after the dogs do their business, and perhaps a leash or two (although it's reasonable to expect the pet owner to provide the leash and harness). And that's about it.

The homeowner is quite likely to have many of these items on hand already and no doubt will share. But you will look much more professional and prepared if you bring your own supplies and equipment—and, of course, your furry charges are much more likely to meet you enthusiastically at the door if they know you have treats in your pocket.

Getting Help

When you launch your pet-sitting or dog-walking business, you're likely initially to be a lone ranger who handles all the work. But experienced pet sitters will tell you that the only way to make the business grow is to hire help, since there's obviously a limit to the number of pets you personally can service in one day. Business owners like Wentz don't even do any pet care anymore—it's all handled by part-time employees (22 of them in his case) who work three shifts that run from as early as 6 A.M. to as late as 10 P.M. With the right advertising and marketing efforts, you could get to that point sooner than you expect, so it pays to think ahead.

We'll discuss how to hire employees in Chapter 13. For now, you'll find it helpful to know that pet-sitter or dog-walker employees are usually paid about $4 to $6 per visit, which for a 25-minute visit works out to better than minimum wage. By the way, it's not uncommon in this industry to give employees a percentage of the pet-sitting fee—from

40 percent to as much as 80 percent in some cases. But as Wentz says, "Why would anyone want to pay out that much [80 percent]? That sets you up for failure. Even in the NHL, payroll is only two-thirds of revenues. You need to have a lower rate of pay so you can add 20 percent to 25 percent on your payroll to cover expenses like workers' comp, unemployment and Social Security."

Setting Rates

Setting a reasonable rate is always a tricky issue for new business owners. You don't want to price your services too high because you could scare off potential clients, but you also don't want to go too low because it will appear as though your work isn't valuable. So here's an easy way to come up with a rate. First, figure out how much money you need to earn to pay your bills. Let's say you need $2,400 a month after taxes to cover your mortgage, utilities, and other living expenses. That means that if you're a sole proprietor, you'd have to earn about $3,000 a month to cover your federal taxes (assuming you're in the 20 percent tax bracket) and cover the household bills. If you charge $16 a visit (the national average), you'll have to make 187.5 visits a month (or 9.375 visits a day if you work 20 days a month). If you charge $12 a visit, you'll have to make 250 visits a month, or 12.5 visits a day. The question is, can you physically handle that many visits a day given the distance you'll have to travel between clients? (Keep in mind those 12.5 visits might be to only six residences a day, since dogs and cats usually require two visits a day.) If not, you'll have to make some adjustments either in your expected earning level or the logistics to make it work.

Startup Costs

The cost to start a new pet-sitting or dog-walking business is quite low—no more than about $3,000 to $5,000, most of which is due to costs incurred when you set up your home office, order business cards, and so on. If you already have a computer or suitable office furniture, you can get under way for less. To give you an idea of what your business expenses may be, check out the "Sample Startup Costs" chart you'll find on the next page, which is for a fictitious, one-person pet-sitting and dog-walking service. You'll also find a worksheet on page 22 that you can use to start figuring your own costs.

Sample Startup Costs

Item	Cost
Basic toolkit (treats, poop scooper, etc.)	$50
Office equipment, furniture, supplies	$985
Business licenses	$20
Phone (line installation charges)	$40
Utility deposits	$0
Employee wages and benefits (first six months)	$0
Personalized polo shirts	$0
Magnetic sign	$60
Startup advertising	$100
Legal services	$200
Vehicle	$0
Insurance (annual cost)	$500
Market research	$250
Membership dues	$140
Publications (annual subscriptions)	$60
Online service	$20
Website design	$800
Web hosting, domain name	$90
Subtotal	$3,315
Miscellaneous expenses (roughly 10 percent of subtotal)	$332
Total	**$3,647**

Startup Costs Worksheet

Item	Cost
Basic toolkit (treats, poop scooper, etc.)	
Office equipment, furniture, supplies	
Business licenses	
Phone (line installation charges)	
Utility deposits	
Employee wages and benefits (first six months)	
Personalized polo shirts	
Magnetic sign	
Startup advertising	
Legal services	
Vehicle	
Insurance (annual cost)	
Market research	
Membership dues	
Publications (annual subscriptions)	
Online service	
Website design	
Web hosting, domain name	
Subtotal	
Miscellaneous expenses (roughly 10 percent of subtotal)	
Total	

3

Dog Training

Dogs have been man's (not to mention woman's) best friend for tens of thousands of years, but during that time they haven't always been models of good behavior. Our canine buddies bark excessively, howl, growl, bite, run away, get underfoot, jump up on people, sniff inappropriately, and exhibit a lot of other occasionally annoying behavior in the fulfillment of their life's work as . . . well, dogs. But if you find dogs endearing no matter what they do and you have the patience and stamina to work with these sometimes unruly, always lovable pets every day, then you could have what it takes to be a dog trainer.

> Tip...
>
> **Smart Tip**
>
> Industry experts say it takes up to five years of study and hands-on dog training to become a capable entry-level trainer. For this reason it's a good idea to apprentice with an experienced trainer and take as many hands-on workshops as you can to gain the competence you need to be successful in the field.

There are several career paths for dog trainers. The most common way to enter the field is as a pet-dog obedience trainer who teaches canines to be model citizens. Such trainers teach in group settings or one on one in either the pet owner's home or a training facility (which can be home-based or site-based). One common type of group training that is utterly charming yet challenging at the same time is puppy training for "youngsters" that are at least four months old, but of course you also can offer group classes to teach new tricks to old dogs of any age.

It's also possible to become a dog trainer who prepares dogs for specialized work outside the realm of pet dog-dom. For instance, trainers are used to teach dogs to handle search-and-rescue missions, police work like tracking, individual and/or property protection work, bomb and narcotics detection, and service work (guide dogs, hearing dogs, therapy dogs, etc.). And, of course, the film and TV industries also use trainers to handle their canine stars.

Finally, you can enter this field as an animal behaviorist, which is a professional who studies animal function, development, and evolution of behavior. This is a scientific field that requires extensive education (often a master's degree or a PhD), and increasingly these professionals are using their applied animal behavior expertise to train pet dogs. Degrees in psychology, like Oak Park, Illinois, trainer Jamie Damato has, can also be helpful when pursuing a career as a dog trainer.

Whichever career path you choose to follow, dog training can be exciting and challenging. Our mission in this chapter is to give you some background and tools to make that pathway a reality.

Basic Training

Dog trainers practice their profession in many locations. Some open training facilities in their own homes and have pet owners drop off their canines for one-on-one sessions or group work, or they'll work with both dog and owner in tandem. This type of business setup has low overhead and ensures a short commute to work for the trainer. Others go to clients' homes for one-on-one sessions. Although it's possible that the owner will just want to teach Fido some manners, often training is requested to correct a behavioral problem, like biting or overcoming separation anxiety. Finally, some trainers offer sessions in a dedicated facility. This type of business has the highest overhead costs since you have to pay for rent or a mortgage, and it is the most likely type of business to have employees.

A trainer's bag of teaching tricks will run the gamut from basic on-leash obedience training (sit, stay, come, heel, and so on) to behavior modification. Trainers often specialize in certain types of services—usually the ones they like doing best. Among the most common services are:

> **Fun Fact**
>
> *Schutzhund* (German for "protection dog") is a sport that develops and trains dogs (usually German Shepherds) to make them useful and happy companions. Its intent is to demonstrate a dog's intelligence, endurance, courage, and ability to scent. The sport focuses on tracking, obedience and protection, and makes Schutzhund-trained dogs perfect for police work.

- On- and off-leash obedience
- Puppy obedience
- Competition obedience (handling techniques for obedience trials at competition)
- Full owner participation training (teaching the owner how to handle the pet)
- Pre-pet awareness (helping owners decide which breed would best fit their lifestyle)
- Hand signal and voice command training

Trainers also offer behavior consultations for problems like:

- Aggression (toward people and other dogs)
- Biting and nipping
- Fear biting (a response to fearful situations that make the dog bite to protect itself)
- Hyperactivity
- Digging and chewing
- Running away/roaming
- Anti-social behavior (including dog fighting in the home)
- Anxiety (such as separation anxiety)
- Fear of loud noises

Finally, trainers offer assistance with housebreaking and build confidence in shy and submissive pets.

Equipment

Dog trainers use a wide variety of training tools to instill good behavior. These humane tools are used for positive reinforcement, not punishment, and some are downright fun for dogs, owners and trainers alike!

Some commonly used equipment includes:

Beware!

Always let someone (your spouse, significant other, parent, or adult child) know where you are when you're conducting a private lesson in a client's home. You may never run into a problem, but it's always better to be safe than sorry. For the same reason, always carry a cell phone with you (set on vibrate).

- *Prong collar*. This looks like a medieval torture device with its series of linking prongs, but some trainers use it because it replicates the way a mother dog reprimands her pups. It's used to teach dogs to walk on a loose leash and to give motivational reinforcement when a dog steps out of line. It's considered completely safe and humane because it fits to the exact size of the dog's neck and won't cut off its airway. Cost: about $10 to $18.
- *Gentle leader*. This is a head halter that resembles the contraption used on horses' heads. It buckles behind the head and doesn't interfere with the dog's ability to bark or drink water. It's used to stop dogs from pulling and to prevent inappropriate sniffing behavior. Cost: about $18.
- *Martingale collar*. Similar to a slip collar (which slips over the head but can just as easily slip off), the Martingale has an extra loop of nylon on the main collar and an attached ring to which the leash is hooked. When the pet pulls, the main collar tightens enough to give the owner control without choking the dog. Cost: about $10 to $16.
- *Six-foot canvas leash*. This is economical, easy to handle and a good length for teaching a dog to heel. Cost: from $5 for nylon; about $20 for leather.
- *Clicker*. When depressed, this simple tool emits a clicking sound. It's used to reinforce positive behavior and is always followed by a treat (the real reinforcement). Cost: about $40 for a 50-pack.
- *Assess-a-hand*. Use this to test the reaction of aggressive dogs, fear biters, and nervous pets. It looks like a man's arm covered by a shirtsleeve, and assesses whether the pet will lash out or bite to defend its food, avoid being leashed, or otherwise protect itself. Cost: $20.
- *Tether*. This short, plastic-coated wire has clips on each end, one of which is attached to the dog's collar and the other to a fixed point, like a stake in the ground. It is helpful as a housebreaking aid because dogs won't soil in the area where they're confined. (But, of course, it should never be used when the dog is unattended.) Cost: about $17.
- *Taste deterrents*. These unpleasant tasting spray or cream foams deter pets from licking, biting, or chewing inappropriately. Cost: about $5.

- *Treats*. Trainers usually have more than one type of this ultimate teaching aid on hand because not all dogs will like the same one. Like human treats, dog treats can be loaded with salt and sugar, so be sure to read the label.
- *Kong*. A hard, heavy-duty rubber toy shaped like a three-tier snowman, it has a small hole on the top and a larger one at the bottom that can be filled with kibble or other food treats like dog sausages and even peanut butter. In addition to being plain fun for dogs to chew on in an attempt to get to the surprise inside, Kongs are great for keeping a dog with separation anxiety busy or for distracting it when there's company in the house. Trainers love them because they're so stimulating for the animal. Cost: around $6 to $9 each, plus $4 per package for liver treats to stuff inside.
- *Toys*. Frisbees, sticks, and other toys can be used to reinforce behavior for dogs that don't respond to food treats. As with dog "yummies," keep the toys nearby while training for immediate reinforcement of appropriate behavior.

As you can see, these tools are not specialty items available only to trainers—they can be purchased in any retail pet store. But carrying them in your training facility or your mobile "office" (that is, your vehicle) when making house calls can be a great way to earn extra income. According to some trainers, the Kong alone is a great item to carry—virtually every pet owner who sees how it keeps his or her pet occupied and happy will want one (and some treats to stuff it with). And, of course, you'll need some of these items to use in your business. You can pretty much get everything you need for less than $100.

One final thing you might consider investing in is some type of uniform for yourself and your employees, if applicable. A collared shirt (no T-shirts—too casual) with your name embroidered on the left breast or the pocket will give you a professional appearance. They're not very expensive—they can cost as little as $14 each from a company like Amsterdam Printing—and you can order as few as six at a time. We've included a few resources in the Appendix that you can explore.

Bright Idea

Trainers typically give the owners in group classes homework to do with their pets between classes. To make the lessons learned "stick," write a description of the behavior learned in class, reiterate the most important points about what was learned, and give some pointers on how the owner should work with his or her pet to reinforce the behavior.

A Day in the Life

While the main part of your workday will be devoted to prepping puppies and their older cousins so they'll mind their manners, being a business owner also means that you'll have to attend to a lot of administrative details. Some of the tasks you can expect to handle on a daily basis will include:

- *Office administration.* Answering the phone, opening mail, handling accounts payable/receivable, paying the bills, processing credit card payments
- *Customer service.* Scheduling appointments, meeting with prospective clients, giving tours of your training facility
- *Purchasing.* Buying supplies for the business (office supplies, training supplies) and products for resale (leashes, collars, pet treats, etc.)
- *Cultivating professional relationships.* Touching base with veterinarians and local business owners who could be the source of future referrals
- *Personnel management.* Hiring, overseeing the work of employees, making up work schedules, conducting performance evaluations

Bright Idea

Promotional items like pens, magnets, and memo pads imprinted with your business name and contact information are a great way to spread the news fast about your new business. And don't forget clickers. Have them personalized and give them to every person who takes clicker training with you.

Getting Help

Not every trainer will need or be able to afford a staff at the genesis of the business. But there may come a day when you'll need assistance with tasks like office management, or you'll need to hire assistant trainers because you have more pets to train than you can handle yourself. That can be a scary moment because employees are a lot of responsibility. But when you no longer have enough time to do the jobs you love and started the business to do, the time has come.

The types of employees you'll need for your business may include a staff trainer or assistant trainer to help you with the group training activities and to handle one-on-one training overflow you don't have time to do yourself; assistants to help during class; an office manager to oversee the actual running of the business (handling payroll, keeping the lights on, etc.); and possibly a receptionist to greet customers, offer coffee to waiting clients, and to call clients to remind them about appointments, and so on.

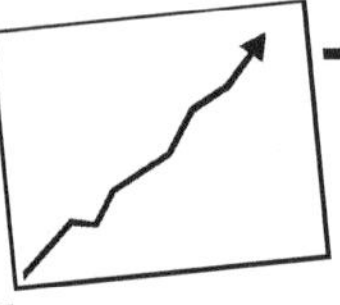

Stat Fact

There are no reliable dog-trainer statistics available. That's because, as Association of Pet Dog Trainers (APDT) president Teoti Anderson says, "Since you don't have to be licensed, anyone can put out a shingle and claim to be a trainer!" What is known is that at 5,000 members, APDT is the largest association of dog trainers worldwide.

Hiring people experienced in any of these areas will make your life easier, especially in a busy business. When it comes to dog trainers, however, you'll probably want to hire people

Dog-torate Degree

When all the good little girls and boys are ready to graduate from Obedience U., what could be more fun than to throw them a graduation party? Owners and dogs alike will love this activity, which can include timed games like relay races and fetch (to see who brings a ball back quickest), as well as games that show off a dog's newly acquired skills, like a contest to determine which dog can do the most "sits." Naturally, there should be prizes for the dogs who win, but every dog should go home with a goody bag or some other token like a small toy.

To make the occasion really special, have a dog parade in which each dog and its owner comes forward to accept a diploma. You can buy award certificates from office superstores that can be personalized on your computer. Affix a gold seal to the front of the certificates, tie them up with ribbons and present them with a flourish. After all, every good dog deserves a pat on the head and something for its trophy case!

who already have the training and experience you need. For this reason, you can expect to pay these employees a higher wage. According to one industry insider, experienced trainers earn $20 to $40 an hour on a contract basis, although trainers like Jamie Damato prefer to pay a set fee per class, plus an incentive for every student enrolled. For instance, you might pay your trainer $200 for a six-week class, plus a $10 incentive for each student, which for a class with six students would add up to $260.

And here's some good news for your bottom line. According to Lexington, South Carolina, trainer Teoti Anderson, "Many beginning trainers apprentice for several years and pay for the privilege of working for an experienced trainer and learning the ropes. Others work for free so they can learn the business and art of training dogs."

If you plan to do all the training yourself, you may still find it helpful to have assistance with general business activities, as Anderson does. She has had up to five assistants at a time, but she rotates them so she has just one per class. These assistants handle general duties like taking attendance, helping owners who are having difficulty in class, giving out handouts and fitting Gentle Leader head collars. These types of helpers can be paid minimum wage or a little better.

While there is no published data on salaries paid to administrative people who work specifically in the dog-training industry, there are general data available that can give you a pretty good idea of what to pay. For instance, the International Association of Administrative Professionals says that in 2005, receptionists earned from $19,800 to

$24,250 a year, while an office manager earned $28,000 to $35,250. Depending on the hours you keep, the amount of business you have, and the part of the country in which you work, you can adjust these figures up or down.

Beware!

When scouting out possible training facilities, be on the lookout for potential pup distractions. Lexington, South Carolina, trainer Teoti Anderson recalls, "I once trained in a gym that had a walking track up on the second floor that circled the entire gym. It was quite a distraction once the dogs noticed the people 'walking on the ceiling'!"

Earnings Potential

The amount your business can earn will depend on a number of factors. To begin with, Anderson says it's not uncommon for trainers to work part time on the side, as the majority of Association of Pet Dog Trainers members do, while holding a different full-time job. (In fact, that's exactly what Anderson does.) So rather than guesstimating how much a new trainer could earn over the course of a year, she offers these typical work scenarios and rates:

In-home private lessons are generally priced higher, both because the trainer must travel to the client's home and because he or she is accommodating the client's schedule. This type of one-on-one training is often necessary to address a specific issue, like aggression, fearful behavior, or separation anxiety. Because of these special circumstances, and because there can be liability issues, in-home trainers can command fees of $30 to $200 an hour.

A lot of new dog-training business owners take out only small stipends at the beginning so they can plow as much as possible back into the business to give the company the best chance at success. Damato, for instance, says she took out "just enough money to eat on" when she launched her business. Today, she takes a biweekly salary that she says is still pretty modest but is enough for her needs.

Setting Rates

To get to the point where you can actually take a salary, you have to set rates for your services that are equitable and appropriate for your target market. This can be difficult at best, and it's also hard for us to give you any hard-and-fast guidelines because rates can vary widely in different parts of the country. You may find that calling around to find out what other trainers are charging is a good way to get a baseline figure for setting your own rates.

Or you can do what Damato did, which was essentially to ignore the other guys on the block and price her services exactly where she wanted them. "We're the most expensive service on the west side of Chicago, and we get what we want because people know

Dog Training Earnings Potential

GROUP CLASSES

3 to 15 classes per week
6 to 10 students per class

Average rates for a 6-to-8-week session:
$60 to $120 per student

Sample earnings:

5 group classes per week x 10 students per class x $60 per student = $3,000 for 6 to 8 weeks

5 group classes per week x 10 students per class x $120 per student = $6,000 for 6 to 8 weeks

PRIVATE LESSONS

2 to 14 one-hour lessons per week

Average rates:
$20 to $80 per lesson

Sample earnings:

10 private lessons per week x $20 an hour = $200

10 private lessons per week x $80 an hour = $800

we're good," she says. "So much of my business comes from referrals that I don't have a lot of price resistance, plus I'm so damned good at what I do there's really no competition!"

There's a good lesson in that approach. You don't necessarily have to beat the competition's prices to get lots of business. Having a reputation as the highest priced service actually can work to your advantage—many people will automatically think you're the best at what you do just because you are so expensive. The bottom line is, you need to figure out how much money you need to pay the business bills and have enough left over to pay your personal obligations (like the mortgage and car payments). Ideally, you'll have a little profit left over after meeting all your expenses, which you can sink back into the business or salt away in a passbook account.

When calculating rates, be sure to include a mileage surcharge if you'll be visiting clients' homes. As of 2008, the IRS allowed a 50.5-cent-per-mile deduction for business-related travel. You can use that same amount to figure how much extra to charge your clients. For example, let's say your target market has a range of 25 miles and you sit somewhere in the center. You might want to include a mileage surcharge of $6 in your rate (12.5 miles x .505 = $6.31) to accommodate those clients who are on the boundaries of your target market. But don't tell your client about the extra charge—build it into your rate so you don't cause any hard feelings. (You are completely within your rights to charge for mileage, but not every client will like it.)

Startup Costs

All in all, the total startup costs for a homebased dog-training business are pretty low. You'll need a computer and other office equipment and supplies to launch the business, as well as services like web hosting and legal and accounting assistance (all discussed in more detail in future chapters). Throw in a business license and possibly some

When the Dog Bites

There's nothing sweeter than a cuddly puppy or well-mannered adult dog curled up by your chair or dancing with glee around your feet when you come home after a long day. So it's sometimes easy to forget that even friendly dogs have the potential to bite if provoked. Certainly no one knows this better than dog trainers, whose gentle but firm ministrations can earn them a disgruntled nip—or worse. As a reminder, here's what the American Veterinary Medical Association (AVMA) recommends you do if you are bitten by a dog in your care:

- Seek immediate medical attention.
- Wash the bite area with soap and water and control bleeding until help is obtained.
- Ask to see a plastic surgeon when you arrive at the emergency room. Serious dog bites can leave a scar, but a board-certified plastic surgeon will know how best to repair the site to minimize scarring.
- Report the incident to the local health department, animal control agency, or police department.
- Speak to the dog's owner about the animal's vaccination record and medical history.

signage for your vehicle if you'll be traveling to clients' homes, and you'll be pretty much ready to roll for as little as $4,000. In fact, Anderson recommends a low-cost startup for the best chance of success. "It is much more economical to start up a dog-training business if you don't lease a space or have your own building, because you don't have to worry about the overhead," she says. "I teach at rec centers—they handle the money and I handle the training. So I don't have any credit card fees or other expenses, and I take checks and cash for the limited retail products I offer."

If you are planning to work out of a commercial facility, or if your home will need expanding or renovating to make it dog-friendly, your costs will be higher. For example, Damato says she spent $15,000 to build out the vet's office where she apprenticed to accommodate her training facility. But you can launch your own business for less simply by renting.

To help you figure out how much it might cost to establish your own business, we've included "Sample Startup Costs" on page 34 that gives typical expenses for two fictitious dog-training businesses. The low-end business, A Matter of Manners Dog Training, is a sole proprietorship whose owner operates out of a home office and travels to clients' homes to train pets. The high-end business, Denehen Dog Academy, is an LLC that operates out of an 800-square-foot facility. It employs one part-time trainer who is paid on a contract basis (five hours a week). Once you've looked over this chart, you can try your hand at estimating some of your own expenses on the worksheet on page 35. The other figures you'll need to complete the worksheet, like the cost of web hosting, will be discussed in future chapters.

Sample Startup Costs

Item	A Matter of Manners Dog Training	Denehen Dog Academy
Mortgage (first six months @ $650/mo.)	$0	$3,900
Basic equipment (collars, treats, etc.)	$100	$100
Startup retail inventory	$0	$400
Office equipment, furniture, supplies	$985	$3,415
Business licenses	$20	$20
Phone (line installation charges)	$40	$40
Utility deposits	$0	$200
Employee wages and benefits (first six months)*	$0	$2,400
Personalized polo shirts	$75	$75
Magnetic sign	$60	$60
Startup advertising	$100	$100
Legal services	$200	$200
Vehicle	$0	$0
Liability insurance (annual cost)	$500	$500
Market research	$250	$250
Membership dues	$100	$100
Publications (annual subscriptions)	$25	$100
Online service	$20	$20
Website design	$800	$800
Web hosting, domain name	$90	$90
Subtotal	$3,365	$12,770
Miscellaneous expenses (roughly 10 percent of subtotal)	$340	$1,300
Total	**$3,705**	**$14,070**

**Contract employee who earns $20 an hour for five one-hour classes a week*

Startup Costs Worksheet

Item	Cost
Mortgage	
Basic equipment (collars, treats, etc.)	
Startup retail inventory	
Office equipment, furniture, supplies	
Business licenses	
Phone (line installation charges)	
Utility deposits	
Employee wages and benefits (first six months)	
Personalized polo shirts	
Magnetic sign	
Startup advertising	
Legal services	
Vehicle	
Liability insurance (annual cost)	
Market research	
Membership dues	
Publications (annual subscriptions)	
Online service	
Website design	
Web hosting, domain name	
Subtotal	
Miscellaneous expenses (roughly 10 percent of subtotal)	
Total	

4

Pet Grooming

When it comes to providing a service that genuinely helps animals, there may be no better profession than that of pet groomer. By virtue of their clippers and skill, pet groomers offer many extrinsic benefits to pets (and their owners!) that go way beyond simply keeping them pretty and clean. Dematting a long-haired dog's or cat's coat helps prevent the discomfort of skin lesions. Bathing and fluffing a pet means that the animal will get cuddled and petted more often. Eradicating fleas makes them healthier. Expressing anal sacs spares pets considerable discomfort. And the list goes on.

> **Smart Tip**
>
> One of the best and most comprehensive grooming sites on the internet is PetGroomer.com, which has phenomenal resources ranging from lists of grooming schools and certification programs to "Grooming 101," a how-to resource that gives grooming, blade, and tool tips for more than 150 dog breeds.

But being a pet groomer entails far more than just having the technical skills to do a lion cut or hand-strip a cairn terrier. Good pet groomers must have gentle hands, a kind heart, and the patience of Job. They must be fearless (although not foolhardy) when confronted with a pet that clearly doesn't want his tail shaved or her nails painted. But above all, they must have a genuine love of animals, as well as a knack for dealing with their owners.

"When people bring an animal in, they need to feel comfortable that you'll treat their pet well," says Barbara Menutes, a Houston cat groomer who also has groomed dogs in her 12-year career. "If clients don't trust you, they won't leave Fifi with you. People tend to be even more obsessive about their pets than they are with their children, so it takes 'people psychology' and good rapport with them to be successful."

It also takes careful attention to detail. "All groomers are artists, but they need clear information so they know what the customer wants," Menutes says. "It's important to take detailed notes so you give the client exactly what they want. You may work more with the animal, but you need to spend a lot of time with the owner, too."

And there should be plenty of work for you. A study by the American Pet Products Association (APPA) predicted that Americans would spend $2.4 billion in 2005 on pet services, a category that encompasses grooming and boarding. It also estimates the average amount dog and cat owners spend on groomers and grooming aids every year is $107 for dogs and $24 for cats. Considering that there were an estimated 90.5 million cats and 73.9 million dogs owned in the United States in 2004, you can see there is a lot of opportunity out there for business owners.

The Business at a Glance

There are three ways you can start your pet-grooming business:

1. *Homebased salon.* If you have a space you can dedicate to the business, like a finished basement or converted garage, or you're willing to put an addition on your home to accommodate your business, then this could be a viable option

for you. Some industry experts say you'll need a minimum of 500 square feet for your business if you're a one-person operation, which will give you enough room for the grooming table, tub, cages, and other equipment you'll need. However, grooming industry product provider John Stazko in Myakka City, Florida, says 500 square feet is generous—he once had two employees in a busy 250-square-foot shop that was more like a closet.

> Tip...
>
> **Smart Tip**
>
> Offering retail items like leashes, flea collars, and brushes for touch-ups between grooming appointments is an easy way to increase sales. Be sure to place these items near the cash registers to tempt pet owners as they're paying for their grooming services.

Chances are you'll have to do some renovation to make this space suitable for the business, including adding plumbing or upgrading the lighting, and adding a nonslip floor that will stand up to the rigors of dripping pets (and possibly dripping groomers). You also will need room for a small reception area and a retail-products area so you can sell the same products you use on Fluffy or Fido. Finally, you'll need an office from which to manage your business. If there's room, this can be in or near your salon, but if the quarters are especially cramped, you may have to establish this office in another area of your home, like a spare bedroom.

2. *Commercial salon*. Whether you set up the business in a stand-alone building, a strip-mall space or a storefront, this can be an expensive proposition. In addition to renovating a commercial space to make it work as a pet salon, you'll also be taking on a monthly mortgage or rent payment, which can quickly eat up your operating capital. You may be able to save on the cost of renovations by searching for a store that was previously used as a pet salon—or a human hair salon, for that matter, since the water and electricity needs are similar. If the previous owner is willing to make a deal for the styling stations and mirrors, so much the better. Today's pet salons are looking more and more like their human counterparts every day, and you'll save a lot of money on the décor and styling equipment if you can simply use what a previous owner left behind or is willing to part with.
3. *Mobile business*. Operated out of a specially outfitted van, this type of pet business goes where the customers are—that is, right to their homes. You simply drive up, collect the pet, take it to your van, and work your magic. There are many companies that retrofit vans or trailers to accommodate a groomer's equipment and tools, or you can purchase a brand-new, fully outfitted van for about $35,000 to $50,000. These vehicles come with everything a groomer needs, from hydraulic tables to dryers, vacuum systems, and cages, as well as

luxury add-ons like sound systems. If that's a little too rich for your blood, you may also be able to purchase a used mobile grooming van. Try doing a search on the internet or check with the conversion van or new grooming van companies to see if they handle used vehicles. You'll find contact information for a few "groommobile" companies in the Appendix.

Professionals in this industry often specialize in grooming a single type of animal—usually dogs, more often than not, because cats are more difficult and take longer to groom. As a result, if you're entering the field in a market that already has a lot of grooming salons, you might want to

Beware!

By law, every establishment that sells retail products must conduct a physical product inventory for tax purposes. To make the job easier, you can use a business software program like QuickBooks to keep track, or you can invest a little extra when you buy your cash register and get a pricing gun that scans barcodes and automatically tracks inventory.

What's a Groomer To Do?

Chances are, if you're considering starting a grooming business, you know a thing or two about pet grooming. Still, when considering how to structure your business, it may help to keep in mind the different types of groomers that might be found in a typical shop. After all, the time for hiring help may come sooner than you expect—and the process will be easier if you know what level of experience will be most helpful to you as you expand your business.

There are three basic types of pet groomers:

1. *Pet bathers or bather/brushers*. These are entry-level groomers who are learning the business from the bottom up but don't yet do any styling. Rather, they prep animals for the groomer while learning about skin and coat care, tools and equipment.
2. *Assistant groomers*. Assistants are those who may have been promoted from bather and do some of the clipping and scissoring under the watchful eye of the professional groomer.
3. *Full-charge pet groomers*. These are the talented stylists who clip and scissor pets from start to finish. As a one-person shop owner, this describes you, at least in the beginning. You will do all the brushing, clipping, nail cutting, ear cleaning, bathing, blow-drying and give the final clip and style.

> **Dollar Stretcher**
>
> If you can, buy products from pet-products distributors, who will come by once you've been in business for a while. Not only will this save you a lot of money on shipping heavy items like gallons of shampoo, but also the supplies will be delivered right to your salon.

specialize in cat grooming since that could mean there would be a lot of work for you, both from the public and from referrals made by dog groomers who prefer not to handle felines.

Obviously, an important consideration for people who wish to start a grooming business is the salary they can hope to earn. Stazko says grooming is a very lucrative business, but it depends on your pricing, expenses, and skills. "You can make a very good profit if you're doing enough animals in a day and your expenses are in line," he says. "It's possible to earn anywhere from $20,000 to $100,000 a year." Mobile groomers can earn approximately $60,000 a year plus tips, according to Wag'n Tails, a converter of mobile grooming vehicles.

Equipment

To make sure you have all your bases covered, here's a brief rundown of the grooming services you could offer followed by the tools you'll need to get started. Services might include:

- Clipping and scissoring
- Bathing
- Dematting
- Carding (to remove dead hair)
- Nail clipping
- Hand stripping
- Expressing anal sacs
- Ear cleaning
- Giving formal show trims
- Applying veterinarian-prescribed bathing treatments (including flea baths)
- Bow making (for those cute toy breeds)

> **Smart Tip**
>
> Wearing a polo shirt embroidered with the name of your mobile business will give you a sharp, professional appearance while you're on the job. In the shop, a smock with your business name on it adds to your professional appeal, while giving you pockets in which to stash combs, clips, and other small items that are easily misplaced.

Of the five types of pet-care businesses discussed in this book, the grooming business is the only one that has significant workroom needs. Grooming schools estimate that you'll need $1,000 to $1,500 worth of basic equipment to launch your business, or more if you want to install hair salon-style workstations with mirrors and cabinets. For a handy chart that lists these tools along with their low- (Barky's Canine Coiffures) and high-end (Molly's Snip and Clip) prices, see the next page. Then use the worksheet on page 44 as you read through the following to get a feel for what you might spend.

The basic tools include:

- *Grooming stations.* You'll need one to two for a one-person grooming business; up to five if you have employees. The centerpiece of your workstation should be a hydraulic table, which can be raised, lowered, and rotated as necessary. The standard table size is 24 inches by 36 inches and will cost $350 to $900. Electric tables are more expensive at $600 to $1,500, but the cost is worth it when you find yourself confronted with a 75-pound dog. Since an electric table goes as low as 18 inches, you won't have to lift those big bruisers—they can just jump up themselves. To keep costs in line, consider buying just one electric table to supplement your hydraulic equipment. Each table also will need a groom post ($20 to $50).
- *Professional grooming tub.* A basic model without a sprayer is $300. A deluxe model with a sprayer, built-in strainer for trapping loose fur, drain stopper, faucet with hot and cold fixtures, and hose hook will put you back a cool $1,100. Purchased separately, the sprayer/hose combination is $70 to $160.
- *Comb-out table.* This is used before bathing to remove as much soil, mats, and hairballs as possible. Combing here rather than at a station also means you won't inadvertently spread dirt to clean pets that are being clipped or dried. A 6-foot banquet table like you can buy at Costco works fine; a table from a pet-care products business is $60 to $140.
- *Stand dryer.* Two different types can be handy: a regular model for small dogs and cats or a heavy-duty model for dogs with heavy coats; $180 to $850.
- *Cage dryer.* Just clip it on the front of the cage to blow-dry the pet; $250 to $450.
- *High-velocity force dryer.* This is for sweeping excess moisture from the coat; $40 to $950.
- *Cages or crates.* You may want to have up to six in different sizes on a table along one wall and at a height that will cause the least amount of strain on your back when you lift pets out. Make sure to include cushiony bedding like easy-to-launder towels and water bowls that cannot be tipped easily as part of the cage décor so waiting pets are as comfortable as possible. Prices range from $50 to $450, depending on the construction of the cage, with multi-tier products being the best value.
- *Tool caddy.* These wheeled carts have drawers to hold all your grooming tools. You can get a professional model from a grooming equipment company for $100

Basic Grooming Equipment and Supplies

Grooming Equipment and Supplies	Barky's Canine Coiffures	Molly's Snip and Clip
Hydraulic table	$350	$700
Electric table	$0	$600
Grooming post	$20	$50
Grooming tub	$300	$300
Comb-out table	$0	$60
Standing floor dryer	$200	$200
Cage dryer	$0	$250
High-velocity dryer (force)	$100	$200
Cages or crates	$600	$600
Tool caddy	$50	$200
Clippers (2) and blades	$225	$450
Scissors	$150	$250
Muzzles and animal-handling gloves	$60	$120
Stool	$0	$100
Anti-fatigue mat	$65	$130
Groomer apparel	$25	$100
Towels	$12	$24
Towel wringer	$0	$120
Miscellaneous grooming tools and products	$150	$200
Washer, dryer	$0	$600
Wet/dry vac	$70	$70
Waiting room furniture/equipment	$0	$0
Service counter stool	$0	$90
Visitor chairs (2)	$0	$250
Retail product display	$0	$100
POS terminal, credit card receipt printer	$0	$500
Brochure/business card holders	$0	$30
Retail products and supplies	$0	$0
Initial inventory	$0	$200
Total Expenses	**$2,377**	**$6,494**

Grooming Equipment and Supplies Worksheet

Item	Cost
Hydraulic table	
Electric table	
Grooming post	
Grooming tub	
Comb-out table	
Standing floor dryer	
Cage dryer	
High-velocity dryer (force)	
Cages or crates	
Tool caddy	
Clippers and blades	
Scissors	
Muzzles and animal-handling gloves	
Stool	
Anti-fatigue mat	
Groomer apparel	
Towels	
Towel wringer	
Miscellaneous grooming tools and products	
Washer, dryer	
Wet/dry vac	
Waiting room furniture/equipment	
Service counter stool	
Visitor chairs	
Retail product display	
POS terminal, credit card receipt printer	
Brochure/business card holders	
Retail products and supplies	
Initial inventory	
Total Expenses	

to $200, but you'll find the type of plastic home storage cabinet sold at department stores like Target or craft shops like Michael's will work just fine for a fraction of the cost.

- *Clippers, blades, and snap-on comb attachments.* Two clippers are recommended so you always have a backup; you'll also need two sets of blades for each clipper. Keep blade wash solution, lubricating spray, and oil handy for maintenance. Prices are $135 to $320 for corded heavy-duty models or $16 to $75 for trimming and finishing clippers. A deluxe 14-piece snap-on comb set will run around $60.
- *Scissors.* Various types are necessary, including 9- or 10-inch for roughing (first clipping before bathing), finishing shears, curved scissors for fine finish work, thinning shears, blunt-tipped scissors, and straight shears (for trimming ears and footpads). About $250 will cover everything you need in the modest price range.
- *Muzzles and animal-handling gloves.* No explanation needed, right? These will run about $4 for a muzzle and up to $50 for Kevlar gloves (bulletproofing for your hands and arms!).
- *Stool.* It can be a little tricky to learn how to groom while sitting, but if you can do it, your feet will thank you. A tall stool like the kind used behind a bar or in a hair salon usually works best. A stool from a pet-care supply business will run from $50 to $140.
- *Anti-fatigue mat.* This is something you'll appreciate when you're on your feet from opening until closing. Mats cushion bare floors to make it more comfortable to stand and clip, comb and spray all day; about $65.
- *Groomer apparel.* A grooming top or smock will give your salon a professional look and protect your clothing at the same time; around $10 to $30.
- *Towels.* You'll need plenty in the course of a day. A dozen basic towels runs $12.
- *Towel wringer.* This is a handy little tool for dealing with piles of wet towels—if you have time to use it; $120.
- *Miscellaneous grooming tools and products.* You'll need various products like ear-cleaning solution, eye drops, styptic powder, coat sprays, cotton balls, nail files, nail trimmers, tweezers, brushes, combs, mat-splitting tools, rakes, shedding blades, first-aid supplies (bandages, hydrogen peroxide, medicated spray, etc.), flea and tick spray, flea bombs, disinfectant (for tables, tools, crates, and the floor), and a box of latex gloves. Finally,

Bright Idea

To make it easier to scissor the paws and legs of black dogs or cats, place a large white towel on the table under the animal. The contrast of fur against terry-cloth will make it much easier to see what you're doing.

Certifiably Capable

Although many states have professional licensing requirements for hair stylists, no such vocational licensing requirements are yet on the books for pet groomers. (But stay tuned—this is a hot and controversial topic among groomers.) Until it happens, it's easy for unqualified groomers to set up shop, and if they do a bad job, it reflects poorly on every other experienced and capable groomer in the vicinity.

Becoming certified is one way you can set yourself apart as competent and professional. Certification sends a message to clients that you're not an amateur and that your skills have passed muster with a recognized certification organization. For this reason, once you've fulfilled all the requirements and passed the test, you'll want to use the certifying organization's logo on your promotional materials (including your business card), as well as on the door of your establishment.

Typically, grooming certification organizations require you to have several years of experience before you are eligible to take the exam, which usually consists of a written test and a hands-on demonstration of ability on live and possibly uncooperative pets. Exams are usually offered around the country, and at least one of the major certifying organizations offers accredited workshops to prepare you for the test.

You'll find information about the nationally recognized certification programs in Chapter 14.

you'll need different types of shampoo (all-purpose, flea and tick, bluing, etc.) and conditioner. Ribbon and elastic for making bows round out the list. About $150 to $200 should set you up.

- *Washer and dryer*. If you have the room, these can be worth their weight in gold (no more grimy pet towels in with your household laundry!). A reasonably priced pair from a retailer like Sears will run about $600. Buy used and save a lot.
- *Wet/dry vac*. A heavy-duty, 5-gallon, 5.5hp model runs about $70 at a home improvement store like Lowe's.
- *Mobile grooming van*. From a basic pull-behind trailer conversion that can be parked as a semi-permanent salon to a fully mobile van conversion salon with a bathroom, air conditioning, 100-gallon water tank, refrigerator, microwave, and more, these units run $35,000 to $50,000 or more.

You can see from the extreme price ranges given here that it's possible to equip your salon on a modest budget or by using every penny in your life's savings. However,

Menutes says that if you're starting a business from scratch and you don't have a lot of experience, it's not necessary to go for the high-priced tools like $400 scissors. "You won't appreciate them immediately," she says. "What would be a better use of your money are tools that can cut down on hand fatigue while giving a better cut, like $200 clippers and one or two basic clipper blades."

And one more thing to consider: Although grooming is a hands-on business that relies on fairly low-tech equipment, you may find that high-tech business management solutions—aka computer software—can make your office and salon administration a little easier. There are a number of software packages made just for groomers that you might wish to investigate. You'll find them listed in Chapter 14 and the Appendix.

A Day In the Life

There will be a number of other tasks that have nothing to do with clipping and snipping that nevertheless will have to be done on a daily basis to keep the business running. Among them are:

- *Salon management.* This will include everything from answering the phone, making appointments, and greeting customers to meeting with prospective clients who want to see your operation for themselves before they entrust Rover to your care. If you decide to sell retail products, you'll have to stock the shelves and artfully display the merchandise in your salon. Collecting cash and processing credit cards also will be an integral part of your workday.
- *Office management.* As the top dog in your business, you'll be in charge of opening the mail, making calls to the companies that supply your shampoo and other products, managing the books, making estimated tax payments, and handling numerous other business tasks that crop up.
- *Purchasing.* In addition to those pet products just mentioned, you'll also be in charge of buying office supplies like computer paper and cartridges.
- *Personnel management.* If you start as a one-person business—as many new grooming business owners do—this won't be an issue. But if you need to hire employees, you'll find they bring with them a whole new set of management responsibilities. In addition to scheduling and training, you may also have to resolve

Bright Idea

Send birthday and holiday cards to the pets you groom, preferably with a percent-off coupon enclosed. This not only charms their owners, but also it reminds them that Fluffy or Fido may be due for a grooming. Likewise, if a pet is ill or dies, a get-well or sympathy card will demonstrate your concern at a difficult time.

conflicts, soothe hurt feelings and referee disputes (always a problem when you're working in fairly close quarters). You'll also have a lot of financial liabilities when you have employees, which we'll discuss in Chapter 13.

- *Connecting with vets.* Any time you work with wriggling animals that are not exactly pleased to be on your table, there's the potential for accidents. You'll want to establish friendly relationships with one or two veterinarians in your area whom you can count on just in case medical care is needed. In addition, vets can be a great source of referrals, so it would be helpful to establish connections with them when you don't need emergency care, then cultivate those relationships. Pet sitter Jerry Wentz in Raleigh, North Carolina, did this successfully by first establishing a friendly relationship with the office staff. He dropped off chocolate and other small gifts along with his business card, then eventually asked to meet the veterinarian. By that time, the office staff loved him so much (or maybe it was the goodies) that they unhesitatingly made an appointment. This approach can work for you, too.

> **Bright Idea**
>
> Communication is key when meeting clients for the first time. Always spend enough time talking with them before you ever pick up your clippers so you understand completely what they want and what their expectations are. That way, your animal friends shouldn't have any "bad hair days" or disappointed owners.

- *Housekeeping.* There's nothing worse than shuffling through mounds of dog and cat hair on your way to bringing in the next furry client. Not only does this send a bad message to your human clients about the cleanliness of your business, the hair also can harbor fleas, mites, and other critters that can be passed along to incoming animals. So in addition to keeping the floor swept and the grooming tables, tubs, and tools disinfected after every grooming customer, you'll also need to keep both odors and the flea population under control. Experienced groomers will tell you it's a good idea to use a fogger product in your shop during flea season—usually as often as once a week. An ionizer and odor-killing sprays like Oust can help keep the air smelling sweet, and a disinfectant like Lysol that kills viruses, bacteria, and funguses should be used to sanitize all work surfaces. It's also a good idea to hire a professional cleaning service to come into your shop about once a week.

Getting Help

If you think all this sounds like a lot of work for one person, you're right—it is. That's why some groomers decide to hire staff to assist them—sometimes right from day one. In a perfect world, you would have a full staff of helpers, which would include:

- Salon manager to assist you with all the tasks in the preceding section
- Pet trimmer/groomer to clip and trim, as well as do finish trims on animals that are started by the assistant pet trimmer/groomer; also responsible for training
- Assistant pet trimmer/groomer to do pre-clipping on the face, stomach, feet, and tail in advance of the finish trim done by the full-charge groomer
- Pet bather to wash, brush, and comb pets; may also clip nails and inspect each pet for parasites like fleas and any lesions or cuts
- A receptionist to greet customers, answer the phones and explain services, receive pets and escort them to the holding area, ring the register and process credit card payments.

Stat Fact

Industry experts say that once your client base reaches about 1,500 clients, you seriously need to consider hiring a salon manager to assist with business management. This frees you up to concentrate on clipping and snipping (if that's your first love) rather than overseeing shop operations, meeting with grooming supply salespeople, and other less interesting tasks.

As you no doubt expect, the more skilled the employee is, the more that person will earn. It's pretty typical in this industry to pay groomers a commission (often as much as 60 percent of each grooming fee), although bathers and receptionists usually earn an hourly wage. The salaries paid vary by region. In Virginia, for instance, typical hourly wages are $25 or more per hour for master groomers, $15 an hour for assistant groomers, and $7 to $11 for bathers. A receptionist might earn $7 an hour.

Setting Prices

The most common way to charge is by the breed, since the amount of time you spend will vary from one pet to the next. Since many groomers prefer not to publish their prices, it can be difficult to get a feel for what the market will bear without calling groomers in your area and discreetly polling them. However, PetGroomer.com publishes an annual Pet Grooming Business Owners survey with results compiled by geographical area, and while they warn that the prices are not to be used to calculate or set your own prices, the survey results will give you some insight.

For instance, according to one of their recent surveys, the overall average grooming service fee by region was:

- *Eastern*: $39.50
- *Central*: $35
- *Mountain*: $36.25
- *Pacific*: $38.25

These prices were up to 2.25 percent higher than the prices reported in the previous year's survey. By comparison, the survey also indicated that a "no pattern" complete grooming for a standard poodle was:

- *Eastern*: $62.50
- *Central*: $48.75
- *Mountain*: $49.50
- *Pacific*: $55.25

Add-on services also make prices go up. Flea baths, tooth brushing, and dematting for extremely matted pets are charged as extra services and can range from low (say, $10 for anal gland expelling) to high (around $50 per hour for hand-stripping or dematting an exceptionally tangled coat).

To help figure out prices, Menutes recommends checking out the demographics of the area and the average age and income of the people who live there. It also helps to find out the prices at the next closest shop to make sure you're not too high—or too low.

And speaking of higher prices, even though mobile businesses offer the same services as site-based salons, their prices tend to be a little higher because of the convenience of bringing the salon right to the pet, because they have significant nonbillable time due to drive time between clients, and because they service fewer pets in one day. Wag'n Tails says it's common for mobile businesses to mark up services $15 to $20 or more.

Another way to charge is to set an hourly rate for your services. Customers generally prefer this method because they'll know exactly how much they'll be charged for, say, a three-hour service. However, unless you are a fairly experienced groomer, you may find it difficult to estimate exactly how long it will take you to perform that service—depending on the condition of the animal's coat, it could take you much longer or shorter than the amount of time you've quoted.

No matter which price structure you choose, your goal should be to determine first how much money you'd like to make, then set a price that allows you to cover your expenses and make an operating profit. An accountant can help you run some numbers and determine what that amount should be.

Startup Costs

Now that you've seen estimates of what the basic materials costs will be to start a grooming business, try your hand at estimating your own costs. Toward that end, take a look at the "Sample Startup Costs" on page 52, which lists expenses for two hypothetical grooming businesses: Barky's Canine Coiffures, which is a one-person sole proprietorship with low expenses, and Molly's Snip and Clip, a high-end S corporation that has a full-time owner and two part-time assistants (one assistant groomer and one bather who each work 20 hours per week). Then use the worksheet on page 53 to pencil in your own projected costs. Other information you'll need for this worksheet, including the cost of professional services, advertising, and other business expenditures, can be found in upcoming chapters. Menutes says it's possible to start a homebased salon with only about $5,000, which will get you the basics necessary to launch the business. Weekly supplies (shampoo, et al) will run in the $50 to $100 range.

Sample Startup Costs

Item	Barky's Canine Coiffures	Molly's Snip and Clip
Mortgage (first six months)	$0	$3,900
Grooming equipment, tools, supplies	$2,377	$6,494
Office equipment, furniture, supplies	$985	$3,415
Business licenses	$20	$20
Phone (line installation charges)	$40	$40
Utility deposits	$0	$200
Employee wages and benefits		
(first six months)*	$0	$8,160
Groomer apparel	$25	$100
Magnetic sign	$60	$60
Startup advertising	$100	$200
Legal services	$200	$900
Insurance		
(professional liability, annual cost)	$500	$500
Market research	$250	$1,000
Membership dues	$75	$175
Publications (annual subscriptions)	$50	$50
Online service	$20	$20
Website design	$800	$1,500
Web hosting, domain name	$90	$90
Subtotal	$5,592	$26,824
Miscellaneous expenses (roughly 10 percent of subtotal)	$550	$2,700
Total	**$6,142**	**$29,524**

**Two 20-hour/week assistants: assistant groomer at $10 per hour; bather at $7 per hour*

Startup Costs Worksheet

Item	Cost
Mortgage (first six months)	
Grooming equipment, tools, supplies	
Office equipment, furniture, supplies	
Business licenses	
Phone (line installation charges)	
Utility deposits	
Employee wages and benefits (first six months)	
Groomer apparel	
Magnetic sign	
Startup advertising	
Legal services	
Insurance (professional liability, annual cost)	
Market research	
Membership dues	
Publications (annual subscriptions)	
Online service	
Website design	
Web hosting, domain name	
Subtotal	
Miscellaneous expenses (roughly 10 percent of subtotal)	
Total	

5

Pet Food

While no business can be considered truly recession-proof, a pet-food business may be the next best thing. After all, "dogs and cats have to eat and people have to buy food year-round," explains internet pet-food retailer John Zambelli of Elmwood Park, New Jersey. "There are no peaks and valleys in this business like with traditional retail stores."

Because of this ready-made market, the pet-food industry was expected to ring up $14.5 billion in 2005, according to APPA, up slightly over 2004 and during a time when interest rates were rising, massive hurricanes had crippled parts of the South, and gasoline prices were soaring. In fact, market research company Business Communications Co. predicts an average annual growth rate of 3.6 percent through 2008, which would make the industry worth $16.7 billion in just a few short years.

There is commercial pet food available for virtually every kind of animal on the planet. Just the Purina Co. alone offers dozens of types of animal feed, from dog chow and cat chow to rabbit chow, cow chow, and pig chow—and who knows, probably aardvark chow. Pet food is available in many forms and formulations, such as all-natural human-grade foods and perishable raw foods (see Snapdata International's "U.S. Pet Food Segmentation" below for a breakdown of the industry). Pet treats also come in many varieties, from pig ears and rawhide bones for dogs to honey sticks for finches. There are even pet bakeries that specialize in homemade, nutritionally balanced treats. The list is endless and the variety is amazing.

Because there is so much variety, many pet-food business owners choose to specialize in a certain type of food. Two of the entrepreneurs interviewed for this book specialize in natural diets for dogs and cats, while another established a business to manufacture a healthy raw pet food.

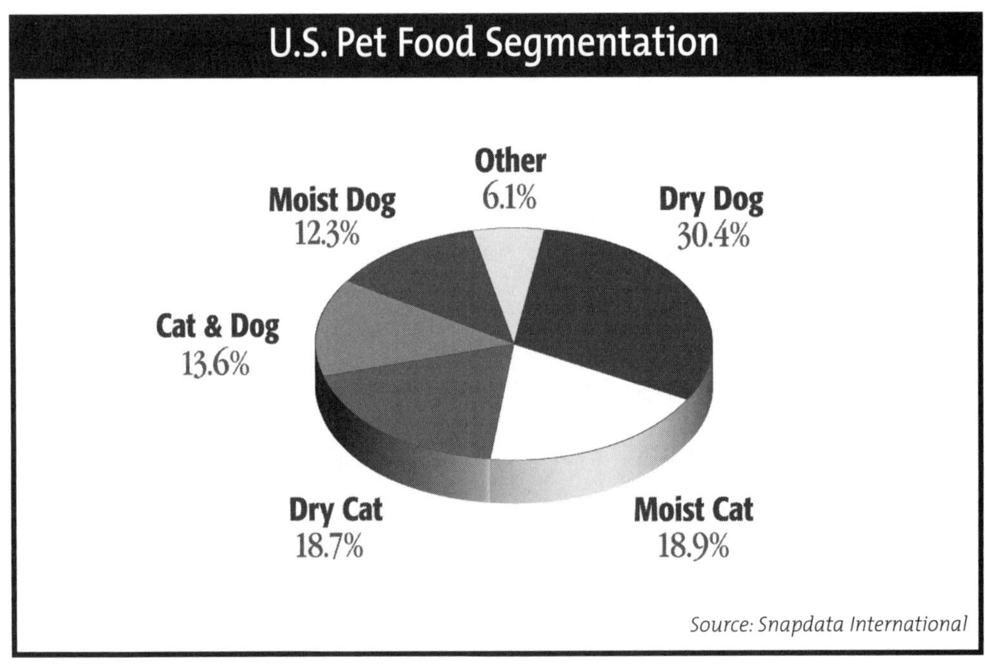

The Choices

There are a number of different ways you can get into the pet-food industry:

- *Bricks-and-mortar store*. This is the traditional type of business, with pet food stocked on the shelves of a commercial building or other retail space. Most pet-food stores of this type cater to small animals like dogs, cats, birds, hamsters, and so on, and carry additional products like pet treats and toys. In rural areas, it's not uncommon to find feed stores that carry livestock vittles, although for the purpose of this book we'll assume that you're planning to sell food for domesticated animals.
- *Internet store*. This is an economical way to do business because you can run a virtual store from your home and store product in your basement or any other dry, cool place you have available. By taking this route you (or your fulfillment center) are responsible for filling the orders that come your way, from processing the order and checking credit to packing and shipping.
- *Drop-shipping*. This is an even more economical way to get into the industry, because not only can you run the business via the internet from your home, but also you don't have to store any inventory. Rather, you forward your customer's order for dog or cat food (or whatever else) to the manufacturer, which ships it for you directly to the customer. You usually have to enter into a distributorship arrangement to be able to drop-ship, which basically means you become an agent for the manufacturer. When you make a sale, you collect the money, handle the paperwork to get the order to the manufacturer, then earn a percentage of the sale as a commission. For instance, Flint River Foods, a dog- and cat-food manufacturer, pays a 19 percent commission to its distributors on each pet-food sale. Many companies offer this type of distributor arrangement, and pet-food business owners like John Zambelli say it's an ideal arrangement, especially if you don't want to start out with any inventory.
- *Pet-treats bakery*. This type of business can be run in a bricks-and-mortar location or via the internet. Be aware that there's more to making doggie treats than just whipping up a batch of biscuits and tying up the packages with pretty bows. Treats (like other pet food) should be nutritionally sound, and because they may be made of perishable ingredients like

> Tip...
>
> **Smart Tip**
>
> To carve out a distinctive spot in the pet-food hierarchy, consider selling a niche product. For instance, since the organic, holistic, and natural pet-food markets are strong now, you might try promoting cat food that includes cranberries to bolster urinary-tract health or a line of kosher pet food.

eggs and cheese, they may require special handling and storage. But if you have any expertise in pet nutrition, this could be the business for you. If you've never made a dog chew before but think it could be your life's work, check to see if your local university has an animal sciences program. You should be able to hook up with an animal nutritionist there who can help you formulate the recipe. A veterinarian who offers specialized diagnostic services and treatment beyond your average pet vaccinations and neutering services also may be able to refer you to someone qualified.

Want to avoid this step entirely? Then purchase treats from a talented and competent baker, mark them up, and sell them yourself over the internet. That's exactly what Santa Fe, New Mexico, upscale pet products retailer/wholesaler Diane Burchard does. The all-natural, fresh-baked treats in her doggy deli are produced by a dog-treat baker in town in the shape of petit fours, tacos, hot dogs, burgers, and French fries. The local dogs (and their owners) literally sit outside the door for free snacks, and Burchard rewards them with a "Frequent Chompers Club" card that gives buyers one free 12-ounce package of dog treats after they buy a dozen bags.

- *Pet-food manufacturing*. OK, this type of business is not for everyone, largely for the same reason that a pet bakery is a more complex business to run: Namely, you need to have pet nutrition expertise or hire someone who does. But if you really want to be a manufacturer, there's no need to buy a factory. Instead, look for a manufacturer who will work with you to make your product. That's what Leonard Green in Woodbridge, New Jersey, did. This entrepreneur already had 13 other companies when he started The Blue Buffalo Co. in 2002; the gourmet pet-food business now grosses $6 million a year and employs 30 people.

Still, your startup costs as a manufacturer will be higher than for the other types of businesses mentioned in this book. Green's startup was $100,000, driven by a huge first order from PetSmart, although it is possible to do it for far less, depending on what you wish to accomplish.

Some pet-food business owners—especially those who specialize in raw-food diets—do manufacture the food they sell. Jennifer Boniface, the Temple Hills, Maryland, entrepreneur, does just that. After a foray into pet nutrition consulting, during which she persuaded well-meaning pet owners to prepare raw food for their pets' meals as a way to address health problems, then didn't

Bright Idea

Consider offering a few add-on impulse products with your pet-food line to increase the dollar value of sales. For example, John Zambelli of Elmwood Park, New Jersey, sells catnip, flea collars, and other nonfood items on his website to complement his natural pet-food line. You'll be surprised how fast even small add-on purchases will add up.

Beware!

In many states, you must obtain a commercial feed license if you wish to manufacture or distribute commercial feed, including pet food. The cost of the annually renewable license usually is nominal. For more information, contact your state's department of agriculture.

see her clients following through, she realized she could do it for them—and a new business was born. She made her first product, Pupplements (a nutritious treat), in her kitchen, then graduated to manufacturing in a facility owned and operated by her company. The rest is, as they say, history, but make no mistake about it, it's a big job. The manufacturing process includes receiving and inspecting raw materials, prepping them, making the frozen food, and cleaning up. Processing orders, shipping, office administration and personnel management (she employs five people to assist with the manufacturing process) rounds out the process of bringing the product to market.

"Our private facility is FDA registered, inspected, and approved for pet-food manufacturing," Boniface says. "We also own our own equipment, and every bit of raw food and treats we sell is produced right here on our own premises. Control over quality and whether or not recipes are followed correctly are far too important to me to place in someone else's hands where I can't personally see what is going on at any time I wish."

A Day in the Life

While your ultimate goal is to sell pet food or treats, there will be a number of tasks you'll have to do to get to that point where you're actually putting the food in the hands of your customer. For example, a typical day in the life of a pet-food business owner may include:

- *Handling office administration.* You're the chief cook and bottle washer when you start up a business, which means you'll be in charge of every little thing, like answering the phone, opening the mail, making calls to suppliers, checking product against invoices, reconciling your accounts, and handling the other 512 things you'll need to do to keep the business running.
- *Purchasing.* Your business will need various tools to run efficiently, including office supplies and the actual products you'll sell to your client, whether you have them on hand in your own storage area or you're drop-shipping.
- *Finding suppliers/wholesalers.* Because your business will continue to grow and evolve throughout its lifetime, your supplier list will have to grow as well. Companies come and go, and you'll not only have to replace those that go out of business, but you'll also want to keep up with the latest nutritional trends and offer the newest products. We'll talk more about finding product suppliers in Chapter 12.

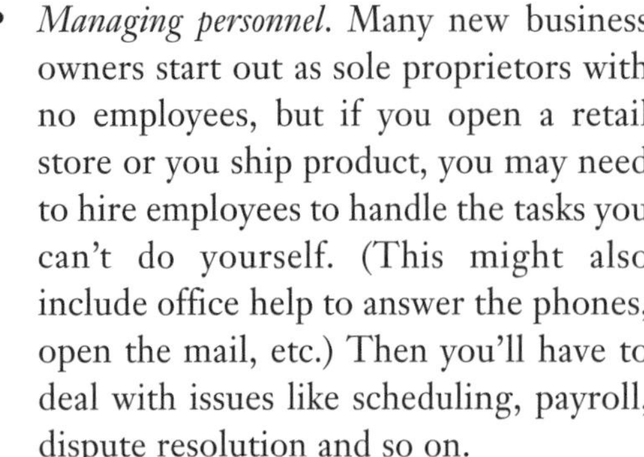

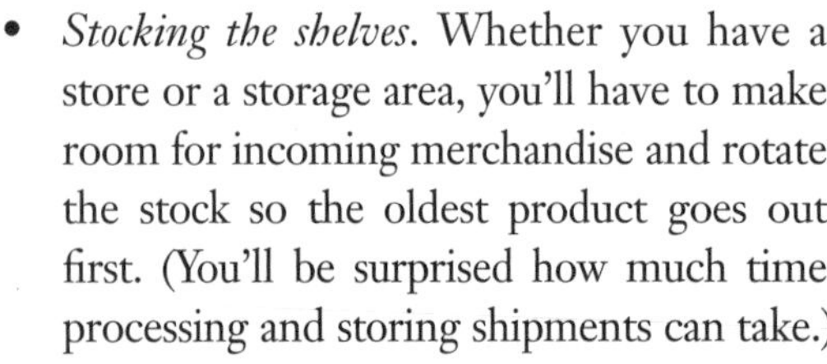

- *Managing personnel.* Many new business owners start out as sole proprietors with no employees, but if you open a retail store or you ship product, you may need to hire employees to handle the tasks you can't do yourself. (This might also include office help to answer the phones, open the mail, etc.) Then you'll have to deal with issues like scheduling, payroll, dispute resolution and so on.
- *Stocking the shelves.* Whether you have a store or a storage area, you'll have to make room for incoming merchandise and rotate the stock so the oldest product goes out first. (You'll be surprised how much time processing and storing shipments can take.)

Stat Fact

Industry experts say that the next hot trend in pet products is private-label brands, and independent retailers are finding ways to manufacture these products. The Private Label Manufacturers Association says store brands now account for 11 percent of cat food and 12 percent of dog food, and people are buying them in droves.

- *Overseeing production.* Obviously, this applies only to businesses that manufacture food products. If you have a dog-treat bakery, you may actually be doing the production work; more likely, if you start a manufacturing business you'll be inspecting your employees' work or the work of the manufacturer you use to keep a close eye on quality control.

  And by the way, entrepreneurs like Leonard Green will tell you that product testing needs to be an important part of the product development process. Recently his company was preparing to launch its newest product, sushi for cats. "It looked nice, the package looked nice, but we tested it and cats didn't like it!" Green says, laughing. "Since cats couldn't tell us why, we went back to the drawing board. The product is so unique, all we had to do is get cats to like it and people would pay a premium for it. We tweaked it and a year later, we were able to launch it."
- *Marketing and advertising.* This is crucial for the success of your business and requires planning and insight. We'll talk about techniques you can use to spread the word about your company in Chapter 15; for now, suffice it to say this is an ongoing process that can take a significant amount of time.

On the Web

As previously mentioned, it's possible to launch your pet-food business as an internet-based enterprise. This is advantageous for several reasons. First, you'll keep your operation costs low, since you can run the business from your home. Second, the sales side of the business is "open" 24/7, which is very appealing to people who like to surf at all hours of the day and night. Finally, you literally can reach consumers around the globe (although whether you actually want your reach to extend that far remains to be seen—shipping internationally can be challenging).

Product descriptions will be an integral part of your website. They should be as detailed as possible, with information like product package size and the major ingredients. If you're selling a particular manufacturer's product, chances are that manufacturer will already have stock language written that you can use on your site. But if you're starting a pet-food company, you'll have to write those descriptions yourself, and they can literally make or break a sale. After all, customers can't touch the product, so the words used to describe it must be precise and appealing. You may want to hire a freelance advertising copywriter to help you write the descriptions. If you're doing business in a part of the country that has a lot of product manufacturers (pet food or otherwise), you may even be able to find a writer who specializes in product or catalog copy. You can find such writers through local business organizations (like the chamber of commerce), university advertising departments, and the Yellow Pages.

Picture Perfect

Selling a product on the internet—even one as simple as pet food—is all about showing the customer what he or she is getting for the money. That's why using sharp and crisp product photos on your website is a must.

Since one bag of dog food looks pretty much like the next, you might want to try taking the photos yourself. But beware. Product photography is not easy, and you could come off looking like an amateur. (To see what effect bad photography could have on your credibility as a businessperson, check out the listings at eBay. You'll easily be able to identify the sellers who are true businesspeople vs. those who are simply clearing out their attic.)

If you need a professional photographer, look for someone who specializes in either product or "tabletop" photography, since there's a knack to doing both that, say, a wedding photographer may not have. But here's a heads-up: You may have to pay a professional as much as $300 per photo. As an alternative, you might want to check with the local art school to see if you can hire a student who will do a good job for quite a bit less money.

There's one final option for getting professional-quality photos. If you're purchasing food and treats from a drop-shipper, you may be able to obtain photos of the product package from the manufacturer. Often those photos will be provided to you at no charge, so it pays to ask.

For more advice and guidance on how to create a website, refer to Chapter 16. You can also check out Entrepreneur's *Start Your Own Online Business*, to learn how to take your business online.

Tip...

Smart Tip

When choosing pet foods to sell in your business, the Animal Protection Institute recommends avoiding food that contains "byproduct meal" or "meat and bone meal" because these are the less expensive sources of animal protein. Also avoid generic brands because they often contain poor-quality ingredients.

At the Store

If your intent is to open a retail location, your startup costs will be higher and your startup activities will take longer. But there's no doubt that opening your own store can be a very satisfying experience. It's a tangible manifestation of your ambition and drive—and if you're a people person who loves animals it's a great place to interact with customers and their pets face to face.

You might think that because your retail store will be filled with colorful bags of kibble and piles of canned food (or possibly occupied by a bakery counter filled with scrumptious pet treats) that you don't have to do much besides set up some shelving units and display racks before you're good to go. But retail selling is a science driven by factors like interior design, traffic flow, and ambience (yes, even if you're selling bird food!). For instance, a brightly lit, neatly stocked store will be more visually appealing and inviting than one stocked to the ceiling with jumbled-up products. In addition, retailers often place advertised products at the back of a store so customers have to walk past all the other inventory to get to the sale merchandise, which ideally will spur additional sales. For this reason, you should seriously consider consulting with an architect, interior designer or other retail-space design professionals to create the optimal shopping environment. See Chapter 11 for additional tips on designing a retail store; and for more in-depth information on how to launch your own retail store, check out Entrepreneur's *Start Your Own Retail Store*.

Storage Solutions

Whether you're selling on-site or online, you're going to need a place to store your pet vittles. If you'll be operating out of a retail location, the obvious thing to do is to designate a spot in your store as a stockroom. But if you'll be selling online and handling the shipping yourself, you'll need a place to store your inventory. Basements and other storage areas (even attic spaces or spare rooms) can be outfitted inexpensively with steel shelving purchased from the local hardware or home improvement store. If you'd prefer to keep the food out of your living spaces, you may find it helpful to rent a storage locker at a self-service storage park (just check to make sure the complex permits food storage—there could be restrictions against it because of the potential to attract unwanted pests). You'll find more specifics about storage options in Chapter 12.

Fulfilling Orders

Once you process orders, you'll have to marshal your forces and send out the pet food or treats in a timely fashion. To do this you'll need boxes and packing materials, a way to produce invoices and mailing labels (QuickBooks can do both), an inventory control system so you don't run out of products, and a shipping service to send the boxes on their way. While it's possible to hire a company known as a fulfillment house to handle all these tasks for you, most new business owners generally choose to do the work themselves—mostly because fulfillment houses can be pretty expensive. (One pet-business owner we know says it can cost $2.50 to $10 per item.) It's helpful to have a dedicated space located near your inventory storage area—perhaps a 6-foot table—where you can spread out all the materials you need. Then all you have to do is box up the food and/or treats, drop in a sales receipt and packing peanuts or newspaper, seal up the box, and call the shipper or cart it to the post office. The Postal Service and commercial shippers like UPS, FedEx, and Airborne will pick up your products right at your home office. All you have to do is sign up for an account with the shipper of your choice. You'll find contact information for several of these shippers in the Appendix.

Getting Help

While it's not uncommon for entrepreneurs to handle every aspect of business management themselves, there may come a time when you need assistance. The types of employees pet-food businesses commonly use include:

- *Clerical help*: to handle office administration, including answering phones and processing paperwork.
- *Fulfillment help*: to pack boxes, generate invoices, deliver packages to the post office, and so on.
- *Retail help*: to staff your store and greet customers, ring the cash register, bag merchandise, and stock shelves.

Additionally, if you're planning to manufacture your own products (either kibble or bakery treats), you'll need skilled labor to mix up the batches, bake it, and package it. If you're using a factory to make your product, you'll need a quality-control person to oversee manufacturing.

With the exception of the skilled labor, these types of jobs typically pay minimum wage (which

Tip...

Smart Tip

"Natural" pet foods preserved with Vitamins C and E are healthier than those that contain chemical preservatives like BHA, BHT, ethoxyquina, and propyl gallate, according to the Animal Protection Institute. You should also look for the "AAFCO guarantee" on the bag, which indicates that the food is complete and balanced as determined by the Association of American Feed Control Officials.

as of July 2009 is $7.25 an hour), or perhaps a little more. You'll probably find that if you up the wages a bit, you'll attract a dedicated employee who is more likely to stay with your company and not jump ship for a 25-cents-an-hour raise. Skilled labor comes at a higher price. Although wage figures aren't available specifically for pet-food manufacturing labor, the Bureau of Labor Statistics' *2007–2008 Occupational Outlook Handbook* says that in 2006, food manufacturing personnel averaged $13.13 an hour, while bakery workers averaged $12.63.

Setting Prices

Depending on where you purchase your products, you may find yourself locked into the retail prices set by the manufacturer. But if you have some wiggle room, you should take a scientific approach to determining prices. One way to do this would be to take all your expenses into account, including product, advertising/marketing, fulfillment costs, shipping and so on, and set your prices accordingly. Some small-business owners such as Zambelli start with the suggested retail price and mark the product up or down accordingly. However, Zambelli says that pet foods in general don't have as high a profit margin as other types of products. You're more likely to make your money on volume than on markup.

Jennifer Boniface, the Maryland pet-food manufacturer, keeps a close eye on costs to determine prices. "I keep a spreadsheet that analyzes my production costs for each item, which helps me keep track of the ups and downs that are a normal part of the marketplace," she says. "I also have a rough idea of how much profit I think is fair for this type of product, and I try to build that much into my final retail price. Once I have established what seems like a fair retail price, I work backward to take a percentage off for wholesale and another percentage off for the distributor to arrive at a final cost."

Earnings Potential

So how much can you earn in the startup phase of a new pet-food business? This is a hard question to answer because a lot depends on how successful your marketing and advertising strategies are when you launch your business into orbit around Planet Profit. Bob Vetere, COO and managing director of the APPMA, says the average weekly sales per employee in retail pet-products businesses (including pet food) is $2,600, of which 19 percent ($494) goes to payroll and benefits. The rest of the money goes to inventory, taxes, licenses, fees, and rent or leases. But just think: If you're drop-shipping, you don't have inventory costs (rather, you'll earn a percentage of sales). If you work out of your home, you don't have to shell out for building leases or rents. That puts more profit in your pocket.

You might be wondering if it's even possible to come anywhere near that $2,600 in sales per week. Not initially, Zambelli says. His first-year sales were in the thousands, which is why he started the business as a part-time venture. But when he came into the business full time, improved his product mix, and spent more money on advertising, the business took off.

Some new business owners choose not to take much out of the business so it has the best chance of growing and succeeding. Boniface, for example, jokingly says that everyone else at her company makes far more money than she does because she sinks all the profits back into the business. "I think to be successful, you have to realize that it takes money to make money," she says. "I would feel guilty if I was rewarding myself and spending lots of money on personal stuff instead of growing my business."

Startup Costs

Now that you have a bird's-eye view of what it takes to start a pet-food business, you can figure out how much scratch you'll need to fund it. If you're launching a homebased internet or drop-ship business, your office costs will be fairly low. Basically, you'll need office equipment and supplies, money for advertising and shipping supplies, and incidentals like accounting services and website design/web hosting (see Chapter 10 for a detailed list). You'll also need startup inventory, which for a pet-food business might be $4,000 to $5,000. But if you're opening a retail store, your costs will be higher because you'll probably need more inventory, plus you'll have a lease or mortgage payment, and numerous other costs associated with a store.

To estimate your startup costs, take a look at the "Sample Startup Costs" on page 66, which gives typical startup costs for two pet-food companies: a fictitious online pet-food business called FurandFinFood.com—a sole proprietorship with one employee (the owner)—and a retail store called The Doggy Diner—an S corporation that has one full-time employee (the owner) and one part-time retail clerk. You'll also find a worksheet on page 67 that you can use to project your own startup costs.

Fun Fact

A recent study by the American Animal Hospital Association shows that 98 percent of respondents would risk their own lives for their pets, while 45 percent said their pets listen to them better than their significant others! No wonder more of today's pet owners are so willing to buy holistic and human-grade pet food at any cost.

Sample Startup Costs

Item	Furand FinFood.com	The Doggy Diner
Mortgage (first six months @ $1,000/mo.)	$0	$6,000
Startup retail inventory	$5,000	$50,000
Startup manufacturing costs	$0	$0
Fulfillment	$0	$0
Office equipment, furniture, supplies	$985	$3,415
Business licenses	$20	$20
Phone (line installation charges)	$40	$40
Utility deposits	$0	$200
Employee wages and benefits (first six months)*	$0	$4,224
Startup advertising	$2,000	$3,000
Legal services	$200	$200
Liability insurance (annual cost)	$500	$1,500
Market research	$250	$250
Membership dues	$0	$1,500
Publications (annual subscriptions)	$0	$0
Online service	$20	$20
Website design	$800	$800
Web hosting, domain name	$90	$90
Subtotal	$9,905	$71,259
Miscellaneous expenses (roughly 10 percent of subtotal)	$1,000	$7,126
Total	**$10,905**	**$78,385**

**20-hour-per-week employee at $8 per hour, plus benefits at 10 percent of salary*

Startup Costs Worksheet

Item	Cost
Mortgage	
Startup retail inventory	
Startup manufacturing costs	
Fulfillment	
Office equipment, furniture, supplies	
Business licenses	
Phone (line installation charges)	
Utility deposits	
Employee wages and benefits (first six months)	
Startup advertising	
Legal services	
Liability insurance (annual cost)	
Market research	
Membership dues	
Publications (annual subscriptions)	
Online service	
Website design	
Web hosting, domain name	
Subtotal	
Miscellaneous expenses (roughly 10 percent of subtotal)	
Total	

6

Upscale Pet Products

When Elizabeth Taylor started putting diamond clips in her Maltese's "hair" and other Hollywood celebrities began carrying their pooches around in designer satchels, a lot of people shook their heads in wonder at the eccentricities of people with too much disposable income. But savvy entrepreneurs recognized the beginning of a lucrative trend, and the upscale pet-products industry was born.

According to *Pet Age* magazine, more than six out of ten U.S. households, or 64.2 million, own at least one pet. Not all these households have designer pet strollers on the driveway or marabou-trimmed beds in the master bedroom, but enough people were buying products to pamper their pooches and kitties to make the pet-supplies industry a $5.86 billion market in 2003. Market research company Business Communications Co. predicts that by 2008, pet supplies will be a $7.05 billion industry, with an average annual growth rate of 3.8 percent. And while there are no statistics available specifically on the upscale pet-products industry, it's safe to say that the people who are selling these products are taking a big bite out of that prosperous market.

Fun Fact

Designers that have segued into the luxury pet market include Burberry, Coach, Chanel, Gucci, Louis Vuitton, Prada, Ralph Lauren, and Tiffany & Co. Even Harley-Davidson makes spiked leather dog collars and shirts. Market research company Dillon Media attributes this trend to the whims of empty nesters, couples without children and other young professionals who consider their pets to be family members.

Upscale pet products run the gamut from the sublime to the sometimes ridiculous. There are ferret hammocks, faux mink dog blankets, and cashmere sweaters, Halloween costumes and Santa suits, and plush beds shaped like Fabergé eggs (the latter is the charming creation of one of the entrepreneurs interviewed for this book). Butter-soft leather tote bags made by famous designers and inhabited by tiny dogs are frequently seen on the arms of starlets and well-heeled consumers alike. There are even tiaras and pearl necklaces, strollers, and car seats. Other upscale pet products now in demand include jewelry (both barrettes and necklaces), wedding dresses and tuxedos, fashion eyewear, elaborate cat condos, stairs and ramps for elderly pets, pet toys and massagers, apparel (sweaters, dresses, and T-shirts), collars, and leashes.

Despite the proliferation of upscale pet products, this really is an industry in its infancy. While there have always been a lot of companies that sold pet products, as recently as 2001 there were very few offering upscale pet fare. Since then, there has been an explosion in the number of companies that sell these pricey products, which has made the industry much more competitive. But if you're a committed pet lover who believes there's a need for what some may consider fripperies, this is an industry in which you can make a good living.

Making Your Mark

There are several ways you can tap into the upscale pet-products industry:

- *Retail store*. In this type of business, you'll buy products from a wholesaler, mark them up, and sell them in your own store. Going the retail route requires a fairly substantial investment, not only in terms of inventory but also for building costs. You'll probably also need employees to help run the store because there's no way you can be there every minute and still hope to have a life.
- *Wholesale outlet*. In this case, you supply products to boutiques and other retail stores (including online stores). This is how Santa Fe, New Mexico, retailer/wholesaler Diane Burchard started selling the pet coats she originally designed and sewed for her little white dog, Teca Tu (the namesake for her "happy little shop," as she calls it). She's still a wholesaler today, but she has turned the sewing over to others. She also uses a pottery studio to create ceramic bowls, a leather belt maker to make pet collars, and even a co-op in Bolivia for hand-knitting sweaters.
- *Internet store*. This is a cost-effective way to enter the world of upscale product sales. You'll need inventory (which you'll buy at wholesale and sell at retail), and you'll have to store it somewhere and package it up as orders come in, but if you operate out of your home, you can save a lot of money on overhead costs. Alternatively, you can sell at wholesale prices to boutiques and other retailers.
- *Drop-shipping*. No room for inventory? Then a business that fulfills orders on a drop-ship basis may be the way to go. Drop-shipping means you strike a deal with a product manufacturer to ship orders from its warehouse or production facility directly to your customer. (This type of arrangement is also known as a distributorship.) You simply get the order, handle the paperwork to get it filled, and receive a percentage of the sale or a flat fee from the grateful supplier. This type of business works well if you're planning to sell really large or bulky items, like pet beds or cat condos, and don't have room to store them yourself.
- *Product manufacturing*. If you're a homebased entrepreneur, you may think this type of business would be outside the realm of possibility. But actually, if you have any design experience or proficiency and you're willing to learn about product manufacturing, this can be a viable business to look into. As you can imagine, manufacturing requires a lot more time upfront to get the business started. Susan Benesh, who runs the Columbia, South Carolina, pet-products manufacturing/wholesale company, says her business was on the drawing board for a year, while wholesaler/manufacturer Amanda Miller of Scottsdale, Arizona, says it took three years to lay the groundwork. You'll also have higher startup costs, but the potential to make a lot of money is excellent.

You don't have to establish your own factory to turn out products. You can contract with a manufacturer to make products to your specifications. That's what all four of the upscale product manufacturers interviewed for this book did when establishing their businesses. For instance, Miller uses a high-quality "people furniture" manufacturer to build her unique pet beds, which is a win-win situation because this company makes her products with the same care and quality as its own. Once you have a manufacturer relationship, you can sell products on a website, advertise in pet-products trade publications, or sell at trade shows.

Just be sure you have products to sell when you get to that point. Exton, Pennsylvania, products manufacturer Joyce Reavey went to her first H.H. Backer trade show—the industry's largest—with just prototypes of her pet beds and brochures to hand out but no production to back her up. "I had read you should test the market before you start manufacturing, but the stores at that show were hungry for product and wanted the beds immediately," she says. "I lost a lot of sales because I didn't have any products ready to ship. Even though it may seem risky, you need to invest in production before you launch so you have something people can buy."

Still, remember that research, development, and manufacturing take time. Benesh says it can take 100 hours to develop a product, including shipping prototypes back and forth, trying out the products on dogs, and so on. "But," she adds, "I love it!"

A Day in the Life

Of course, running an upscale products business involves more than just picking out or manufacturing cool toys and market-testing them (with the able assistance of your own precious pets, most likely). There are a number of tasks you'll have to undertake on a daily basis to keep the business running smoothly and efficiently:

- *Office administration*. As the nerve center of your fledgling pet-products empire, your homebased office (or possibly an office at your store or manufacturing facility) will be the place where all the action takes place, from talking to customers and suppliers to balancing the books, planning advertising campaigns, and, in short, handling all the various details involved in running a small business. For this reason, you'll want to outfit your workspace with appropriate office furniture and equipment so you can do your job efficiently. We'll detail everything you'll need in Chapter 10.
- *Product research*. With the internet, the process of finding new and exciting products—or inspirations for your own

Beware!

Outsourcing product manufacturing overseas can help you save on production costs because labor is cheaper, but you usually must have a pretty high volume to take advantage of those economies of scale. Also, freight and duty charges can be very high, and you won't always be able to speak to your foreign counterparts during U.S. business hours.

creations—is much easier. Business owners often spend hours a day just on keeping abreast of what's new on the market. You'll find an in-depth discussion on how to find product suppliers in Chapter 12.

> **Smart Tip**
>
> If you're interested in manufacturing products abroad but don't know where to get started, try contacting your local SCORE office (score.org). A partner of the SBA, SCORE is staffed nationwide by retired executives from all types of businesses. They'll either have the expertise you seek or be able refer you to the right people.

- *Purchasing*. Obviously your assortment of products will be the engine that makes your business machine go, so you'll have to devote a fair amount of time talking to sales and manufacturers' reps. (One entrepreneur says that once you've been to a trade show, you'll start getting cold calls from reps eager to sell you product for your bricks-and-mortar or internet store.) You'll also have to buy supplies for your office, like computer paper and paper clips, and packaging materials like boxes, packing peanuts, and sealing tape. Finally, you'll have to purchase the raw materials that will become your pet beds, towers, collars, and so on. This may entail traveling to places like the Los Angeles or New York garment and fabric districts, since there's no substitute for actually touching and holding the materials that will become your upscale products.
- *Personnel management*. Even if you're a one-person band, you may one day find yourself in need of help to ship out a big order or unload a truckload of holiday merchandise. If you have employees (either on your payroll or contract workers), you have to oversee their work. You'll have to come up with work schedules, process the payroll, and handle personality conflicts. You'll also have to find and actually hire these people, then do the considerable IRS paperwork that comes with having employees.
- *Inventory control and stocking*. Unless you're drop-shipping, the product you sell has to go somewhere, and that somewhere is the shelves in your home storage area or the display areas or stockroom in your store. This is tedious, physical work that many business owners prefer to delegate to someone else, but if you're on a tight budget you may find yourself hefting those pet beds onto the top shelf or hanging the pet sweaters on racks in your store.
- *Production*. If you decide to manufacture products to your own specifications, you'll be spending a fair amount of time on product design. You'll inspect and approve prototypes. Then when the assembly line fires up, you'll oversee production to make sure it meets your exacting standards. All this may take place in a city far, far away—like Beijing, for instance, or Hong Kong, which means you'll have to factor travel time into your schedule.

Holiday Magic

All right, class—what time of year puts a twinkle in the eyes of retailers from coast to coast? Why, the November-December holiday season, of course. According to a recent American Pet Products Manufacturers Association survey, nearly 154 million pet owners spent an estimated $2.6 billion on pet gifts during the 2005 holiday season, which means there's plenty of opportunity for you to take a bite out of the market.

When planning your pet business, make sure you time its debut well in advance of the start of that all-important holiday season. Since it takes a while for people to respond to advertisements (and repetition is key, especially for new product or new store launches), you'll want to have your ad campaign in full swing in the early fall, if not sooner. Ditto your key words if you're an internet retailer. Pick them early and start paying for them right away so you'll get as many hits as possible.

But don't just stock up on toys and clothes. Make sure you add two of the hottest pet products to your line: Holiday pet bags and greeting cards. Wholesaler CMI makes a gift bag with flashing LED lights and pictures of puppies, kittens and birds that "sing" Jingle Bells, while Avanti Press is offering a line of dog-themed cards.

Of course, Americans are so enamored with their pets that the gift giving doesn't stop in December. Pet lovers are showering their significant others with Valentine's Day presents, rabbit ears at Easter, and Halloween costumes. You'll want to include a mix of these products in your retail line to spur new sales for every gift-giving occasion possible.

- *Trade shows*. Speaking of travel time, you're likely to want to display your products at pet trade shows to generate interest, build name recognition, and hopefully make a buck. This can take up several days and thousands of dollars, but in the long run you may find it's time and money well-spent. Susan Benesh is a big believer in the importance of trade shows, but she doesn't attend them herself anymore. Instead, she uses a company that provides trade representatives to sell for her. The company earns a 25 percent commission ("Which is a great incentive to make sure they sell for us," she says), and she's a big winner, too—she attributes 30 percent of her sales to this arrangement.
- *Marketing and advertising*. Trade shows, ads in publications, news releases and your website are all viable outlets for promoting your business, and it's crucial

Stat Fact

There are nearly 7 million horses in the United States, of which nearly 3 million are recreational animals, according to the Horse Council. So if you have a yearning to offer luxury products for pretty palominos or the people who love them, you should have a ready and receptive market. And don't overlook the horseless—those who may not own a horse but wish they did can be big consumers of these products, too.

that you plan the scope and timing of these efforts carefully to maximize their impact. You're likely to be thinking about these tasks literally every business day—and, no doubt, even in your sleep.

On the Web

Because it can be expensive and more time-consuming to launch a new business in a bricks-and-mortar location, many upscale-products business owners prefer to sell their wares from a virtual store on the internet. The cost to establish such a store is quite low—usually no more than the cost of web hosting and website design, two things we'll discuss at length in Chapter 16; it beats shelling out for a mortgage payment and utilities, shoveling snow in winter, and repaving your parking lot every few years.

There are other significant advantages to having an internet store. It's always open, even when you're asleep or on vacation or at your daughter's dance recital. It also can attract orders from all over the world, which means you need to decide upfront whether you're willing to ship to Sri Lanka and deal with currency conversion issues and the complexities of overseas shipping.

Because your website is your conduit to sales, it's important to design a site that includes as much information about your products as possible. To begin with, you need to have excellent product photographs, both to tempt people to buy and so prospects can see exactly what they're buying. Benesh goes so far as to post a photograph of every product she sells in every color it comes in to make it as easy as possible for the customer to make an informed decision. (In fact, she has hundreds of photos on her site.) In addition, you'll also need detailed product descriptions that include product size, materials used, and shipping weight.

"Don't ever take your product photos lightly," adds Joyce Reavey. "They're your image, so they have to be crisp, clean, and professional."

Bright Idea

Susan Benesh in Columbia, South Carolina, spends a lot of time on major tasks like overseeing manufacturing, but she's such a stickler for quality control that she still checks every order before it's sealed up. She also boxes the high-end merchandise herself. "I like to see what's going out, which is why I'm working 80 hours a week," she says, laughing.

Since your website is your personal sales representative, you should make it look as professional as possible. Unless you have excellent photographic and copywriting skills, you should hire a product photographer to take the pictures and a copywriter or catalog copy specialist to write the descriptions. This will be expensive (Benesh says each product shot costs her $300), but it's money well-spent. Just think of it as an investment in your company's future—that you'll be able to write off as an expense on your business taxes, to boot.

If you're not convinced you need to go to that trouble and expense, especially when it comes to photography, take a few minutes to surf through the listings on an auction website like eBay. You'll clearly see the difference between companies that had their products professionally photographed and the people who are just trying to make a few bucks by listing stuff they no longer use. (This is especially obvious in the clothing listings, particularly when the item for sale is dark-colored. Without proper lighting, the garments look like blobs.)

To find a copywriter, contact local business organizations (like the chamber of commerce) or university advertising departments for leads, or check out the Yellow Pages. Likewise, you can find a professional photographer in the Yellow Pages. Look for one who specializes in product or tabletop photography. (No wedding photographers need apply! The skills don't transfer to product photography.) We'll discuss the overall process involved in creating a website in Chapter 16.

Once you've sold a product, your final task is to get it into the hands of your customers. There are companies called fulfillment houses that can handle the packing and shipping for you, but with all your other startup expenses you may find the cost prohibitive. (It can cost $2.50 to $10.50 per item for the fulfillment alone—postage is extra.) To go into the fulfillment business yourself, all you'll need are boxes and shipping materials like popcorn and sealing tape, as well as customer receipts and mailing labels (both of which can be produced using a software program such as QuickBooks), and perhaps a table on which you can spread all your stuff. A six-foot banquet table (which you can buy at a party-supply store) is a good choice.

> Tip...
>
> **Smart Tip**
>
> If you're concerned about using packing materials that will end up in landfills, try using earth-friendly materials like packaging peanuts made from natural vegetable starches. They're both nontoxic and biodegradable, and they dissolve on contact with water. Your customers will appreciate your concern for the environment, so be sure to tell them about it in your company literature.

A word of caution: Be careful to select the appropriate shipping supplies. Reavey says in the beginning she made the mistake of shipping five-pound pet beds in boxes meant to hold 30 pounds. The result? "I paid out of the nose on shipping costs," she says. "I eventually had to buy all new boxes in the right size, but that couple of inches saved me a lot of money."

Once you've packed up your customers' orders, you can either take them to the post office or a mailing center like The UPS Store, or call for a pickup. Companies like UPS and FedEx (and even the post office) will come to your home to pick up packages, but they may have minimum orders or extra weekly charges for the service. You'll also need to establish a shipping account with any of the services you use. Check out the Appendix for a list of shippers.

For everything you need to know to take your business online, you can also check out Entrepreneur's startup guide *No. 1819, Online Business.*

At the Store

As mentioned earlier, starting a retail store can be a time-consuming and expensive proposition. But some people are not cut out to be internet retailers—they prefer hands-on management and sales, as well as face-to-face interaction with people and their pets. If you're this type of person, you may be thinking about establishing a site-based pet boutique.

Probably the most important thing you need to consider when establishing a store (possibly even more important than inventory selection) is location. Since the type of products you'll be selling will be pricey—think $350 for a pet bed or $125 for a pet stroller—you can't put your store just anywhere. You have to go where the disposable income is, and if you do your market research (see Chapter 7) you will have a pretty good idea where that will be. But keep in mind that just because a location has a lot of high-end homes or a thriving local economy, it doesn't necessarily mean the area will sustain your business. For example, it's reasonable to assume that the denizens of the conservative Hamptons or old-money Grosse Pointe will not flock to your store—they may be too conventional and thus not likely to put pearls on their Persians. But a retail store situated in or near a luxury resort, in an upscale shopping area, or near a high-end day spa might indeed thrive. And, of course, locations with high disposable income and well-heeled visitors (like, say, New York City, Los Angeles, or Miami) should also be good choices for your business. So what can you do if this doesn't sound like your marketplace? To be frank, you might want

Stat Fact

A recent survey by the American Pet Products Manufacturers Association indicates that 100 percent of retailers believe competition from mass retailers threatens their business. So to make your mark, don't even try to fight with the big boys—emphasize the personal service and product knowledge you offer instead.

to start with an internet business to test the waters before you take the plunge into retail store ownership.

Retail-store design is of critical importance when you're selling upscale products. To begin with, ambience will be very important—your shop will have to be beautifully designed and merchandised. In addition, you can't use the garden-variety type of retail displays (i.e., adjustable painted steel shelving) when you're showcasing products with high price tags. Rather, you'll have to invest a significant amount of

Thanks for the Memories

As you have seen, pets are big business—and so are any products or services sold to commemorate, glorify, or otherwise enshrine them in their owners' hearts. Here are a few more ways you can tap into Americans' love affair with their pets:

- *Pet photography*. "People" photographers are usually game to photograph pets, too, but they'll be the first to tell you that it can be a challenging process. As a result, there's a real market for pet lovers who specialize in pet photography. And all pets are fair game—if it will sit long enough to smile for the birdie, you can photograph it.
- *Pet pics*. Speaking of photos, you can parlay photography into a business even if you're not a photographer by starting a pet T-shirt or jewelry business. There is equipment available that will allow you to transfer a scanned photo of a pet onto apparel, keychains, necklaces, and other jewelry. These items are affordable and especially in demand around the holidays.
- *Pet scrapbooking and memory books*. Scrapbooking continues to be a strong hobby, and now might be a great time to consider creating pet-themed materials, including stickers, paper, stamps, and other embellishments. This would be a perfect internet business, since the cost to mail these featherlight supplies will be fairly reasonable. Along the same lines, now would be a good time to offer a line of memory books that could be used to commemorate the life of a cherished pet.
- *Pet parties*. A birthday party for a beagle? An anniversary bash for a pair of ferret mates? It's all within the realm of possibility. Doggy day cares have been throwing festive parties for their charges for years, complete with dog-food cakes and party hats. There's a real potential to build a business around this concept, especially as many pets are considered family members.

money on your product displays, racks and sales counter. We recommend that you hire an architect, interior designer or other retail space design professional to help you create the optimal sales environment. If you can find someone who has experience designing for the upscale products market, so much the better. You'll find additional tips on designing a retail store in Chapter 11. You can also get lots of in-depth information on how to launch your own retail business in Entrepreneur's startup guide *No. 1821, Retail Store*.

Incidentally, Diane Burchard hit on a novel way to display her products when she started her retail business in 1995. She rented a window in a historic Santa Fe hotel that's a tourist attraction. Although the hotel is about four blocks from her shop, she says it's one of the best forms of advertising she has, and at $205 a month it's a bargain, particularly since it doesn't take long for people who see the display to spend $200 in her shop (her pet beds alone top out at $1,350).

Storage Solutions

Unless you are drop-shipping merchandise, you're going to need a place to store all the pet beds, tiaras, and other products you'll be selling. If you plan to open a store, you can designate a part of the space as a stockroom where you can stash your overstock. But if you're running a homebased internet store, you will have to carve out a storage space in your house. Depending on what you're selling, you may be able to appropriate a closet or pantry, then outfit it with shelving to store merchandise safely. Some entrepreneurs install shelving units in their home office or a spare room to serve as Inventory Central.

If you'll be selling large products—those designer pet beds or elaborate cat towers, for example—you're going to need more space. A lot more space. A dry basement or garage can fit the bill, or you might even consider adding a room onto your home, as Amanda Miller's partner, Cathy Miller, did. Her 1,000-square-foot "warehouse" is a bare-bones room with electricity, climate control, and little else. If that's not an option, you could rent a storage locker in a self-service storage park. For more specifics about these storage options, see Chapter 12.

Getting Help

Although you're probably starting your business with the intention of handling virtually everything yourself, there may come a time—possibly sooner than you think—when you'll need some help. (That point usually comes when you decide you need to sleep and have a personal life in addition to running your business.) If you're operating a retail store, you may need a sales clerk or two to greet customers, work the cash register, and stock shelves. When the business really ramps up, you may also need someone to help handle paperwork in the office and answer the phone. If you're doing business over the internet, your primary need will probably be for people to help with order fulfillment and to cart packages to your shipper on the days when you don't meet the minimum number requirement. An office assistant who can answer phones, handle paperwork, and process orders can also be a big help when you're out on buying trips or overseeing production at the factory.

> Tip...
>
> **Smart Tip**
>
> When calculating costs and setting production schedules prior to launching your business, pet-products business owner Joyce Reavey recommends using the "three times" rule—everything will cost three times as much and take three times longer to produce than you thought.

As we've said, it can be very expensive to add people to your payroll. In addition to paying a fair wage (probably minimum wage or a little more for the types of jobs outlined here), you also have to pay a whole bunch of employment taxes and file paperwork when sending your payments off to the appropriate taxing authority. For these reasons, many business owners opt for contract labor rather than regular employees. Benesh, for instance, uses three part-time contract workers on an as-needed basis, both because she doesn't have a steady stream of work and because she doesn't want to keep up with the paperwork required by the IRS when it comes to employees. Even so, there are some strict IRS definitions about what constitutes a legitimate employer-contractor relationship. For more guidance on this subject, see Chapter 13.

A final option for finding help is to contact a temporary staffing agency. It can be expensive to hire these temporary workers—you'll usually pay $3 to $5 hourly or more above minimum wage, depending on your location, even for entry-level workers. However, on a short-term basis, this can be a good option for finding qualified and prescreened help. An added bonus is that if the person works out well, you can hire him or her after paying the agency a "finder's fee" that is usually equivalent to a percentage of the worker's projected income. We'll discuss these options and more in greater detail in Chapter 13.

Setting Prices

If you're manufacturing your own products, you'll have some control over the prices you charge. They should be based on an equation that takes into account all your expenses, from materials costs to packaging. But if you're purchasing products to resell, your retail prices will be based on the cost set by the wholesaler or supplier, plus a markup that covers your business costs and profit margin. Susan Benesh suggests looking at your costs, seeing what other companies are charging for similar prices, and splitting the difference. She says, "If you have a superior product, can bring it to the market faster than anyone else, and offer excellent customer service, you're in."

Earnings Potential

It's not uncommon for a startup upscale pet-products business to have gross revenues as high as six figures in the first full year of business. However, after ponying up for product, fulfillment, office management, insurance, and myriad other expenses required to run a business, the net revenue will be considerably lower—maybe even minuscule. This is why it's not unusual for startup entrepreneurs who have working spouses or significant others with health-care benefits simply to plow all the revenue back into the business for the first couple of years, which gives the business the best chance of success.

Susan Benesh, for example, takes just a small salary because her company is still in a growth curve. "If you want to take a salary immediately, the amount you take has a direct relationship to how much you want the business to grow," she says. Others, like Diane Burchard, depend on other income to make ends meet. When she started her business, she was a working mixed-media artist who had artwork in galleries around the country. The sales of that artwork helped to pay her monthly bills so she could sink everything else into the retail business.

This is not to say that you can't depend on your business for a salary. According to Bob Vetere of the APPA, the average weekly sales per employee in a retail pet-products business are $2,600, or $135,200 per year. Of that amount, an average of 19 percent usually goes to payroll and benefits, while 44.5 percent goes to inventory. The rest goes to taxes, licenses, fees, rent, and/or leases. Of course, if you're drop-shipping, you won't actually have money tied up in inventory; rather, you'll get a percentage of the amount of the sale. That all becomes pure profit. And if you're working out of your home rather than a bricks-and-mortar facility, you pocket the rent money as well. Or more likely, you'll put that money back into the business until it's on stable ground.

Obviously you won't spring right from the box earning that average $2,600 per week. It takes time to develop your market and get the word out. So until then, it's really important to have a nest egg equivalent to 6 to 12 months of living expenses to carry you through those lean early months. This can be money from personal savings, from a home equity loan, or from a business startup loan. Just be sure you have enough cash readily available (not locked up in long-term investments) so you don't have to shut down the business prematurely because you can't make ends meet. "This is what it takes if you want your business to grow," says Benesh. "If you want to take a salary immediately, your business will grow slower, so you might want to arrange for other financing like a bank loan to carry you through."

Some entrepreneurs find it works well to take a small regular salary but decrease the amount at certain times of the year according to seasonal demands. For instance, Joyce Reavey, who is part of a two-career family, takes very little out of the business in the summer when she's gearing up for the holiday season. "Summer is the bleakest time for

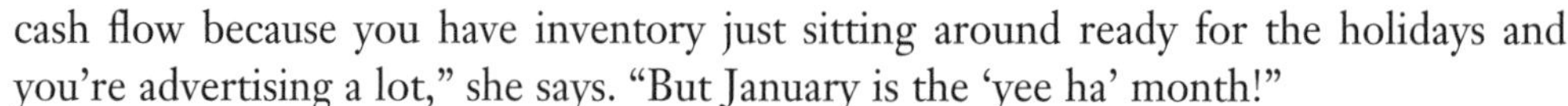

cash flow because you have inventory just sitting around ready for the holidays and you're advertising a lot," she says. "But January is the 'yee ha' month!"

Startup Costs

As you can see, there are a lot of varied costs involved in starting an upscale pet-products business. A homebased business owner will have the lowest outlay of cash since the overhead costs will be much lower than those of a site-based merchant. Susan Benesh, for instance, shelled out just a few thousand dollars for a "juiced-up laptop," as she calls it, and basic office supplies and equipment (including a color printer/scanner/fax machine). But no matter where you do business, your most substantial cost will be for the inventory you purchase or manufacture. If you're buying product to resell, you probably will need $15,000 to $30,000 in inventory to get started; if you're homebased, you could start for less. If you're going the manufacturing route, your startup inventory costs could be at least $30,000—or considerably more, depending on what you're producing. One of the entrepreneurs interviewed for this book says her startup inventory costs were $500,000, which included manufacturing, etc. Today, she's shipping 60 to 100 orders a day, so the initial outlay definitely paid off. Another entrepreneur launched her business with a loan from the SBA for $45,000, fortified by $5,000 of her own savings and $5,000 from her brother and sister-in-law—and she could have used more, she says.

Fun Fact

You never know when you might hit it big. Bob Vetere of the American Pet Products Manufacturers Association knows one entrepreneur who used a sewing machine to stitch gloves that remove pet hair simply by petting the animal. The product was featured on the *Today* show, and the entrepreneur, who started his company for $1,000, eventually sold it for millions.

To help you estimate how much you'll need for product and business operation expenses, we've included "Sample Startup Costs" on the next page that give the typical expenses for two businesses: The Pet Emporium, a one-person, homebased sole proprietorship that buys at wholesale and sells at retail from a website; and The Snazzy Pet, an internet-based corporation that manufactures the high-end products it sells. After looking over the sample, you might want to try your hand at estimating your own costs using the worksheet on page 84. We'll discuss a lot of the other costs you'll need to estimate, like advertising and website costs, in later chapters.

Sample Startup Costs

Item	The Pet Emporium	The Snazzy Pet
Mortgage	$0	$0
Startup retail inventory	$5,000	$0
Startup manufacturing costs and inventory	$0	$75,000
Fulfillment	$0	$0
Office equipment, furniture, supplies	$985	$3,415
Business licenses	$20	$20
Phone (line installation charges)	$40	$40
Utility deposits	$0	$200
Employee wages and benefits (first six months)*	$0	$7,680
Startup advertising	$1,000	$3,000
Legal services	$200	$200
Liability insurance (annual cost)	$0	$1,500
Market research	$250	$250
Membership dues	$0	$1,500
Publications (annual subscriptions)	$0	$0
Online service	$20	$20
Website design	$800	$800
Web hosting, domain name	$90	$90
Trade shows (attendance at 2 per year)	$6,000	$6,000
Trade shows (exhibiting at 2 per year) **	$0	$10,000
Subtotal	$14,405	$109,715
Miscellaneous expenses (roughly 10 percent of subtotal)	$1,440	$11,000
Total	**$15,845**	**$120,715**

**Two 20-hour-per-week independent contractors at $8 per hour*

***Booth cost $2,000; travel and expenses $3,000 per show*

Startup Costs Worksheet

Item	**Cost**
Mortgage	
Startup retail inventory	
Startup manufacturing costs and inventory	
Fulfillment	
Office equipment, furniture, supplies	
Business licenses	
Phone (line installation charges)	
Utility deposits	
Employee wages and benefits (first six months)	
Startup advertising	
Legal services	
Liability insurance (annual cost)	
Market research	
Membership dues	
Publications (annual subscriptions)	
Online service	
Website design	
Web hosting, domain name	
Trade shows (attendance)	
Trade shows (exhibiting)	
Subtotal	
Miscellaneous expenses (roughly 10 percent of subtotal)	
Total	

7

The Scoop on the Market

If you've ever been a buyer or a seller in the real estate market, you've probably heard the old cliché that "location, location, location" are the three most important factors that determine the price of a home or a piece of real estate. The same concept applies to your new pet-care business. Depending on which type of business you're starting, you'll need a location that's convenient for both you and your customers, that's visible enough to attract new business, and that isn't in competition with too many similar businesses.

The only type of business discussed in this book whose fortunes are not so closely tied to physical location is an internet-based pet-product business, since customers will not come to you—only their checks and PayPal payments will. But pet sitters, dog walkers, dog trainers, pet groomers, and providers of pet food and products, whether home-based or site-based, all must be concerned with location when setting up their businesses. To determine whether you can make a living in your chosen area, nothing beats targeted market research.

Market research involves identifying and understanding the needs of your customers, then creating a business to serve them. Here's a for-instance: Let's say you're a dog walker. If you want to set up shop in the Washington, DC, area, you'd be better off choosing Georgetown or Falls Church, Virginia, as the target for your midday dog-walking services rather than DC itself, since the latter has a lot of government buildings (and presumably not too many dogs), plus demographics show that the people who live there have less disposable income and therefore are probably more likely to walk their own pets. And what if Georgetown has ten times more dog walkers than Falls Church? Then you would likely be more successful doing business in Falls Church, where there's less competition.

The only way to know about these potential pitfalls and opportunities before you open your business is by doing some market research. This chapter will give you some doggoned good insight into what to consider and how to use market research knowledge to your best advantage. Please don't yawn and skip ahead to the next chapter. One of the main reasons why new businesses fail is because their owners failed to understand their market. Don't let that happen to you.

Setting Your Sights

There are three main things you need to determine upfront to give your business the best chance of success. You need to identify the people who are most likely to want and need your services; figure out whether your target market area can actually sustain the business; uncover any potential pitfalls that could derail your enterprise. Armed with this information, you must create a plan of attack that will improve the likelihood that your business will flourish.

To get started, study the demographics of the area you're targeting. Demographics refers to the specific characteristics that influence your potential customers' buying habits. For example, age is an important demographic to consider. If you are trying to set up that dog-walking business in an area with young families, you might be out of luck, since presumably they'll be so energetic, active, and short on cash that they'll prefer to walk their own dogs, thank you. Other demographics to consider because of their potential impact on that hypothetical dog-walking business include:

- *Income*. Do residents earn enough, on average, to warrant paying for a value-added service like dog walking? In addition, what is the local employment rate? If you have an area with high unemployment, it's obviously not a good place to base a business that provides a "nice to have" rather than a "gotta have" service.
- *Mobility*. How far do residents in this area travel to work on average? Lengthy travel time equals less time to walk the dog.
- *Educational level*. What is their highest level of education? It could be argued that more educated people would see the wisdom of paying someone to exercise their dog so they could do other things instead. In addition, people with higher education also may have higher level corporate jobs that take them away on business or keep them in the office for long periods of time—two more reasons why they might use a dog walker.
- *Home ownership*. Homeowners can have just about any pets they want, within reason, while people who lease apartments often cannot. So you'd target the homeowners.

> Tip...
>
> **Smart Tip**
>
> In addition to analyzing your competitors in terms of price (an important benchmark), also be sure to consider their location, the service they offer, the quality of that service or product, and the way they advertise. Studying these factors can give you insight into what strategies might work for your own business.

Other useful data to consider include the percentage of people who are employed full time (it's reasonable to assume they have more disposable income than part-time workers); the types of jobs they hold (you might want to target white-collar employees for the same reason); population growth (a city in decline is not likely to be a good market); and overall population, since cities or other areas with high-density business and residential districts are probably better markets than a rural community with one gas station and a post office. But if you think creatively, even that rural market could work out pretty well. For instance, if you add livestock care to your business mix you could have the makings of a prosperous business there after all.

It's actually pretty easy to gather all this information. The U.S. Census Bureau is the logical place to start—especially since you can access information online anytime and for free at census.gov. In addition, your local chamber of commerce, economic development office, utility companies, or state or municipal government office are all likely to have such information, and you'll probably be able to access it free of charge or for a nominal fee. In particular, the chamber of commerce can be a mother lode of

Bright Idea

An inexpensive way to gather insider information about customer needs is by conducting a focus group. Invite six to ten people to your shop or a neutral location and ask questions related to your product or service line. In a 90-minute session, you should be able to cover about five or six questions. To encourage participation, offer a small honorarium (say, $25).

information, since it usually conducts its own periodic reviews of local demographic trends and population growth, information that can be invaluable for your business. You may have to join the chamber for full access to the information, but it will be worth it, especially since you also can use the organization as a networking venue.

On Your Mark

While demographic information will tell you a lot, you'll also want to conduct a little market research of your own using both primary and secondary research tools. Primary research involves collecting data yourself—you ask prospective clients exactly what kinds of business services they'd want, as well as whether they would even consider paying for them in the first place. (Don't be surprised if a certain percentage of your respondents say they wouldn't pay for your services or products even if they cost just 10 cents. You can't please everyone—so focus on pleasing only those who indicate a sincere interest in your service or product.) Surveys conducted on paper or by phone (aka telemarketing) are examples of primary research tools. You also can collect primary research data through observation; for example, you can learn a lot by staking out the local pet store and casually observing the buying habits of pet-supply customers.

Secondary research consists of data collected by others, which you can analyze to come to some decisions about your own prospective business. Secondary research tools include all that demographic information we discussed earlier in this chapter, as well as information in authoritative industry publications.

Smart Tip

Tip...

An excellent source of demographic information is the U.S. Census Bureau's American FactFinder website at factfinder.census.gov. Just type in the city and state you're interested in researching, and you'll get a fact sheet with data like social, economic, and housing characteristics at no charge. Better still, the site is even easier to use than the Bureau's main website at census.gov.

Scoping Out the Market

Kick off your information fact-finding mission with a little primary research work by checking the Yellow Pages in your target market. Find out how many businesses like yours are already operating in the area. Is the area saturated with sitters or walkers or trainers or pet-product sellers, or does it look like there's room for one more (you)? Keep in mind, though, that not everyone who is operating a pet business will be listed in the phone book—you must have a business telephone line to be in the book, and not every small-business owner is willing to take on the not-inconsiderable expense. So there actually could be far more people operating your type of business than you think. But you can still get a grip on the local situation by looking at the book, then estimate high to include those folks who rely on word-of-mouth advertising rather than an ad in the big yellow book. And don't forget the chamber of commerce when you're trying to get a

Searching High and Low

To help you in your quest for market research information—both the primary and secondary varieties—check out the following SBA recommendations:

- *Analyze competitors' ads.* This is a great way to learn about what your competition perceives to be its target market, as well as its market position, product features, benefits, costs, and so on.
- *Surf the internet.* In addition to learning more about specific products or services, you may be able to get a gander at what your competitors are up to, as well as what they are charging.
- *Make personal visits.* Drop in on your competitors' location(s) to check out everything from employee/customer interactions to shop layout and displays.
- *Attend presentations.* If you hear that one of your competitors will be making a speech or presentation in your community, you should be in the front row to observe and ask questions.
- *Check out trade-show displays.* Besides learning which trade shows and industry events your competition considers important, you should stop by their trade-show booths or other displays for an inside look at what they're doing.
- *Devour industry- and business-related publications.* To get a well-rounded business education, read widely. Among the materials you should peruse are general business magazines, marketing, and advertising publications, local newspapers and business journals, industry and trade association publications, and industry research and surveys. Also be sure to search computer databases, including the business-only databases available at many public libraries.

handle on how many pet businesses are operating—they may be able to tell you without batting an eye, or you might be able to browse an online membership directory.

Next, call any pet-related businesses in your area that are not in the exact same business that you're exploring and ask what they think the demand might be for another player, as well as whether they think there's enough room in the market for a newbie. For instance, if you're a groomer, talk to the local dog trainers; if you're a pet sitter, call the pet stores; if you're a pet-products seller, call the kennel.

And no matter which business you're starting, you can certainly feel free to talk to veterinarians, since they probably won't be partial to any of the businesses. In fact, vets can be a great ally for a new pet-care business owner, so do whatever you can to forge a friendly relationship with them, up to and including asking them to recommend your services if one of their clients asks for a referral. By the way, vets actually may play another important role in your pet-sitting, dog-walking, dog-training, and pet-grooming businesses—namely that of savior, since there's always the possibility that a pet could be injured while in your charge.

While you're talking to these various business owners, you can even explore the idea of forming a partnership of some kind with them in the future, like dog walker and pet sitter David Lipschultz of Oak Park, Illinois, does. He attaches dog treats to business cards, heaps them in a basket, and drops them off at vet offices, groomers, and retail stores of all types. "It's an easy way to get a steady source of new clients," he says.

You should also Google your industry and find out what people are selling and what people are buying. This is how Columbia, South Carolina, wholesaler/manufacturer Susan Benesh gathered information before going to luxury dog boutiques and other stores to talk to the owners.

Straight to the Source

Go right to the people in your community who might be prospective customers and ask them what they think about what your new business will offer them. You can do this by surveying people in person or by mail, or by conducting a telemarketing campaign. Certainly the easiest way to survey people is by mailing them a questionnaire, which is also less expensive than telemarketing. (Incidentally, you also can use your questionnaire as a telemarketing script if you ever get to the point where you want to try that type of market research.)

On that questionnaire, you can ask as many questions as you'd like—but be reasonable. People are not going to have a lot of patience with a multiple-page questionnaire unless they perceive there's something in it for them when they fill it out (i.e., peace of mind when they need a pet sitter for that trip to Turks and Caicos). That's why some surveyors actually include a dollar bill or a money-off coupon with their surveys. Even such a small token can greatly increase response, according to experienced direct marketers.

If giving away Washingtons is too rich for your blood in the startup phase, just try to keep the questionnaire short (about one page) and to the point (with short answers and check-off boxes), and you should be able to get about a 1 percent response, which is considered good in the direct-mail industry.

> **Smart Tip**
>
> Market research should be done on an ongoing basis throughout all stages of your business's life, not just when you start up. Keeping in touch with customers is paramount for continued success, so be sure to schedule regular research campaigns—say, once every couple of years—to make sure you understand your target market's needs.

Because direct-mail questionnaires can be a little tricky to write, you might want to get some professional assistance. A good source of low-to-no-cost help is the business school at your local university. One professor we know of at a major state university charges $1,000 to write a survey questionnaire himself, but he's also been known to assign the questionnaire as a class project, then gives the surveys to the business owner at no charge (sans red ink). Alternatively, you could see if you can find a business marketing major who will do it for less. But try to get a senior—hopefully he or she will have a fair amount of experience creating surveys by then.

Survey questions should be short, to the point, and open-ended, meaning they can't be answered with a simple "yes" or "no." Here's an example of a closed-ended question:

- Do you ever buy gourmet cat food?

  ___yes ___no

No matter which answer the respondent checks, you haven't learned much. Wouldn't it be more useful to know what kind he or she buys? So here's an open-ended question:

- Which brands of gourmet cat food do you buy?

  _______name ________name ________name _______ other (specify)

A checkmark beside any of these choices gives you information that can be useful for determining which brands to carry in your inventory.

So what exactly should you ask in your survey? Anything relating to how you might want to run the business, from which hours would be good for a prospective client to the scope of products or services you should offer (i.e., does your target market want just dog-walking services, or would they also want someone to water the plants, change the cat litter, etc.?) and how much would they pay for your products or services. You should jot down a list of these kinds of questions before you speak to the person who will help you write the survey so you can be sure to cover every issue that's important to you.

Get Set

Once your questionnaire has been committed to paper, you're ready to mail it out to a randomly selected number of households in your target market area. To do this, you'll need to buy a mailing list. Such lists are available from any number of companies and organizations, including some that are right in your target market. (Remember that the next time you're tempted to enter a drawing for a Ford Expedition or a gym membership—your name and contact information will go into the company's database, which in turn can be sold to business owners who want to get their advertising message

Survey Says

If you really want to find out what potential customers think of your product or service idea and you like talking to people, go right to where they shop and conduct a mall intercept survey. Mall intercepts are widely used to capture information from a large and broad-based population. In fact, the Council of American Survey Research Organizations says that about 25 percent of all marketing research and 64 percent of personal interviews are conducted at the nation's malls.

Mall intercepts are conducted by approaching a certain number of people passing by and asking them questions from a prepared script. These surveys are valuable for a number of reasons. First, you can actually listen to what respondents have to say. Second, you can ask open-ended questions that will yield much more useful information than closed-ended yes/no responses. Finally, you don't have to invest much money to conduct them. Basically you need a clipboard and some paper surveys, although it does help to have a supply of small "rewards" to give to those who consent to be interviewed, such as candy bars, dollar bills, or even pet-food samples.

There are some disadvantages to intercepts, however. Because malls tend to be in major metropolitan areas, you're less likely to get input from people in smaller markets who also may be part of your target audience. Also, the sample can be demographically skewed, since mall shoppers tend to be young, female, and middle-income. Finally, it can be hard to get a random sample, because you may find many more people will turn you down than will talk to you.

Even so, mall intercepts can be a good way to gather primary research that can help you plan your marketing strategy. Just be sure to obtain permission from the mall management office before launching your survey.

out.) These lists are usually organized into categories according to demographics, which makes it easy for you to pick market segments such as heads of households aged 40 and up or couples with combined annual incomes of $80,000 or more.

Just about every company that has customer contact maintains a mailing list (there's gold in them thar lists), from local homeowners or realtor associations to daily newspapers. To find a very specific list (i.e., *Cat Fancy* subscribers or members of the Dogs Rule Admiration Society), flip through the pages of the *Standard Rate and Data Service* directory, published by VNU, or the *Encyclopedia of Associations* (Gale Research). You'll find copies of both in large libraries.

Mailing lists are typically rented for one-time use at a flat rate of anywhere from $40 to $100 per 1,000 names, which are available to you either on pressure-sensitive labels or CD-ROM. To be scientific about the sample you get, you should have the list compiler remove every nth label (as in 4th or 10th) from its master file until you get the number you want.

When producing the survey, make sure it's neatly formatted and that all the words are spelled correctly. (A grammar check is also recommended.) Then print it on high-quality paper (take it to FedEx Kinkos, OfficeMax, or somewhere similar) and insert the copies into envelopes with typed addresses and real stamps in the corner. (Both make the envelope look more like it contains correspondence and less like junk mail.)

Go!

Hopefully you'll receive a zillion responses to your questionnaires, and you'll have a pretty good idea of how well your new business will fare in your marketplace. Once you have that information in hand, your next step should be to do a little introspective thinking about where you want to take the business and what you hope to accomplish with it. An easy way to start the process is by writing a mission statement.

A mission statement is a brief description of the reason you're in business, what you hope to accomplish, and how you'll get there. One of the most famous mission statements in history is Pepsi's brief and concise statement, "Beat Coke." But while you'll probably need a few more words to describe your mission and purpose, you won't need as many as Jerry Maguire had—30 pages!—in the 1996 movie of the

Dollar Stretcher

The website ResearchInfo.com offers various free market research resources, including demos, freeware, and shareware you can use for everything from creating marketing surveys to analyzing data. You can access these tools at researchinfo.com/docs/software/index.cfm.

same name. If you recall, Jerry got himself fired over that mission statement because it was too honest, too critical, and too in-your-face. But Jerry had the right idea—and it's an idea you can copy.

Your mission statement should consist of a few sentences in which you describe your company's purpose and goals. It also should address who your customer will be and can include the qualifications you possess to make your goals happen. A simple mission statement for a pet-products business owner might say:

> Glamour Puss will provide one-of-a-kind and luxury daywear, bags, beds, jewelry, toys, and other feline products to Southern California's affluent pet owners through an online store. Excellent customer service and low overhead will result in first-year sales of $60,000.

Here's the mission statement John Zambelli, the Elmwood Park, New Jersey, pet-food business owner, uses:

> NaturesPet.Com is dedicated to providing its customers with the highest quality line of natural, nutritious and holistic products that enhance and extend the lives of their pets. It is our goal to promote the wellness of pets by not only providing natural and holistic products and information to pet owners but by also donating a portion of the corporation's sales to organizations that support the wellness and the ethical treatment of animals.

And here's the mission statement for Susan Benesh's wholesale/manufacturing business:

> To promote animal welfare and jobs creation through the sale of high fashion and luxury adornments for the cultured canine and the humans who love them.

Now, in case you're saying, "Why bother with a mission statement? I just want to click train German Shepherds!" consider this. You probably already know that committing your plan and goals to paper is a tried-and-true way to make them happen. Reviewing your mission statement periodically also can help make sure your business is moving in the right direction. For example, let's say you refer to your mission statement midway through your first year and realize that you've only earned $23,000 when you expected to be at $30,000, or half of your first-year goal. There would still be time to make adjustments to your business plan (like ratcheting up your advertising or running a clearance sale on merchandise that's not moving) so you can nudge those sales up and meet your first-year goals.

Now it's your turn to try writing a mission statement. There's a worksheet on the next page that you can use to generate some ideas and draft that all-important statement.

Mission Statement Worksheet

To draft a mission statement, answer the following questions:

Why do you want to start a _______________ business?

____

Who are your customers? (be specific) _______________

____

What product or service will you sell? _______________

Where is your market area? _______________

____

What will make your company different from the rest? _______________

____

What special qualifications and skills do you bring to the business? (include education and service/product skills) _______________

____

What is your financial objective? _______________

What is your vision for success? Where do you think you'll be in one, two, and five years? _______________

____

Using this information, write your mission statement on the lines below. But don't try to cram in all the above information—use what you perceive to be most crucial for setting a direction for your business.

Mission Statement

____

____

____

____

8

Paper Training

Here's where things start getting interesting. Up until now, everything we've discussed has dealt with ideas, planning, and due diligence. Now we'll get down to the business of actually establishing your very own business.

There are a number of things you need to do to stake out your place in the pet-business marketplace. Among them are establishing an office space where work can be done—even if you don't seem to have a lot of room to spare in your home—and creating a business plan, which is a must to keep your pet enterprise on track. You'll also need to choose a business name and register it with the appropriate local government entity, select a legal form of operation, and obtain any licenses and/or permits that are necessary in your community. (Professional licensing is not necessary to be a dog groomer, photographer, or any other type of pet-business owner—least, not yet; give the bureaucrats time.)

Home Sweet Home Base

One of the first tasks you should undertake when starting your business is to set up a physical space in which to do it. Whether you conduct your animal activities in your own home, your clients' homes, or a store, you'll need to have a dedicated space where you can attend to the behind-the-scenes tasks and paperwork related to your business. In most cases, that place will be an office in your home. Having a home office has several benefits. First, it helps keep your overhead and expenses to a minimum during your startup phase. It helps you stay solvent even when business is slow because you're not forking over precious operating funds for office rent and utilities. It also gives you a place to handle all those necessary administrative details without commuting to an office or having to stick to a traditional nine-to-five schedule. Imagine being able to do your bookkeeping or your advertising planning in the wee hours when your creative juices are flowing, and in your pajamas, no less. Is that a great life, or what?

There's one more important benefit of owning a home business: It's quite likely your home office will be tax-deductible, either on your business taxes or on your Schedule C if you're a sole proprietor. Since there are some IRS restrictions on what and how much can be deducted, you'll want to check with your accountant or income tax preparer to verify whether your home-office expenses qualify, but the chances are good. And by the way, you shouldn't be shy about taking the home-office deduction if all the expenses are legitimate. It used to be that this type of deduction raised a red flag for the IRS that said, "Hey, audit me!" But the IRS grudgingly loosened up its stranglehold on home-office deductions a few years ago, so small-business owners like you shouldn't be afraid to take every deduction to which you're entitled. Just make sure you have documentation and receipts (i.e., canceled checks for utility bills and the bills themselves, receipts for mortgage payments, etc.) to substantiate any deductions you claim.

Tip...

Smart Tip

Planning to park your grooming-mobile in your neighborhood or even in your driveway? Be sure to check with your local government to make sure there are no zoning restrictions. Many municipalities won't allow businesses to park commercial vehicles in areas zoned for residential.

There is one little IRS requirement you should keep in mind if you're planning to deduct that office: The space must be dedicated solely to the business. That means you can't store off-season clothes or your sewing projects in the closet, let the kids watch TV in the room, or allow family members to use your business computer. Who's to know? Well, it is a matter of trust, and as an ethical businessperson you should play by the rules. (Not to mention it's not beyond the realm of possibility that an auditor could stop by to check out the setup.) So if you can't devote a space entirely to business, then you should forgo taking the deduction. And don't even think about trying to deduct that cozy little corner of your living room that serves as your work area or the closet with a bifold door that houses your incredibly efficient workstation. The IRS' definition of a home office is basically a room with a door. Period.

Having said that, we do want to stress that a dedicated work space is an integral part of doing business whether you can deduct the cost or not, and no matter where the office space is. Every business owner needs a place where business can be conducted effectively and efficiently—and optimally it will be that room we talked about earlier. Outfit it with a desk, a comfortable chair, a file cabinet and/or bookcase, a computer, a high-quality telephone, and everything else you'll need to get your job done, and you'll bring a level of professionalism to the job that is crucial. (We'll talk more about the things you'll need in your office in Chapter 10.)

In addition to making you more efficient and productive while you're working, having a dedicated office space has important psychological benefits. It's like a little island of productivity in your home where you go every day to get your work done. It says that when you're in that space, you're at work and unavailable to chat with the neighbors, surf the power tool websites, or decorate cookies for a school bake sale. It also gives you a place to leave at the end of the day, an act that helps you maintain a healthy balance between home and work life.

Lexington, South Carolina, dog trainer Teoti Anderson found this out the hard way when she started her business and took phone calls practically around the clock. "That was a big mistake! [The business] took over my life," she says. "People would call at all hours of the day and night, and it was very disruptive. I really believe it's healthier to keep your personal life and business separate, especially if you have a family. I now have a voice-mail box that features a greeting with basic information. Folks leave a message and I return calls Monday through Friday in the

Dollar Stretcher

If you qualify for a home-office deduction, you can deduct a percentage of your mortgage interest and taxes (or rent), electricity and heat bills, trash removal, and even cleaning services. To figure out the amount, divide the square footage of the office by the square footage of the house. The resulting number is the percentage you can deduct from your bills.

evenings. I've found that setting boundaries keeps you going longer . . . a lot of times when you're first starting out, you devote everything to a business. It's easy to get burned out that way."

> **Smart Tip**
>
> For a little light reading about the IRS' many regulations concerning home-office deductions, see IRS Publication 587, *Business Use of Your Home*. While you're at it, you might want to review Publication 4035, *Home-Based Business Tax Avoidance Schemes*, so you don't run afoul of the Feds. They're available at irs.gov.

Even if you truly can't spare a whole room in your house, condo, or apartment for the business, you should still carve out a niche you can devote solely to the business. This can be a corner of the living room that can be partitioned off from the living area with a decorative screen, or that closet-turned-workstation we mentioned earlier. Other alternatives include hutches made specifically to house computer equipment (big bonus: they can be closed up at the end of the workday), or a workstation built into a corner of the kitchen or pantry. But the key is to place your work area in a place that's out of the mainstream of family traffic or you'll be distracted by every family feud or phone call. Then you must educate your spouse and children to respect the time you spend in that space. Plus if you choose to invest in a dedicated phone line for your business (recommended!), make sure everyone knows that you're the only one who is allowed to answer it. Some callers may be charmed when the phone line is answered "Hi, Gamma" by a two-year-old, but it really makes you seem unprofessional and bush-league.

If you're planning to bring clients' animals into your home, you'll also need a pet-friendly area separate from your office space. For instance, if you're a dog or cat groomer, you'll need a worktable, a water source, grounded electrical outlets for clippers and other equipment, and a cabinet for storing supplies and other tools of your trade. Likewise, a homebased pet photographer will need studio space, while a pet sitter will need a secure area for the "clients" to run and frolic. A fenced backyard or a converted basement or garage may be just what you need. These and other possibilities are discussed in detail in Chapter 12.

It's a Plan

Want a surefire way to create endless frustration and needless extra work for yourself? Then start up your venture without a business plan.

A business plan is a crucial tool in a fledgling entrepreneur's business toolbox. It should outline every step you plan to take to build a viable business, from concept ("What are my goals in this line of work?") to execution ("What do I do with the customers I've drummed up?"). In between, it should touch on your plans, goals, and strategies for the business in clear and concise detail.

Now, we know it can be tempting to skip this step, especially if you're an enthusiastic solo entrepreneur who's more interested in petting cats than massaging marketing plans. But you wouldn't set out on a road trip without a map and an itinerary, would you? You wouldn't plan a wedding without a list of tasks and the necessary resources to get the bride to the church on time, right? Your journey into self-employment deserves the same level of planning.

You can get additional free help and information from a Small Business Development Center (found in the federal section of the Yellow Pages under the SBA or by logging onto sba.gov/sbdc). For additional insight, tap into the free resources at your local library, which should have current books and software that can make the business-plan-writing task less onerous. Finally, you'll find a wealth of published business resources on sites like Amazon.com and eBay. If you do end up investing some of your startup dollars in such resources, never fear—these materials are tax-deductible business expenses (just keep those receipts!).

One final word about your business plan: Don't let it languish in a drawer. Rather, once you have your plan on paper (or in an electronic file), you should refer to it periodically to judge how well your strategies are working and whether you're on course to reach your goals. Then if you're falling short or something has changed that is impacting your progress, you can adjust your plans accordingly—again, in writing—as a way to keep moving in the right direction.

Making It Legal

Another thing you need to consider early on in the development of your pet-care business is the legal form it should take. This, of course, is another one of those annoying but necessary IRS tasks. But unlike many other IRS requirements, there will be a reward for your efforts in this area: You will be entitled to tax breaks. You'll want to decide early on which legal form is best for your particular situation, since the decision you make will impact every dollar you earn.

Beware!

Your community may have restrictions on the number of people who can gather in your home at one time for business purposes, as well as on how many cars you can have on your property (or in front of the house) at the same time. Check with the local zoning department to find out if you need a special permit or a variance.

There are four basic legal structures: sole proprietorship (the choice of many new small-business owners), partnership, corporation, and limited liability company (LLC). The differences among them basically come down to the amount of risk you are prepared and willing to take. Many small-business owners start out as sole proprietors because it's the easiest type of business for them to form—there's no paperwork involved, other than one additional form for the IRS (Schedule C) at tax time.

Santa Fe, New Mexico, retailer/wholesaler Diane Burchard had yet another reason to choose this form of business. "I'm a control freak," she confesses. "I previously was a partner in an imported knitting business in Dallas with a dear friend, and when she wanted to leave the company to travel after three years, I had to close down the business. Even though she was and still is a close friend, you run a lot of risks with partners."

In addition, if you're sued for any reason, you could lose not only your business, but also you could lose your home and other personal assets. Considering that you're working with people's prized pets and may have access to their homes, you may feel more comfortable as a C corporation, S corporation, or LLC, all of which give you more protection. (Having the right business insurance can also provide a measure of security; see Chapter 9 for more information.)

Joyce Reavey, the Exton, Pennsylvania, pet-products business owner, went with an LLC precisely for that peace of mind. "Actually, it was a toss-up between an LLC and a corporation," she says. "I talked to a lawyer, and he said an LLC was good for small business and less complicated, so that became my choice."

"I chose an LLC because it was flexible yet offered me practical liability protection," adds Testi Anderson. "Unfortunately in today's society, lawsuits can come at the drop of a hat. Although I am very careful, there is always a chance when working with dogs that something could happen. So now my personal assets are protected."

To determine which form of ownership is best for your particular situation, consult with an attorney and/or accountant. You'll find some tips on how to find both in the next chapter.

What's in a Name?

What parent doesn't relish the thought of naming a new baby? No doubt the same sense of pride will overcome you when naming your new business. The trouble is, in this day of trend-setting celebrities giving their children unusual names like "Apple" and "Bagel" (just kidding about that one), it can be tempting to come up with a name that's just too precious for words (an occupational hazard in a field that services cute and cuddly little animals). It's always better to strive for professional and businesslike over excessively cute. Besides, if you get too cute, you could end up obscuring your real business purpose, as the owners of the following actual pet-walker and pet-sitter businesses have done, no doubt unintentionally:

- Cruisin' Canines (How do they see over the steering wheel?)
- Geaux Pets (Another espresso, garçon!)

- Fetch (Then roll over and think up another name.)
- Zoolatry Inc. (The word means "animal worship," but who's going to look it up?)
- Midnight Sun Critter Comforts (And your point would be?)
- Your Furry Godmother (Electrolysis can help.)
- Keeping Tracks (Especially when working on the railroad.)

When choosing a clever name, try to make the business function as clear as possible. Actual pet-business names that are creative and yet effective include "Paw-pourri Pet Care," "Whiskers and Wags Pet Sitting," and "For Pet's Sake Pet Sitting." Don't be afraid to try out a lot of names before you pick one. Reavey and her marketing director at the time brainstormed a list of 50 names, each of which they put into a search engine to see if they were already in use. They ended up with five variations of one name, which eventually morphed into Pawsitively Posh.

Once you select a name, practice saying it out loud several times, preferably on the phone so someone else can get the full effect. Stay away from names with too much alliteration, which can kill your diction (try saying "Sandee's Swedish Fish Spa" 40 times a day), as well as names that are too long ("Trixie's Pet Sitting, Dog Walking and Veterinarian Taxi Service"), which are too hard to say.

In your quest for an unusual and memorable name, don't underestimate the power of your own name. It is simple, powerful, and straight to the point, which is always a good idea when you're launching a new business. However, using initials can sometimes be a problem. One small-business owner we know of uses her initials, K.C., in her business name. The trouble is, clients can't distinguish between the initials and the word "Casey" when they hear the name spoken. The result has been checks written to the wrong company name and unhappy customers who have to tear up the first check and write a new one.

Inspiration for a catchy name can be as close as the Yellow Pages, although it might be better to check out the big books in metro areas other than your own so you don't duplicate names. In addition, you'll find a worksheet on the next page that you can use to brainstorm names for your new business.

Officially Yours

There's one more thing you have to do before you can start using your new company name: You have to claim it officially by filing paperwork to establish an assumed or fictitious name (commonly known as a DBA, for "doing business as"). Usually, you register your DBA with the county, parish, or borough in which you'll be doing business. The cost to do so is typically quite nominal—as little as $10 in some parts of the country. What this gets you is the right to use the name for a period of about three years and the assurance that no one else in your market area is using the same trade name. (The name is infinitely renewable once you've snagged it.) The government entity

Naming Worksheet

It's pretty common for pet-care business owners to choose a clever or cute name for the business. It's best not to get too precious because it can turn off some customers. But a memorable name is always a good idea, especially since it becomes the cornerstone of the "brand" you are establishing. Use this worksheet as a tool to brainstorm some ideas that can be turned into the perfect name.

List three adjectives that come to mind when you think of the type of business you're forming (think "natural" and "holistic" for pet food; "reliable" and "trustworthy" for a pet sitter):

1. ______________________________
2. ______________________________
3. ______________________________

List the top three things you think of when you consider the type of pet your business will serve (words like "best friend" for dogs, "finicky" or "elegant" for cats, or "mischievous" for ferrets):

1. ______________________________
2. ______________________________
3. ______________________________

List three unique landmarks or other distinguishing features that characterize your city, state or regional area (like the Pike Place Market or Martha's Vineyard):

1. ______________________________
2. ______________________________
3. ______________________________

Now try to combine the various elements from the sections above in different ways:

1. ______________________________
2. ______________________________
3. ______________________________

It may take more tries than this, but eventually you'll hit on just the right combination. But before you order business cards, take your name out for a spin. Say it out loud several times to make sure it's easy to say and easily understood, both in person and on the phone. You should also check your local Yellow Pages and plug the name into a web browser to see if it's already in use. If all looks good, head down to the county seat or other official registrar to file a DBA, and you'll officially be in business.

where you file will do a name search to verify that it's unique, and if it is, it's yours. If it isn't unique, you'll have to try a different name, so it's always a good idea to have a backup in reserve. And by the way, a DBA is still necessary even if you choose to use your own name as your business name. You never know how many dog-training Larry Pamplemousses there are out there.

Another type of license you may need to launch your new venture is a business license, which is also issued by the local government agency where you're doing business. Since

Tip...

Smart Tip

As soon as your DBA registration has been approved, head down to your bank and open a commercial business account in your new business name so you'll immediately be able to accept checks from your clients.

Claim to Name

Once you've picked the perfect moniker for your little pride and joy, you might want to consider having it federally trademarked. A trademark is a word, symbol, or design registered with the United States Patent and Trademark Office (USPTO) used to identify a company's product or service and to distinguish it from those sold by another company. It's meant to help consumers understand where the product or service comes from.

While you can't trademark ideas (as in a clay substance that cats use to deposit bodily waste), you can trademark products and their names (as in Lowe's Kitty Litter, registration number 0719809, which is described as "ground clay used for litters for small animals, such as cats, rats, mice, and hamsters"). And even though you're probably going to be running a very small operation at the beginning, you may still want to consider trademarking your name. Otherwise, you run the risk of receiving a cease-and-desist order down the road from an attorney representing another company whose name you inadvertently used.

It's easy to apply for a trademark. Log on to uspto.gov, where you'll find an online directory of trademarks you can search to see if the name you have chosen is available. If it is, all you need to do is to fill in an electronic filing fee form and pony up for the initial trademark application fee of $325 using a credit card, automated deposit account, or electronic funds transfer. (Never fear, you can file on paper, as well. You'll find contact information in the Appendix.) Keep in mind filing the form won't automatically secure the name you've chosen—you'll need to wait for the USPTO to do an in-depth search before it grants your trademark. But once it clears, it's all yours.

pet-care businesses are not state-regulated in the same way as professional businesses like hair salons or general contractors, all you're likely to need is a standard business license, which gives you permission to operate your homebased or site-based business legally. The cost is around $10 and the license is renewable annually. In some communities, a license isn't even necessary, but don't assume anything—ask about and then comply with any regulations that exist in your area so you will be a good corporate citizen.

9

Professional Handlers

Now that you have the start of a plan for persuading busy pet owners to turn over some aspects of their pets' care to you, it's time to think about relinquishing certain things related to the care of your business to other professionals. Does that surprise you, considering your status as a one-person business with limited startup funds? It shouldn't, because just think about it: Do you really want to practice law—or walk dogs? Are you willing to stay up late crunching numbers instead of getting a good night's sleep the night before you sell pet toys at a trade show? You're bound to appreciate the wisdom of adding an attorney, accountant, insurance agent, and computer expert to your business management team on an as-needed basis.

These business professionals are invaluable for several reasons. First, they free you from the more mundane aspects of running the business, like invoicing or reading contracts, so you can do what you like and are best qualified to do. They take over inescapable tasks that would otherwise eat up an inordinate amount of your time, like filing taxes. They help you avoid common startup blunders. They help you make the best use of your time, which will be at a premium considering all the things you'll need to handle personally to keep your business running efficiently. And finally, and perhaps most important, having these pros on your management team will help make your business seem much more stable and solid, which can be comforting to potential customers who check your references and to bankers you approach to obtain financing.

Your Legal Champion

American author and philosopher Ralph Waldo Emerson said, "The good lawyer is . . . the man who . . . throws himself on your part so heartily that he can get you out of a scrape." And that, in a nutshell, is why you need an attorney on your side. As mentioned previously, an attorney can help you deal with myriad legal issues, including deciphering documents you may not understand, helping you form a partnership or corporation, or otherwise unraveling the intricacies of the law. He or she also can help you immeasurably in the fairly unlikely event of litigation, as in the case of a usually stellar employee who shows up drunk and disorderly at The Poodle Parlor while you're at lunch and gives Fifi a mohawk.

In addition, if you're contemplating signing a contract for a lot of money or one that will cover a long period of time (say, a long-term lease on a bricks-and-mortar storefront for your catnip business), or if you need help with tax planning, loan negotiations, employee contracts, and other tasks, an attorney is an invaluable source of legal knowledge and expertise.

Obviously, that knowledge and expertise comes at a price, which is why many small-business owners shy away from hiring a legal

> Tip...
>
> **Smart Tip**
>
> Thanks to a ruling by the U.S. Supreme Court, there is no such thing as a recommended fee schedule for attorneys. So basically the sky's the limit, which is why it's so important to determine upfront exactly how much your legal eagle is going to charge you for his or her expertise.

gunslinger. But believe it or not, it's possible to find a legal eagle whose fees you can afford. To begin with, try searching for an attorney who specializes in small-business law, since he or she is more likely to be sensitive to an owner's need to keep costs down (as well as more knowledgeable about small-business issues). You'll also find that the rates of an attorney in a one- or two-person office are likely to be more manageable than those of a lawyer in a large firm (this is especially true in major metropolitan areas where business service costs tend to be higher to begin with).

Tip...

Smart Tip

If you are going into business with members of your family, you absolutely need an attorney to help you figure out a family succession plan and address other ownership issues (like profit allocation). Too often family businesses fail when someone leaves the business and the rest of the family ends up squabbling bitterly over what remains.

Since fees vary widely, it pays to shop around. The most common fee arrangement is by the hour, which may range from $100 to $450. Alternatively, an attorney who charges a flat fee for routine work, such as writing letters or setting up a corporation, or someone who offers a business startup package will be much more affordable.

Probably the best way to locate an attorney you trust and respect is by asking other small-business owners, friends, or relatives for referrals. Organizations like the chamber

Cost Cutters

Containing costs is always important for startup businesses, particularly when it comes to services like legal fees, which can add up fast. One easy way to keep attorney costs under control is simply by being organized. "Do your own legwork to gather information you need beforehand, then limit the number of office visits you must make," advises Daniel H. Minkus, past chairman of the business law section of the State Bar of Michigan and a member of the business practice group Clark Hill PLC in Detroit. "You also should limit the phone calls to your attorney, because you'll be charged for those, too."

Before meeting with or calling your attorney, it's helpful to prepare a written list of questions or general issues you wish to cover so you don't stray off track. (Keep in mind that small talk is billed at the same rate as discussions about incorporation or liability!) Then keep an eye on the clock while you talk. It's easy to forget how much billable time is flying by when you're speaking about matters for which you have a personal passion.

of commerce also may be willing to share resources. If you come up short, however, try calling your local attorney service bureau or referral service, both of which are listed in the Yellow Pages under "Attorneys." (Ask for referrals to business-law attorneys or attorneys who practice general law.) Other reliable sources for leads include the American Bar Association (findlegalhelp.org), the Find an Attorney service (findanattor ney.com) or the Martindale-Hubbell Law Directory (martindale.com).

Number Crunchers

Even if you're not quite convinced yet that you need to spend money on an attorney, chances are you'll be much more open to the idea of hiring an accountant. In general, there are two kinds of people: Those who love working with numbers because they're good at it, and those who don't and aren't. If you're in the latter group, you should hire an accountant because now is definitely not the time to risk making a mistake that can impact your entire financial future.

Among the tasks your accountant can help you with is establishing an effective recordkeeping system, or, better yet, taking charge of the books so you don't have to. They can give you advice to help keep expenses in line and monitor cash flow. They can advise you on ever-changing IRS issues, which tend to be very complicated, and they can expertly file your business taxes (or your personal tax return and Schedule C if you're a sole proprietor) with nary a groan or grimace, even if you're using the shoebox method of accounting. They can even help you with retirement planning (as in helping you figure out the amount of money you can deposit to your simplified employee pension plan or IRA annually and still afford basement waterproofing and life's other necessities).

The best way to find an accountant is by asking your lawyer, your banker, or other small-business owners for referrals. The American Institute of Certified Public Accountants' branch in your state can also refer you to a qualified number jockey. (Check the Yellow Pages or go to aicpa.org). Stick with someone in a small practice who has experience with small-business clients both to keep bills down and increase the chances he or she will be tuned into your tax and financial situation.

The going rate for accountants' services is $75 to $125 an hour and up. To avoid paying a small fortune to someone to wade through a jumbled pile of records and receipts at the end of

> Tip...
>
> **Smart Tip**
>
> There are two types of accountants: certified public accountants, or CPAs, who are degreed and must pass a rigorous certification examination before practicing; and public accountants, who do not have to be certified or state-licensed. They usually charge less, but may not be able to represent you before the IRS if you're called in for an audit.

the month or at tax time, set up your own simple filing system and organize your records yourself. That way, you'll pay the big bucks for actual accounting work, not document handling.

If you're really on a budget and feel you can handle your own accounting when you launch your business, you can try using a business accounting software package. Two of the top accounting packages are QuickBooks Pro 2006 by Intuit and Peachtree from Sage Software, both of which are available online and from office supply stores. These easy-to-use programs are useful for keeping accurate financial records, writing checks to suppliers, generating invoices and so on. QuickBooks is especially useful for a small-business owner because it allows you (or your accountant) to download financial records and other information entered into your worksheets directly to TurboTax business tax software, which is a great time-saver. Even if you do plan to hire an accountant, you still should keep an eye on your fiscal health regularly, and one of these programs can help.

> Tip...
>
> **Smart Tip**
>
> The accounting methods most commonly used by small businesses include the cash method, in which you record income you receive and expenses you pay; and the accrual method, in which you record income from a sale when it happens, not when you receive the money. Your accountant can advise you on which method makes more sense for your business.

Keyboard Captain

If the sum of your knowledge about computers consists of knowing how to turn on the power, type, then turn everything off again, you undoubtedly would benefit from having a computer expert on your business team. In addition to rescuing you from the Blue Screen of Death, computer consultants will install peripherals and software, run diagnostics to improve performance, and teach you how to use hardware like scanners. They also can help you figure out the mysteries of the internet if you're new to the Cyber Universe.

Computer consultants usually charge by the hour (possibly $50 an hour or more). You should ante up and pay whatever it takes to get a consultant who makes house calls, because then you won't have to unhook myriad computer cables that feed the beast (and possibly mix them up). Finally, you should choose someone who can translate computer-ese into plain English if you want to have any chance of being able to follow his or her directions.

Insuring Success

Who would think that in a business where you're dealing with cuddly little animals you'd have to worry about protecting yourself from lawsuits and other risks? But let's face it: The tail-waggers are not the ones you have to worry about. It's their moms and dads. So although business insurance is not a requirement when you start a pet-care business, it's highly advisable. And for advice on how much and what kinds of insurance you should carry, you need to call on the expertise of a professional insurance agent or broker.

An insurance agent differs from an insurance broker in that he or she sells insurance products from a single company. A broker, on the other hand, sells many different insurance products from several different companies. As a result, he or she will be able to compare many different policies and levels of coverage against each other, then present you with choices that give you the best product at the best price.

Disaster Relief

A business loss cause by, for instance, fire or flood can be catastrophic for a small-business owner, as evidenced by the mayhem caused in the wake of Hurricanes Katrina and Rita in fall 2005. But there are simple things you can do to make it easier to rebuild after suffering a major business setback.

First, be sure to keep receipts for every item you purchase for the business, from the smallest box of paper clips to the hydraulic table for your grooming salon. Not only will you need these receipts at tax time, but you'll also be able to prove to the insurance company what the item was worth when you bought it. Insurance companies generally pay replacement cost—but they may want to pay for the cheapest possible replacement, not the high-end item you ate tuna casserole for two years to afford. Because many receipts are on thermal paper that fades to bupkis in a few months, photocopy every receipt before filing it. (In fact, make two copies—one for your accountant, one for your personal records.)

Second, use a video camera to make a photographic record on DVD of every major item you use for business. This includes office furniture, computer, phone, grooming equipment, shelving for your inventory, etc. (A receipt will do for the smaller stuff like office supplies and clickers.) You don't have to put this video to music (although "YMCA" is nice), but you should narrate and give details about cost, purchase date, etc.

Store both the photocopied receipts and the DVD in a safe place, like a safe deposit box or an off-site location so your only copies of these important documents don't go up in smoke, get washed away, or become shredded by a tornado along with all the rest of your worldly business possessions.

Another good reason to choose a broker over an agent is that businesses like pet sitting are rather new in the market and have such specific insurance needs that the major insurance companies don't know what to do with the owners who need insurance. Since a broker can shop around, he is more likely to turn up exactly the insurance you need.

Both insurance agents and brokers abound, so you'll want to ask your business acquaintances or attorney for leads to a reputable professional. As mentioned before, it's best to select a professional who understands the concerns of a small-business owner. Ask to see a client list when you interview prospective agents or brokers to get a feel for the types of clients they service.

Bright Idea

If you are leaving a corporate position (either voluntarily or after a layoff) to start your pet-care business, consider using your COBRA insurance benefits for health care, at least temporarily. The cost may be significantly higher than what you paid while employed, but at least you won't have to go looking for health insurance immediately.

Once you've chosen an insurance provider, work with that person to determine exactly how much coverage you need. Here's a simple way to figure that out: Consider how much risk you're willing and financially able to take, then shell out for the appropriate policy, no matter how difficult that may be. Without sufficient coverage, you may one day find your entire investment and livelihood has been wiped out by an unforeseen and uncontrollable event.

Another way to get insurance is to go through the pet-care associations that offer insurance policies to their members. For example, Pet Sitters International and The National Association of Professional Pet Sitters both offer liability protection policies at group rates tailored specifically for their members' needs. You have to be a member to qualify for the coverage, however. Refer to Chapter 14 for more information about these and other such organizations. By the way, several of the entrepreneurs interviewed for this book said it can be hard to get insurance any other way, so you might want to start with these professional organizations when you kick off your insurance search.

Once you see the dizzying array of insurance options available to cover any contingency related to your home office and business, you might just wonder why you didn't decide on a career in the insurance industry rather than pet care. There truly is a policy to protect against any type of loss, but buying all of them would insurance you right out of business. So instead, purchase just enough insurance to offset risk that potentially could force your company into bankruptcy or cause serious financial problems.

Pet-care business owners are most likely to need general liability insurance, dishonesty bonding, business interruption insurance, auto insurance, and workers' compensation (if you have employees). Pet-products business owners, trainers, and groomers who have a bricks-and-mortar location also should have property and casualty insurance.

General Liability

This is the single most important type of coverage you will need for your pet business. Liability insurance covers negligence, accidental damage, and personal injury (including from dog bites), which you'll need if: a) your business takes you into clients' homes, or b) you are housed in a building or other location where clients, pets, or employees may be injured. And we don't mean hair clipper accidents—we're talking events like slip-and-fall accidents (both human and animal) or even injuries sustained when a customer spills a cup of hot coffee while waiting for a hair cut. In addition, pet sitters must be very sure they have sufficient coverage to protect them no matter where they are—in clients' homes, in their own homes, in the park, etc.

Until recently, pets were considered property and were not covered under general liability policies. But insurers have come to realize that pedigreed or show animals can cost thousands of dollars, so they're more likely to be covered under liability policies if they're injured or lost or if they die while you're caring for them. Be sure to ask about this distinction when you shop for liability insurance from any company other than a pet association. At the very least, you may need a rider to your general liability policy to cover your four-footed, feathered, or finned friends.

In this litigious society of ours, people often win large awards in injury cases, so don't cheap out on your liability insurance. Insurance industry experts recommend buying $1 million to $2 million in liability insurance, which will cost around $500 a year for a homebased business.

Property

Also known as casualty insurance, this type of insurance protects both the building you're working out of and its contents, which is very important if you are housing your business anywhere other than your home. Property insurance protects your property against major disasters (like acts of God), fire, theft, vandalism and so on, and the amount of coverage is calculated based on property value as determined by an appraiser who will check out your property before giving a quote. Keep in mind that flood insurance is not covered in most standard policies. If you feel you need protection against flood-related damages, you'll need a separate policy (which can be quite costly) or at the very least a rider on your main policy.

Even if you're homebased, you should consider property insurance, since you'll have

Beware!

Your health insurance plan must be established under your business name if you will be taking the self-employed health insurance deduction. In addition, the IRS says the deduction may be allowed if you pay the premium yourself (as a sole proprietor) or your partnership or S corporation pays it.

equipment, furniture, and other stuff related to your business that should be covered. Rather than purchasing a separate policy, however, it may be possible to pay extra for a rider to your homeowners policy that will cover your business. Your broker can tell you whether this is possible and how much it would cost.

Dishonesty (Surety) Bonding

This type of insurance protects you against loss if your employees (including independent contractors) steal from your clients. According to Raleigh, North Carolina, pet-sitter business owner Jerry Wentz, bonding is a useful marketing tool even for businesses with no employees, since it can send a signal to clients that they're honest and trustworthy. This sets clients' minds at ease (after all, they're giving you the keys to their homes) and can be a selling point when you pitch your services. A $5,000 dishonesty bond is about $100 annually.

Business Interruption

Disaster can befall a business at any time, and this type of insurance will help you pay the bills while you recover from the loss. Both natural disasters like hurricanes and tornadoes and man-made disasters like fire and theft are usually covered by this type of policy, which pays the cost of your normal business expenses, including equipment replacement and facility rental. It also will replace lost income. A pet-business owner who has a facility and/or employees is probably more likely to need this type of insurance. Ask your broker about whether you should have business interruption insurance and how much it would cost.

Auto

If you have an insured vehicle, you're already covered against accidents that might happen on the way to or from a job site. However, if you plan to pick up or transport pets, you should check with your insurance broker to make sure you'll be covered in the event of an accident or property damage. Also, if you're a mobile groomer with a dedicated vehicle, it goes without saying that you'll need insurance. Work out the details with your broker.

Workers' Compensation

Although every person who cares for animals should seriously consider carrying at least some of the insurance policies discussed above, they're not mandatory. But workers' compensation is. Every state has some form of workers' comp, which is a type of no-fault insurance that pays benefits to employees who have work-related injuries, diseases, and illnesses.

Workers' comp is a complicated issue with provisions that vary by state. Be sure to talk to your broker to determine how much coverage you need. Incidentally, only employees on your payroll must be covered by workers' comp. Independent contractors and temporary helpers are not covered. Likewise, as the owner you don't count as an employee in your business, so you can't be covered by workers' comp. For this reason, it might be a good idea to purchase both business interruption and health insurance policies for yourself.

Other Types of Insurance

If you're the main wage earner in your family, you might want to consider having some or all of the following types of insurance coverage:

- *Disability insurance*. This coverage replaces a percentage of your gross income if you can't work due to injury or illness. Since you, the owner, are not covered by workers' comp, this is a good way to make sure you will have an income if by chance you are sidelined for a time.
- *Health insurance*. These days, no one should be without health insurance, and Uncle Sam helps make it affordable by allowing self-employed persons who report a net profit on Schedule C, C-EZ, or F to deduct 100 percent of their health insurance premiums. This includes medical and dental insurance, as well as qualified long-term care insurance for yourself, your spouse, and your dependents. See IRS Publication 535, *Business Expenses*, for more information.
- *Life insurance*. Besides providing funds to your family or significant other in the event of your death, a life insurance policy will come in handy if you're planning to approach a bank for business financing, since it can be a requirement to cinch the deal.

As mentioned earlier, it's really important to have an insurance broker or agent on your team to help you sort through the various insurance options and premiums. In the meantime, use the insurance planning worksheet on the next page to help you get the decision-making process under way.

Business Insurance Planning Worksheet

Type	Required?	Premium
General liability		
Property		
Dishonesty (surety) bond		
Business interruption		
Auto		
Workers' compensation		
Disability		
Health		
Life		
Other		
Total Annual Cost		

10

Kibbles and Bytes

Now that you're on the verge of becoming the CEO of your very own company, it's time to start putting together the various tools you'll need to conduct business. If your plan is to start out working from home, you've likely given some serious consideration to exactly where in your home you'll locate your enterprise's nerve center. As mentioned previously, it's really important for a fledgling entrepreneur to have a dedicated space in which to work, even if it's only a corner of the living room. It's just as important to have all the basic tools you need to make the business run effectively and efficiently. So in this chapter, we'll talk about the furnishings, supplies, and other accoutrements that are essential to keep your office humming.

Before we get into the specifics, however, it bears mentioning that it's not necessary to dash out to the office superstore and gleefully fill your cart with tax-deductible supplies and computer equipment. We strongly recommend that if you already have any of the basics in your home—anything from a computer to Post-Its™—that you use them first. Deferring even those small purchases will help keep your startup costs low, which is always helpful in the early days of a new business venture. Short on supplies? Not to worry—since your initial needs really are modest, you should be able to get what you need without breaking the bank.

To help you estimate exactly how much you'll need to outfit your home office, we've included startup costs for two hypothetical pet-grooming businesses on page 130. (Fear not—even though we've chosen pet-grooming businesses as examples, you'll find their office needs are pretty much the same as those of any new pet-business owner, whether you're clipping, training, or selling.) The low-end business, Barky's Canine Coiffures, is a one-person sole proprietorship, while the high-end company, Molly's Snip and Clip, is an S corporation with two part-time assistants. After looking over the expenses, you can try your hand at estimating your own costs using the worksheet on page 131.

Equipment

The main item you'll need in your home office is a sturdy desk. If you have the capital, feel free to hit a home-furnishings store for a sleek Danish contemporary desk or stop by your favorite antique store to find the perfect period piece. (Sure beats the battered old metal desk you may have left behind at your last job in corporate America.) But if you're trying to contain costs, head over to one of the office supply superstores or even a retailer like Target or Ikea. Both types of stores carry a wide selection of affordable, attractive furniture that will keep you fiscally responsible. Typically, a basic desk will run $50 to $200.

A computer hutch is a great alternative to a desk, especially for home offices that are set up in the corner of a room. Hutches give you more room to spread out and often come with useful little cubbyholes and extra drawers for files and supplies. If your budget allows, opt for a hutch with doors that can be closed at the end of your workday. It will keep the room looking tidier, plus the physical act of closing away work detritus when you're finished for the day can help you make the transition from work

Comfort Zones

Whether you'll be spending a lot of time in your home office cooking up new deals and products or simply crunching the numbers at the end of the day, your workspace should be as comfortable and pleasant as possible. This will not only improve your productivity, but it will also keep your energy high and your commitment level in the zone.

Take temperature, for instance. It's easy to put on a sweater if it's too cold or peel off layers when the temperature rises, but your stress level only increases when you're uncomfortable. Even if you have central air and heat, you may want to consider buying a space heater to keep the temperature comfortable in the winter or a fan or even an extra window air conditioner to keep your temper below simmer in the summer. Make sure you have sufficient task lighting. Sitting in a pool of light that's concentrated only on your work area will give you eye strain and possibly a doozy of a headache. Invest in good overhead lighting so both your work area and the room around you are equally well-lit.

Control distracting outside noise by installing floor-length lined draperies that can be drawn when the neighborhood kids get too noisy. Noise-cancelling headphones (available anywhere electronics are sold) are a good alternative if you don't want to shut the sun out. If your basement or attic work center echoes or amplifies the sound of whatever you're doing, install carpeting with a thick pile and a substantial pad to absorb the noise.

to home life. Hutches do cost more than standard desks (a good furniture-quality piece can run $700 or more), but the extra space and features that will keep you more organized may be worth it.

If your furniture budget is so tight it squeaks, you can make your Jacksons and Hamiltons go further by buying used furniture. (Since you're unlikely to entertain clients other than the four-footed kind, who's to know?) Both thrift stores and newspaper want ads can be great sources of inexpensive yet good-quality furniture. Finally, don't forget to check out eBay and the other online auction houses for furniture. A recent eBay search on "desk" yielded 1,452 hits and included used items like a large solid wood desk with six drawers for $48. New items, all of which required at least some assembly, included a black metal/beech wood computer office workstation desk ($49, plus $89 shipping), an oak finish Mission-style desk and chair set for $229 ($65 shipping), and a handsome executive desk for $370 (free shipping). Sellers sometimes will allow you to pick up items you've won so you can save the delivery charge if they happen to be local. Just be sure to read the item description carefully before bidding to make sure it's possible. Likewise, if a seller is located out of your geographical area, verify that he or she will indeed ship the desk to you. Some sellers prefer local pickup only and will say so in their listing.

Other office basics you'll need are a two- or four-drawer file cabinet with drawers that extend fully (so you can easily retrieve folders from way in the back) and possibly a bookcase for neatly storing reference books, computer software, and other materials. File cabinets cost $40 to $100 each; a four-shelf bookcase will run $70 to $100.

Then there's your chair. Although you can economize on the desk, you should buy the best chair you can afford since you'll be spending a lot of time in it. Likewise, while you can certainly purchase a chair out of a catalog or off eBay, it's preferable to try out any chair you're considering so you can make sure it's comfortable and has adequate back and lumbar support. The height of the chair in relation to the desk is important, too, because if you're sitting too high or too low in relation to the desktop while you're typing, you could run the risk of developing carpal tunnel syndrome. If you can't try the desk and chair out at the same time, spend a little extra money (up to $200) to get a chair with an adjustable height control so you can adjust it to the proper height. It's worth it. Trust us.

Computer

A computer is a must in today's information age. Your computer will help you manage your business, serve as a gateway to the internet, and generally keep your life organized. A good business computer with a hard drive, monitor, mouse, modem, and printer, runs about $2,000 and up. It pays to shop around for the best deal. Companies such as Dell often offer outrageously low prices on great entry-level systems. For example, Dell recently offered a 2.80GHz computer that came with a free flat-panel monitor for just $599.

Useful system add-ons that can make your work easier include a 17-inch high-resolution display monitor (up to $400) or a 19-inch monitor (up to $600), a scanner ($100 to $150 or more), a CD-RW burner ($60 for an internal model, $100 for an external), and an external hard drive for long-term storage, like client records you refer to only occasionally ($100 to $200). If you need to carry electronic files around with you (say, when you take home work from your retail store to download on your home computer), a flash drive (aka jump drive) is very useful and affordable.

When it comes to pet-grooming, pet-food, and pet-products businesses, a digital camera is a must for taking before and after pictures of your furry clients or the products you're selling. These photos can be posted to your website for prospective customers to see or used in printed materials like brochures or catalogs. On the low end, a digital camera will run $130 to $250. If you have cash to spare, you might want to opt for a 6.1 megapixel model for about $350, since it will take sharper photos (an important consideration if you're selling over the internet). A USB cable is required to download digital photos to your computer and costs as little as $2.

If you're printing instead, you can use virtually any inkjet printer, but a digital photo printer is now so affordable, compact, and easy to use that you might want to invest in one. They run about $200 to $250, while the photographic paper costs $39.95 for a box of 50 sheets of 8.5-by-11-inch paper and inkjet print cartridges are $39.95. If you're in the products business, however, you might want to eschew the idea of taking product photos yourself and hire a professional. Product photography can be very difficult, and your pictures can come off looking very amateurish.

Tip...

Smart Tip

A laptop is very useful for keeping track of details while on the go. At around $1,000, they can be a little pricey for a new business owner, so a handheld device like a Palm or a BlackBerry may be a good alternative. A Palm starts at around $299, while a BlackBerry is $449.

Software

The bundled Microsoft Office package is the best-known and most widely used office productivity software around. For $499, the Microsoft Office Professional package

Mum's the Word

Working out of your home brings with it special circumstances—not least of which is the need to keep personal information private. Just as you probably won't want to give out your home phone number to a lot of people, you probably won't want to tell clients where you live, either. (Let's face it: There are a lot of stalkers and other crazies out there, as well as people who may feel compelled to leave a box of newborn kitties or a puppy on your doorstep because you're a pet lover.) So keep your contact information generic on your website (simply publishing the city name is sufficient if you really feel it's important to note your geographical location), and unless you are grooming or training pets in your home, you should seriously consider renting a post office box or a mailbox at a place like Mail Boxes Etc. so business mail has a home away from your home. You can expect to pay $10 to $20 a month at a shipping store, while post office box rates vary depending on the location of the post office and the size of the box. But whatever the cost, it buys a lot of peace of mind.

includes Word, Excel, PowerPoint (for generating presentations), Access (for database management) and Outlook e-mail. One great bonus you get with Office is online access to a variety of business and productivity document templates that you can customize for your own use. Among them are marketing materials and sales and customer tracking tools, as well as templates for cash-flow statements, independent contractor contracts, product brochures and more. For a full list, go to Microsoft Office Online (office.microsoft.com).

Since you're likely to be handling at least the basics when it comes to business accounting, you'll need a good accounting software package. The most popular package is QuickBooks because it can handle such a wide variety of accounting tasks, from tracking receivables and invoicing to check printing. QuickBooks Pro retails for $199.95, although if you have an earlier version already you can upgrade for just $99.95.

There is a fairly diverse selection of pet industry-specific software available to help you with the management of your business. But if you're on a shoestring budget, forgo them for now and instead create your own customized worksheets, schedules, and other business materials using Microsoft Word or Excel.

Fax Machine

Now that e-mail is so commonplace, fax machines aren't quite as prevalent as they once were. However, if you will be selling pet products, you may find that having a fax machine can be very useful—especially when it comes to sending pages of orders to wholesalers or manufacturers. Many computers come with a fax card already on board, but not only will you have to scan in any documents you want to send, you'll also have to leave your computer on 24/7 so it's ready to receive faxes at all times. You may find it more practical to invest in a stand-alone fax machine. Plain-paper faxes are quite affordable these days at around $100. Starting at about $200, you can pick up a multifunction machine that faxes, copies, prints, cooks dinner, and washes your laundry (just kidding about the faxing part).

Tip...

Smart Tip

To cut down on the number of unwanted telemarketing calls you get on your business line, put your number on the national Do Not Call list (donotcall.gov). Also, using a call-blocker device like the TeleZapper will cut down on the number of computer-dialed calls you'll receive.

Phones

One way you can tell the professionalism of a small-business owner is by his or her phone. So ditch the yellow princess phone and pick up a professional-quality business phone, which will give you clearer sound and have useful features like speed dial and a hold button for those side

Bright Idea

If you expect to be on the phone a lot taking orders or making appointments, you might want to select a phone that's headset-compatible. You'll appreciate being able to work hands-free, plus you'll save your neck from the muscle strain that can result when you cradle a phone receiver between your neck and shoulder too long.

conversations with your kids. A two-line speakerphone with auto-redial, memory dial, mute button, and more will come in at $40 to $150. A great source for high-quality phones is Hello Direct (see Appendix), which carries the Polycom line of professional business telephones.

Chances are you already have a cell phone. If so, you'll need to start keeping records on what percentage of the phone is used for business since that will be a legitimate business expense. If you don't have a phone or you would like to have a separate line only for business use, you can expect to pay a monthly service charge of around $40 a month plus activation fees unless you sign up for a contract of one to three years. Tack on another $100 or so for a basic cell phone, or better yet, look for service plans that offer a free basic phone along with packages that include hundreds of minutes of calling time and unlimited night and weekend minutes. The latter is a big plus since you'll probably be working plenty of nights and weekends.

Whether you're out and about or deskbound taking and fulfilling orders, an answering machine is a must. They cost as little as $15 to $65 for a basic model or up to $200 for one with advanced features. Today's high-tech equivalent of the answering machine is voice mail, a bargain at about $12 to $18 a month. Its chief benefit is that it will take messages even while you're on the phone booking appointments or if you're using dial-up internet service—an important consideration because people can get pretty impatient with busy signals and you don't want to risk losing a client.

Finally, a pager is a low-cost way to stay connected with both clients and employees. You can get one practically for pocket change—around $20—then you'll pay about $72 per year for service. Spring for an alphanumeric pager and clients will be able to send you text messages using a computer.

Copy Machine

If you're starting a pet-service business, you probably won't need a copier of your own at first. But product business owners may find it convenient to have a machine right in the office for photocopying orders, packing slips, and other documents. A stand-alone copier, which tends to be rather large, can be as much as $2,000, while a personal desktop model is quite affordable at $100 to $500. Even the less expensive models will enlarge and reduce documents, but if you need features like collating and duplex (two-sided) printing, you'll have to ante up a few more bucks. Toner cartridges will put you back about $10 to $15 each.

Postage

Depending on how much mailing you plan to do, either to promote your business or ship products, you may find it convenient to have your own postage meter. The cost to lease a meter is about $20 a month for a standard model, or $20 to $120 a month for a postage meter/electronic scale combo. And here's the good news: You can save time by purchasing postage online at usps.com, or you can make the trek to the local post office if you prefer. If there are bulk mailings in your future, you'll also need a renewable permit, which costs $150 annually.

Tip...

Smart Tip

U.S. Postal Service regulations do not allow business owners to own postage machines outright. So if you want to have one of these time-savers on the premises, you'll have to rent it from either the Postal Service or an authorized postage meter manufacturer.

The other tool a pet-products business owner should have is a postage scale so you don't inadvertently put too little or too much postage on the letters and packages you send out. While you can pick up a mechanical scale for just $10 to $25, you may find it more convenient to have a programmable electronic scale instead. This $70-to-$250 item is especially useful if you'll be using priority or expedited mailing services regularly.

Point-of-Sale Equipment

Here's a news flash for pet-products business owners, particularly those who plan to sell online: You definitely are candidates for point-of-sale (POS) equipment. A POS terminal is the little box you use to verify electronically whether a customer's credit is good before you pack up the goods, and it is used with a credit card receipt printer. These items cost $299 and $195, respectively. If all your counter space will be taken up with rhinestone collars and fur-trimmed doggy jogging suits, you might prefer a terminal like the Hypercom T7P Standard instead, which has a thermal printer built right in. This type of POS unit starts at around $229. But products business owners aren't the only ones who will find a POS terminal handy. Mobile groomers can beef up their bottom lines by accepting credit cards. A wireless POS terminal you can use anywhere starts at around $995. You also will need cellular service to be able to use your POS equipment.

If you are more likely to be processing charges at your desk rather than in the front seat of a van or behind the counter of a retail shop, then you can skip the hardware altogether and invest in POS software instead. Both PC- and Mac-based versions are available and allow you to check credit viability and print out a receipt with ease. Some well-known POS packages include PcCharge (GO Software Inc., as low as $199 from discounters), Chargem Software (Capital Merchant Solutions, $349) and ICVerify (ICVerify, $335). For the names of companies that sell both POS equipment and software, refer to the Appendix.

Since you'll probably already be carrying a cell phone on the job, why not make it work even harder for you by processing sales through it? Nextel's Creditel PowerSwipe processing equipment attaches right to the side of several of its Java-enabled phones. But all this convenience doesn't come cheap. The card reader, cable, and software will cost about $600, plus you'll pay various monthly fees to process transactions. For more specific information and costs, contact your local Nextel dealer.

The last thing you'll need to power your POS equipment is a merchant account, which is an electronic clearinghouse that allows you to clear credit and debit transactions. Merchant account costs can vary widely, but in general you can expect to pay around $100 to establish a new merchant account, plus per-transaction fees.

Vehicle

One of the perks of being a small-business owner is being able to deduct the depreciated cost of a company vehicle as well as the costs associated with operating it. If you already have reliable wheels in presentable condition that you can use to travel to and from clients' homes or your bricks-and-mortar location, great—you can use it for the business and save your startup dollars for something else. The cost of gasoline, oil changes, and other maintenance are all deductible business expenses, but if your business vehicle doubles as your personal transportation, you'll need to keep careful records about vehicle usage, since only the percentage that is actually used in the commission of your work is deductible. (Check with your accountant or financial advisor for advice.) In the same way, you are permitted to take a deduction for mileage driven for the business, which was 50.5 cents per mile in 2008. The IRS requires written records documenting how many miles you drive for business to grant this deduction. So pick up an auto mileage logbook, which is available at any office supply store, and jot down the beginning and ending odometer reading for every trip you make for business.

> Tip...
>
> **Smart Tip**
>
> Uncle Sam will allow you to deduct your transportation costs if you use mass transit to get to your business appointments. Just keep a written log of the trips you make and note the amount you spend on subway tokens, bus passes, and taxis, and tuck away any receipts you might get as proof of purchase.

Supplies

Plan to budget about $150 for the office supplies you'll need to start up the business, such as legal pads, pens, file folders, Post-It™ notes, and so on. Better still, try going on a scavenger hunt around the house to locate as many of these items as you can in your personal stash so you don't have to wipe out your startup funds on these basics. Other necessities include:

- Schedule book for keeping track of appointments (as little as $15)
- Computer and copier paper ($25 to $50 per case of 10 reams)
- Extra printer cartridges ($25 to $80, or more for laser printer cartridges)
- Extra fax cartridges ($30 to $90)
- Paper shredder ($25 to $30 for a light-duty model; $80 to $180 for handling heavier loads)
- Self-inking rubber stamp for imprinting bank deposit information on the back of checks (customized by an office supply store for around $10)

Dollar Stretcher

The next time you need office supplies, shop online so you can save a trip to the office supply store. You'll save even more nonbillable time when you buy from a chain store like OfficeMax or Office Depot, both of which will deliver orders of $50 or more right to your house within 24 hours at no charge.

You'll also need business cards and imprinted stationery with matching envelopes for business correspondence. Even though you're in a warm and fuzzy business, your documents shouldn't have the warm and fuzzy (read: unprofessional) look. So avoid the do-it-yourself kits at the local office supply store and purchase professionally printed materials that portray you as the serious business professional you are. Cards and stationery printed on high-quality white, cream, or gray laid or linen paper will cost only $200 to $400 when printed by a quickie print shop like FedEx Kinko's or an office supply store. The internet is also a good source for good-looking printed materials at reasonable prices. Refer to the Appendix for a list of printers you can check out.

Finally, a brochure that details the services you provide is another must for your new business. It can do double duty as the piece you give customers who request additional information about your services and as a direct-mail piece you send out to prospects to drum up new business. As with your stationery, it pays in the long run to have a nice brochure designed on good-quality paper rather than just whipping something up on your computer and printing it on standard computer paper. If you need layout help, you may wish to use a quick-print shop to do the job. But if you can handle the design work (which is actually pretty easy when you use one of the Microsoft Publisher

Dollar Stretcher

To get the most mileage out of printed materials like brochures, don't include the prices of your services or products. Not only will your materials need to be updated every time you raise your prices, but people also tend to tuck promo material away for future reference, which means the prices could be outdated by the time they call.

templates), you might try searching for a low-cost printer on the internet. A recent casual search uncovered several companies that will print 1,000 full-color, 8.5-by-11-inch brochures on good-quality paper for around $350. All you do is design your brochure and transmit it to the printer electronically. See the Appendix for contact information for a few online printers that will give you an idea of what's available out there.

Services

As a new pet-business owner, you can expect to incur a number of telecommunications expenses to get your business connected and ready to roll. Chief among these are the cell phone, pager, and voice-mail costs discussed earlier in this chapter. But equally important is the cost of a business telephone line. With a $40 to $60 installation fee and $150 to $400 per line for small-business phone service, a business line may seem pretty pricey, and in fact that's the reason why many sole proprietors choose to install a second residential phone line to use as a business line when they start out. But we do recommend that you install that dedicated business line—or a second residential line at the very least—even in those lean early days, especially if you have small children who like to grab the phone when it rings or teenagers who like to monopolize the line. Besides, do you really want to give out your home phone number to a bunch of people you know only casually as clients? Of course you can circumvent this problem entirely by using your cell phone as your business line, and you have the added benefit of being able to carry your business phone around with you whenever you're on the clock. Just be sure to get voice-mail service to pick up those after-hours calls so you never miss one.

Another necessary service charge you'll incur is for internet access. If you wish, economize by using a dial-up service from a company like AOL or EarthLink, which charge $20 to $25 a month for unlimited online time. But as you probably know, these connections can be slow during peak use times. Many business owners prefer faster connections like an ISDN (Integrated Services Digital Network) line, which will run about $200 for the setup fee, $250 for a terminal or modem, and $50 per month; or a DSL line, with a $100 installation fee, $200 to $500 for the terminal or modem, and a monthly service fee of $30 to $40. If you have cable TV, you probably have the option of Broadband service, which gives you lightning-fast connections and processing. The setup fee for Broadband is around $100, plus you'll have to purchase or lease a modem from the cable company (as much as $300), then pay a monthly fee of about $40.

Assuming you already have a vehicle you can use, you'll find that the other costs necessary to start up your homebased pet business will be pretty reasonable. If you haven't done so already, you might want to enter your projected costs now on the worksheet on page 131 to get an idea of how your startup picture looks. As part of that exercise, don't forget to include the startup costs related to your particular business (found in Chapters 2 through 6). Is the number a little higher than you expected?

Sample Office Equipment Costs

Item	Barky's Canine Coiffures	Molly's Snip and Clip
Office equipment		
Computer, printer	$0	$1,500
Microsoft Office	$0	$0
QuickBooks	$200	$200
Surge protector	$15	$15
Multipurpose fax/scanner/copier	$0	$200
Copy machine	$0	$150
Phone	$50	$150
Cell phone	$0	$100
Pager	$0	$0
Answering machine	$25	$25
Digital camera	$250	$350
Office furniture		
Desk	$50	$150
Chair	$100	$200
File cabinet(s)	$50	$75
Bookcase(s)	$0	$70
Office supplies		
Business cards	$50	$50
Service brochures	$350	$350
Miscellaneous supplies (pens, folders, etc.)	$60	$160
Computer/copier paper	$25	$25
Extra printer cartridges	$50	$50
Extra fax cartridges	$0	$50
Extra copier toner	$0	$90
CD-RW disks	$0	$20
Mouse pad	$5	$5
Total	**$1,280**	**$3,985**

Office Equipment Worksheet

Item	Cost
Office equipment	
Computer, printer	
Microsoft Office	
QuickBooks	
Surge protector	
Multipurpose fax/scanner/copier	
Copy machine	
Phone	
Cell phone	
Pager	
Answering machine	
Digital camera	
Office furniture	
Desk	
Chair	
File cabinet(s)	
Bookcase(s)	
Office supplies	
Business cards	
Service brochures	
Miscellaneous supplies (pens, folders, etc.)	
Computer/copier paper	
Extra printer cartridges	
Extra fax cartridges	
Extra copier toner	
CD-RW disks	
Mouse pad	
Total	

11

Pet Shop Talk

While it's possible to start any of the five businesses discussed in this book as a homebased enterprise, every one except pet sitting/walking has at least a fair probability either now or in the future of being located in a commercial space rather than in the home. This is not to say you can't train pets in your basement or fulfill orders for leashes and sweaters from your spare bedroom. In fact, we'd really recommend you do just that at the genesis of your business to keep costs manageable. But depending on how large an operation you'll be running, you may find it easier and more convenient to conduct business and store product outside your home. This chapter addresses the ins and outs of commercial spaces, and the next chapter details places where you can store your inventory and supplies. And hey, all you pet sitters, feel free to skip ahead to Chapter 13, which talks about personnel. We'll meet you there in a little while.

Building Basics

There are three types of establishments that can be suitable for your pet-care or products business: a free-standing building, a storefront property, or a shopping center location (we'll talk about storage facilities a little later in this chapter). As you probably know, each of these requires a serious outlay of cash. There are a number of factors that will influence the cost, including facility size, availability of retail space, type of community (if you're setting up shop in a trendy town, for instance, the cost will be higher), and condition (a fixer-upper will be more affordable than new construction or a remodeled facility).

A free-standing building has many advantages, whether you're training, grooming, or selling. First, it gives you much more room to work in than you'd typically have in a homebased space. It also sends a message to customers that you're a serious business owner—after all, you've made a visible commitment to the business when you dole out money every month on a mortgage or lease. A free-standing location also makes you an integral part of the local community, which can be a plus among people who prefer to do business where they live and work.

While you may find it's more affordable to lease than to own a building, owning has some important benefits. You can customize the building to suit your needs, including adding a water source exactly where you need it for your grooming business or installing custom display cases for your pet products. Likewise, you can decorate as you wish, and you can control overhead costs like utilities (at last—the perfect temperature!) and even the terms of the mortgage (refinance to your heart's delight). You also don't have to pay the common-area fees associated with leasing a space in a strip mall, which may include the cost of snow removal, advertising

> Tip...
>
> **Smart Tip**
>
> If you decide to lease a facility, try to negotiate the shortest term possible, like one or two years with an option to renew. Because a lease is virtually unbreakable, you'll be liable for the full lease amount if you decide to relocate—so a shorter lease means you won't be stuck with a huge bill.

and security. Finally, you have the tax advantages of owning the building.

Leasing your building is also something to consider. Although you will have a landlord to deal with, that can be a plus when there's a building problem like a leaky roof that needs attention. In addition, it's usually somewhat less expensive to lease than to buy, and some of the utility costs like water may be included in your lease payment. Be sure to negotiate terms upfront for the best chance at getting a lease you can live with.

> **Smart Tip**
>
> Tip...
>
> When shopping for a commercial space to buy or lease, put good parking high on your list of requirements. Customers who can't find a parking space will leave in frustration, and they may never come back. If you don't have a parking lot or convenient street parking, choose a location near a parking structure, then validate those parking tickets to build customer goodwill.

If you're more inclined to leave building maintenance to someone else, a rented storefront property like in a strip mall or in a downtown business district may be a better choice. Strip mall stores usually are readily available, quite possibly because a lot of the small businesses that start out in those locations don't last. (We'll discuss failure factors and strategies to make sure that doesn't happen to you in later chapters.) Space in downtown business districts can be a little harder to come by, particularly if the area is thriving, and they're also likely to be somewhat more expensive, especially if they're in a bustling area or a resort town with year-round activities. However, the visibility you'll gain for your business may be worth the extra cost.

One last viable choice, especially for a products-based or pet food business, is a mall location. Now, we won't kid you—these types of stores are among the most expensive of all the choices available. (One pet-business entrepreneur we know pays $4,600 a month.) But malls also attract a lot of people who have cash or credit cards in hand. And since people love their pets, they're susceptible to your subtle attempts to part them from their cash. Create a cute window display or invite a homeless cat to be your shop cat/greeter, and you'll pull in lookers who can turn into buyers. If you're running a service business, a mall location can be a good choice for you, too, if you can obtain a location with an outside entrance that faces a busy street. An interior location (like between Sears and an exercise equipment store) isn't optimal because customers are unlikely to want to take their pet though a busy mall. In addition, there may be restrictions against animals in the public space. Check with mall management if you're interested in this type of space.

As with strip malls, marketing and maintenance fees are often part and parcel of renting or leasing a mall location. Be very sure to get specific details about costs upfront and how they're paid so you don't get a nasty shock when you're browsing through the bills at month end.

Of special note to groomers: Try searching for a space that was previously used as a grooming business, which is likely to have the expensive water lines, drains, and electrical wiring you'll need already in place. There has never been a pet groomer in your community? No problem—look for a former hair salon location instead, or even a restaurant. In addition to those water and electrical hookups we mentioned, you might even be lucky enough to score a sales counter as part of the building design. All this can save you big bucks on renovation/retrofitting costs.

> Tip...
>
> **Smart Tip**
>
> It's usually a good idea to take an attorney along when you meet with a landlord to negotiate terms. That way you won't get any nasty surprises later when you discover there was a condition embedded in the lease that you don't agree with. At the very least, have him or her review the paperwork.

There's one more way you can set up shop in the mall while ducking the high lease cost. Many malls lease kiosks or carts from which you can sell your products and pet food. Contact your local mall's management office for more information about kiosk/cart availability and cost.

Groomer/Trainer Shop Design

Figuring out how much room you'll need for your shop is almost as important as finding the ideal location. If you're a groomer, industry experts say you need at least a 500-square-foot work area for a one-groomer operation. You'll also need room for a waiting area, a retail area, a break room/office/storage room, and room for the crates and cages that pets arrive in or are safely penned up in while you do your magic on your other furry clients. Finally, space for a washer and dryer is a necessity so you don't have to transport all those wet towels home every night. Considering all this stuff, that 500-square-foot space looks better all the time.

A trainer's needs may be even more expansive, depending on the type of business you establish. Like a groomer, you'll need a waiting room, retail space if you choose to sell training products, and an office/breakroom. But more important, you'll need adequate space to hold the obedience classes. Optimally this training space should be soundproofed so your furry clients don't disturb the day spa or dental office located next door.

Here are some general space guidelines for allocating service/products space:

Grooming:

- Work area: 70 percent

- Retail area: 15 percent
- Office/laundry space: 10 percent
- Waiting area: 5 percent

Training:

- Work area: 80 percent
- Office space: 15 percent
- Waiting area: 5 percent

Bright Idea

Working on a concrete floor for many hours a day can be really hard on your "dogs." Anti-fatigue mats at each pet-grooming station or behind the sales counter of your retail store will make a world of difference. Cushiony gel insoles that make your feet feel like they're floating on air can also be helpful.

Working the Room

Grooming businesses have significant workroom needs. These include:

- *Central pump system*. This specialty system dispenses both temperature-controlled water and shampoo through hoses.
- *Nonslip flooring*. With all the water that will be slung around by wet pets intent on shaking their booties, this is a must. You can save money by having a laminate finish applied to the floor rather than investing in special flooring.
- *Electrical outlets*. One per station is necessary for obvious reasons.
- *Overhead lighting*. Fluorescent lighting is pretty common in commercial spaces, but if by chance the space is lit by something other than fluorescent lights or if there aren't enough of them, you should have them installed right away. One light over each workstation will suffice. Task lighting is also helpful both to increase visibility and to chase any shadows. Some grooming experts recommend having four task lights per station as a way to approximate daylight conditions.
- *Central vacuum system*. This can be one of the most valuable investments you make. Built-in vac systems are more powerful than standard household models, which makes cleanup faster and easier. When the system is installed, make sure there are inlets in the bathing area, in the area where clipping is done, and in the reception area to keep the floor free of hair shed by nervous pets.

Happily, dog trainers have few needs when it comes to location. If you're working at home, a basement or garage will do nicely and can be configured to accommodate an area for selling retail products if you're so inclined. However, you'll probably want to establish your office elsewhere, both to free up the space in your training area as well as to keep your computer and other business tools out of the way of traffic.

If you're planning to open in a commercial location, your facility can be as grand as the budget allows. Oak Park, Illinois, dog trainer Jamie Damato built a 1,200-square-foot building onto a veterinarian's office to serve as Training Central, but you can make do with less space if that's what the budget will bear. Rec centers, gymnasiums, groomer's salons, and an outside space will do—just keep the poop scoop handy to leave the area clean and sanitary for the next user.

Good Reception

The waiting area for both grooming and training businesses should be tastefully decorated and brightly lit, with an attractive reception desk, one or two stools for employees and comfortable seating for a couple of clients. Because these clients will have their pets in tow, it's a good idea to spread out the seating so fights don't ensue (either human or mammalian). Subscribe to a few pet magazines (you'll find an extensive list in the Appendix) and tuck them into an attractive display rack, which takes up less room than a table. If you think you'll often have clients waiting to pick up their pooches or other pets, offer complimentary coffee from a small table in a corner of the waiting room. Just be sure to keep an eye on brew levels so the pot never runs dry (or burns up!). And by the way, easy-care vinyl flooring is a necessity because: a) there will be accidents, and b) rainy and snowy days mean muddy paws. Don't even think about installing carpeting, and avoid tile because you'll have to expend a lot of elbow grease to keep the grout clean. And it's not worth the time it takes to scrub floors when you're trying to make money plying your craft.

Finally, some grooming salons also install safety gates at the entrance to the salon area if there's not already a standard door there. The first time you have a wet dog slip his grooming tether, leap off the table and streak for the front door you'll know why these gates are invaluable.

The reception desk/sales counter should be large enough to accommodate your computer or cash register, credit-card equipment, telephone, and maybe a pooch or feline or two in case clients decide just to hand Buster or Fluffy over the counter. There also should be enough room on the counter for a client to write a check or open a planner to check availability for Fifi's next appointment. If there's any space left you can also set up a small display of a "featured item" or other product you'd like to sell more of.

> **Bright Idea**
>
> If at all possible, separate your reception area from the grooming area so incoming pets can't see the other animals. Not only will this keep the waiting pets from becoming agitated, it will keep the groomer safe from animals that get excited when a newcomer arrives.

And what if the space you are buying or leasing doesn't come with a reception desk? Then check with a beauty salon or restaurant supply company. You can buy everything from granite-topped stunners to glass and metal art pieces. But frankly, given the type of business you're in, a nice utilitarian wood model like you can buy at Target will work just fine.

Retail products for grooming and training businesses, if any, should also be displayed in your waiting area. Invest in some attractive shelving, which can either stand-alone or be mounted to the wall. Both can be purchased at a reasonable cost at a home superstore like Home Depot. Depending on the type of reception desk you install, you may be able to display products on top or in shelving that's built into the desk. Just be sure to keep products neat and clean, even if it means quickly straightening them several times a day.

Pet Product/Pet Food Store Design

Lucky you if you're a product or pet-food business owner—no need to worry about tubs and water hookups and safety gates. What you do need is a spacious shop that gives you the appearance of prosperity, an important consideration when you're selling upscale products. Or to put it another way: Does your target market consist of clients who search for bargains at flea markets or discerning customers who frequent Nordstrom? Not to put too fine a point on it, a small, jumbled shop just doesn't project the image you're going for with your high-end products. You should buy or lease the largest space you can afford, then fill it with high-quality display pieces that will show your products to their advantage, whether you're selling cashmere horse blankets or designer kibble.

Optimally, your retail space should be allocated as follows: Sales area, 80 percent; break room/stockroom, 10 percent; office space, 10 percent. Optimize your sales area space by using not just the wall space around the perimeter of your shop for display shelves and cases, but central areas of the shop as well. An interior designer experienced in retail space design or a window display professional would be great resources for assistance. Check the Yellow Pages for leads, or ask a store owner whose shop you admire for a referral.

As far as size goes, there's a whole science to retail-store development that can't be covered in detail here. (For all the details on setting up a retail store, see Entrepreneur's startup guide *Start Your Own Retail Store*.) Suffice it to say that a good starting point for an attractively organized and appealing "Main Street" store is about 1,000 square feet, according to the Institute for Local Self-Reliance (ILSR), a national nonprofit research and educational organization. That will give you plenty of room for display areas for either pet food or pet products, customer browsing, office space, and inventory storage—but we'll admit that's huge, especially for a startup. You may find that 500 to 700 square feet will suit your needs just fine, although Diane Burchard, the Santa Fe, New Mexico, retailer/wholesaler, found herself bursting out of her first 500-square-foot shop in no time. Four moves later, she now has 1,800 square feet to call her own.

Among the factors you should consider when mapping out store design are:

- *Traffic flow*. Wide aisles and signage will keep people moving; displays that don't reach the ceiling will give the store a wide-open feel.
- *Inventory*. Upscale products will invite touching more than dog food will, so you'll want to place products at arm's length and on shelves that aren't too high so customers can reach them.
- *Aisles*. The store should have a main aisle, and the products or pet food you want to sell most should be displayed along this aisle. Make sure all aisles are wide enough for people to walk down them comfortably and so merchandise doesn't look crowded.
- *Cash register*. This should be centrally located and well-marked so customers can find it quickly. Interestingly, studies have shown that cashiers who have to bend over to find the right size bag will ring fewer sales per hour, so make sure the counter is designed so bags can be placed right at hand.
- *Color*. If you're selling pet food, bright white walls will give the appearance of freshness and simplicity. If you're selling pet products, however, you might want to select rich and sumptuous colors like jewel tones to emphasize the deluxe quality of your merchandise.
- *Lighting*. Bright light is preferred, although a common complaint among customers is that fluorescent lights make products and even pet food look different than they do in natural light. This can be problematic if you're selling pet clothing or bedding that is meant to match the owner's boudoir. In an upscale shop, you might instead install fancy lighting like a chandelier to play up the exclusivity of the shop and to simulate natural light better.
- *Display fixtures*. You'll need fixtures for display (like glass cases or shelves), self-service selection (like clothing racks) and overstock (for inventory). Display fixtures can be very expensive, so you might consider renting or buying them used to keep the cost down.

Counter Point

When installing a sales counter, consider both the size of the shop and the merchandise that will be located near it. In a smaller shop, the counter should be near the back of the store so customers have to pass by all your delightful merchandise or tempting pet food to get there. In a larger store, you should place the counter near the center of the shop and display your most desirable and pricey merchandise (including "designer" dog food) closer to the front. Even though this means the merchandise at the back won't get as much attention, it's important to think of customer convenience first. One way to entice them to the rear of the store is to make sure the displays that are visible to the customers standing at the counter are both attractive and uncluttered. Alternatively, you

Location Checklist

Cost should never be the only factor when choosing a location for your pet service or product business. Also be sure to consider:

- ❑ Is the location easily accessible (i.e., on or near a main thoroughfare)?
- ❑ Is there plenty of traffic in the area—both vehicular and pedestrian? (Everyone who drives or walks by is a potential customer!)
- ❑ Does the building have enough parking, either free or metered? (You can't sell your products or services if your customers don't have a place to park.)
- ❑ Is it possible to erect a large sign that will be clearly visible from the street?
- ❑ Is the area attractive, well-lit, and safe?
- ❑ Are there other retail businesses nearby? (They'll help pull customers into your shop, too.)
- ❑ Is there a veterinary practice nearby? (Your business will naturally catch the eye of pet owners on their way to the vet.)
- ❑ Is there another groomer/pet-supply/dog-training business nearby? If so, are you sure the market can support another business like yours? (Be sure to do your due diligence as discussed in Chapter 7 to find out.)

could put additional quantities of the "signature" product for which your store is noted near the back, both as a reminder and as bait to get customers to walk through the entire store.

As we mentioned in the service business section earlier, beauty salon and restaurant supply companies are excellent sources for attractive sales counters. Check the Appendix for leads on a few companies.

Designed for Success

For any of the businesses discussed here, there are some other things to consider when designing your shop. For instance, do you need a break room? If you're running a one-person shop, you can use your onsite office as your break room. But if you have employees, you should set aside a small area—perhaps 5 to 10 percent of the total area—near the rear of the shop for this purpose. It should contain a sink, a small table and chairs, a microwave, a refrigerator, and locking storage for personal possessions. To keep costs down, buy compact-sized appliances and used furniture.

> **Bright Idea**
>
> Before you even open your doors, contact the local merchants association to see what kinds of benefits it offers member business owners. These associations have a lot more clout collectively than you would individually, especially when it comes to petitioning city hall for municipal services and improvements. The organization may even offer money-saving group advertising and insurance programs.

Alas, when you're starting a small business it's often hard to find quarters for your retail product overstock and basic cleaning supplies—and if you're a groomer, possibly a washer and dryer, as well. As a result, the most you'll probably have room for in the way of office furniture probably will be a desk with a phone, an office chair, one visitor chair, and possibly a filing cabinet or bookcase. If your office is also the storeroom, keep retail products organized by having sturdy shelves installed along one wall so you can see what you have at a glance (this also helps you to rotate product like shampoo so it doesn't get old). Alternatively, a tall pantry cabinet can be a great place to keep product overstock neat and organized.

While you may be sharing space with the training clickers, nail clippers, and fish treats, you still should make your office/storeroom as bright and cheerful as possible. Hang a few pictures on the walls, and make sure you have sufficient lighting. Recessed lighting is especially nice in a small work area, since standard fixtures that drop down from the ceiling can make the space appear even smaller.

Keeping Up Appearances

There's a tendency among some pet-service owners to keep their surroundings spartan and unadorned. While there's a lot to be said for having such a neat work environment, there's no reason why you can't make your pet salon or training facility bright and interesting. For instance, why not install mirrors to give your grooming emporium the appearance of a beauty salon? A fresh coat of paint, wall art, and shiny, clean floors also add to the professional look of your facility. Likewise, a pet-products store should be well-decorated and bright. Flourishes like a vase of carefully arranged garden flowers on the counter near the rhinestone-encrusted leashes or designer coats add a fresh and appealing touch.

Although your color-blind feline and canine friends won't be very interested in the paint color, your human clients may notice, so pick colors judiciously. Cool colors like blues and greens are calming and soothing, while warm colors like reds and yellows are energizing and actually make an area look larger, according to the Color Marketing Group. And remember those mirrors we mentioned earlier? When placed strategically they can make even compact areas seem larger. Finally, spotlights and track lighting are great for emphasizing areas like product displays.

> **Tip...**
>
> **Smart Tip**
>
> Even your furry customers may sometimes need to use the facilities. Establishing a designated dog run and potty area outside your building or home will help keep things neat and tidy. Put up a discreet sign that shows where to go, then provide free poop bags, scoopers, and a place to deposit the deposits.

It goes without saying that your place of business should be kept scrupulously clean, no matter which type of business you're engaged in. If you have employees, you should stress that each person is responsible for tidying up his or her own work area. Likewise, the break room should be kept neat and uncluttered, and the bathroom should be sanitized regularly. Buy brooms, trashcans, and garbage bags, and show employees where they are. For bigger jobs like scrubbing floors in grooming salons or washing windows in a retail establishment, you might consider hiring an outside cleaning service (better than doing it yourself at the end of a long day, eh?). Such a service might cost $50 an hour or more, depending on your geographic location, but it's worth it. A once-a-week once-over is usually sufficient.

Sign of Good Things

The last thing you'll need before you can throw open the doors is exterior signage. Signs serve a dual purpose: They unerringly usher your customers to the front door, and they advertise your business to potential customers who are passing by. Your exterior sign should be large enough to be easily seen from the street, and it should have type that's easy to read (no fancy script typefaces, please). Illuminated signs are always preferable to metal or plastic, since they are clearly visible even at night or when the weather is inclement. Unless your business name includes the type of service you offer ("Luke's Dog Grooming Emporium"), you should include a brief description of the products/services you offer on your sign. For instance, a pet-food company called The Doggy Diner should have "Gourmet Pet Food and Treats" in smaller letters under the name or adoring owners might phone for dinner reservations for Fido's birthday.

And speaking of phone numbers, you can include your phone number on your building sign, or you can have a custom-made neon sign made up to go into your window. Just make sure it doesn't entirely block the view into the facility or store. Some prospects can be enticed to come inside strictly on the basis of a peek through the front window.

While signage can be fairly costly, it's definitely worth the price. But be sure to check with the local zoning commission and/or your landlord before commissioning a sign.

There may be local ordinances relating to the size, design, or style (for example, flush mounted vs. hanging). And here's a tip for potential tenants in historic preservation districts: Do not pass go and do not collect $200 until you check with the doyens of the local historical society. It is their manifest destiny to preserve the historic integrity of the area, meaning you must adhere to their edicts on size, shape, configuration, and colors of signs, not to mention a million other building details. Finding out these requirements upfront can save you a bundle of money.

12

Good Stock

Now that you're on the way to selecting a suitable location for your pet-products business—either bricks-and-mortar or virtual—it's time to give some thought to the products you'll be ordering to stock the shelves. And you don't have to be a budding retail magnate to need this information: All you dog trainers and pet groomers also may be interested in this chapter if you would like to sell retail products from your mobile "field office" or a retail area in your grooming salon or training facility.

Buying Time

It's common knowledge among retailers that the way to make money on your products is through shrewd purchasing decisions. The idea is to get a good enough price on products so you can mark them up and pocket the difference as profit. Then if you have to discount something to move it off your shelves, it's no problem as long as you still sell above the price at which you obtained the goods. The way to do this, of course, is to find reliable and affordable manufacturers and suppliers to provide the products you wish to carry in your inventory.

But finding these supply sources can be challenging, especially for a newly minted pet-business entrepreneur. Sometimes it can be difficult to get a business to sell to you because you're not buying in the huge quantities of the local PetSmart. Rest assured that there are enough companies around that will be more than happy to ship you their goods, so don't be discouraged if you encounter suppliers who are more interested in selling a gross of something than a dozen. Just politely decline and keep looking.

All the Right Places

Among the places you can find merchandise for your site-based or virtual business are:

- *Manufacturers*. It's possible to purchase product directly from the manufacturers once you find out where they live. Use the internet to research the various types of products you want to sell, from pet treats to pet jewelry, then contact the sales office directly and ask to speak to a manufacturer's representative. This kind of direct relationship is great because there's no middle person involved, which means you usually can negotiate better prices on the goods. Whenever possible (and this could be iffy because you are a small operator), work out a 30-day financing arrangement with the manufacturers. That way you'll have plenty of time to sell the items in question, make a profit and repay the supplier in a timely fashion. An association like the American Pet Products Association

Beware!

Don't attempt to buy from too many sources when setting up your supply chain. You'll find it's a labor-intensive process to track inventory, keep up with invoices, and manage other details of the business when you're trying to juggle too many companies with different terms and accounting systems.

(APPA) is an excellent source for finding companies that manufacture the products you want.

- *Wholesalers.* Buying from a wholesaler can be advantageous because it will give you access to an array of products from many manufacturers. That can be a big time-saver because you won't have to make direct contacts with a whole lot of suppliers on your own. Once again, the internet can be a fantastic resource for locating wholesalers. And interestingly enough, wholesalers are even using eBay to sell product lots. As you probably know, product availability and quantities vary on eBay, so there may not be anything you'd be interested in buying for months. But it's worth checking it out from time to time to see what pops up.
- *Merchandise marts.* Retailer-only merchandise markets are a great place to discover new products or inspiration and can be found nationwide. For a partial list of some to check out, see "Shopping List" on page 148.
- *Resident buying offices.* Usually found around merchandise marts, resident buying offices are made up of national and/or international buyers who shop the marts regularly, then report back to retailers on products they feel might be of interest. They also can choose and purchase merchandise for you on a contract basis. These buying offices are especially useful for identifying purchase trends, pinpointing potentially hot products, and otherwise serving as your eyes and ears. To find a resident buying office, check the merchandising services category in the Yellow Pages directory that covers the area where the marts are located, or see if your library has a copy of *Sheldon's Major Stores & Chains & Resident Buying Offices* (Pheldon, Sheldon & Marsar).
- *Trade shows.* Pet-industry and consumer trade shows can be wonderful sources of information about new pet products and pet food on the market. Vendors and manufacturers alike often come to these shows in the hopes of selling product, and you'll be speaking directly to a manufacturers rep when you stop by their booths. Make sure to bring a good supply of your business cards to these shows, and pick up as many product catalogs and cards as possible from the vendors you might be interested in speaking to later. You'll find the names of some of the larger pet-industry trade shows in the Appendix. By the way, you can also use trade shows as

Bright Idea

When shopping at the trade shows or merchandise marts, make notes on the back of each vendor's card to remind yourself what product he or she was selling. Information like minimum orders and turnaround time can also be useful when you get back to your office and can't remember why you were interested in a particular company's wares.

venues to sell your own merchandise if you're a manufacturer. You'll find information about the various trade shows you may wish to consider in Chapter 14.

- *Private-label manufacturers*. If you're planning a career selling pet food, you definitely should make some contacts among private-label pet-food manufacturers. These companies may have their own online or bricks-and-mortar stores, but Bob Vetere, COO and managing director of the APPA, says the smaller private-label companies don't turn away much business and will be more than willing to sell to you. You can find the names of 42 U.S. pet-food manufacturers in a report from the University of Massachusetts Dartmouth called "A Market Analysis of the U.S. Pet Food Industry to Determine New Opportunities for the

Shopping List

There are quite a few wholesale merchandise markets located around the United States that are accessible only to retailers. Some are quite specialized, like the Atlanta Apparel Mart, which carries—surprise!—women's, men's, and children's apparel and accessories. But there are many general marts that could be great sources of pet products. Among the general marts to check out are:

- ❍ AmericasMart Atlanta (americasmart.com/)
- ❍ Charlotte Merchandise Mart (North Carolina) (carolinasmart.com)
- ❍ Chicago Gift & Home Market (merchandisemart.com)
- ❍ Dallas Market Center (dallasmarketcenter.com)
- ❍ Denver Merchandise Mart (denvermart.com)
- ❍ Kansas City Gift Mart (kcgiftmart.com)
- ❍ L.A. Mart (merchandisemart.com/lamart)
- ❍ Miami International Merchandise Mart (miamimart.net)
- ❍ Minneapolis Gift Mart (mplsgiftmart.com)
- ❍ New York Gift Mart (merchandisemart.com/7w34)
- ❍ Northeast Market Center, Bedford, Massachusetts (thegiftcenter.com)
- ❍ San Francisco Giftcenter and Jewelrymart (gcjm.com)
- ❍ Seattle Gift Center (seattlegiftcenter.com)

It's not hard to get these marts to sell to small companies like yours—just as long as you buy sufficient quantities and have that official sales tax license.

Cranberry Industry." The report is located at umassd.edu/cbr/studies/cranbpetfood.pdf.

Beware!

Before you form any partnerships or enter into exclusive marketing relationships with vendors, have your attorney review contracts thoroughly. You need to make sure you're not giving away the farm with your signature or jeopardizing any future agreements you might wish to make with other suppliers.

- *Artisans.* Anyone can sell a designer dog handbag in supple leather. But for a one-of-a-kind product the likes of which a Hollywood starlet might crave, try enlisting the talents of artisans in your community. For instance, perhaps you know a genius with knitting needles who, if provided with the finest cashmere and silk yarn, could handcraft $500 "receiving blankets" for newborn puppies. Or perhaps you're acquainted with a seamstress who has a flair for fashion and could whip up designer carry-all bags for pooches. (Think Kate Spade—she started making her own bags and voilà! She's famous and rich.) Because these items would be handmade and custom-crafted, you wouldn't have many to sell, which would make them oh-so chic and command higher prices.

  This technique has worked well for Diane Burchard, the Santa Fe, New Mexico, pet-products retailer. She uses a number of different artisans, including a sewer who makes her pet coats; a co-op in Bolivia that hand-knits sweaters; a potter who creates the pet bowls; and a leather-belt maker who makes the collars. "This way you don't have to plunk out hundreds of thousands of dollars in inventory and hope it will sell," she says. "I also like the idea of supporting local artisans in New Mexico, plus I can control quality better."

  If you don't know any creative people personally, try calling the gift marts in major cities for leads (you'll find the major ones listed on page 148). Arts and craft shows are also good sources of specialty items or people who may be willing to make them for you. Finally, you can find leads to small businesses across the country through the National Craft Association website (craftassoc.com), which offers various useful resources, like an online wholesale source directory and an arts and craft show listing page.
- *Contract facilities.* As mentioned earlier, it's possible to get a contract manufacturer or packager to make products to your specifications—and it's not as hard or expensive as it might seem. "You can get your product and your formula produced without going into debt because there are bakeries and factories with excess capacity that would be happy to manufacture products for you," says Leonard Green, the Woodbridge, New Jersey, entrepreneur. "In fact, part of entrepreneurship says don't take on employees, buildings, or assets and put all

your money into marketing instead, and that's a model you can follow successfully."

As you may recall from earlier chapters, several of the business owners interviewed for this book also subscribe to this philosophy and have contracted with factories to produce their pet products. You may have to pound the pavement to find the right manufacturer who will work with a small company like yours, but they are definitely out there.

Tip...

Smart Tip

Merchandise marts and other product wholesalers will expect you to pay with a check drawn on a business checking account when you make purchases. They also usually require a second piece of identification to prove you're a retailer. Bringing along a copy of your sales tax license and your business card will usually do the trick.

Stashing Your Loot

Once you've picked out the inventory you wish to carry, you need to have a way to get it to your store—and a place to park it until it goes on the shelves (or in the mail if you're an internet merchant). To begin with, you should establish a few relationships with both freight carriers (for larger items) and shipping companies so deliveries can be made to your home, store, or storage facility in a timely fashion. You probably already know the big players in the shipping industry—companies like FedEx, UPS, DHL, and Airborne. All you have to do to use any of those services is call their local office and set up a business account. Then it's a simple matter of giving your account number to a supplier when the company is ready to ship merchandise to you. You'll find contact information for ground shippers in the Appendix.

Tip...

Smart Tip

Retailers commonly stock three times as many products as they need during periods of normal demand to reach the sales level they want. For example, if you want to sell $1,000 worth of dog tiaras, you should have $3,000 worth of inventory on hand. During peak selling seasons, you might need a higher ratio of merchandise—say, 5:1.

Once merchandise arrives at your home or store, always be sure to check the packing slip against the number of products in the shipment, and call the supplier immediately if there is a discrepancy. If you're planning to store merchandise in your retail location, you will need to establish a stockroom area that is off limits to the general public and preferably secured by a locking door. This stockroom should be outfitted with heavy-duty open shelving like the type sold at home-improvement stores, as well as with storage cabinets for smaller items. Rubbermaid has a line of heavy-duty storage cabinets made specifically for workrooms and garages that are both attractive and affordable (around $120 for a 72-by-36-by-18-inch cabinet

Dropping In

Looking for a way to make a good living selling pet products without ever having to store inventory, box it for shipment, or take it to the post office to mail it to customers? Then consider drop-shipping, in which you arrange for a manufacturer or distributor of a product you're interested in selling to send it out for you. You do all the work finding the customers, taking the orders and collecting the cash. Then you send the order to the drop-shipper, who boxes up the merchandise, sends it off using your shipping label, and bills you for the wholesale price of the product, plus shipping and handling.

The advantages of drop-shipping are numerous. First, you can offer brand-name and pricey products on your website without having to worry about a high outlay of precious startup dollars on inventory or finding the room to store products until they sell. You won't be stuck with leftover items that you'll have to sell at a deep discount. Finally, you can add and drop merchandise from your product mix almost instantaneously.

To find companies that drop-ship, contact manufacturers directly. Not every company will want to deal with you, however, so your next step would be to contact distributors who work with the manufacturers. You can find both manufacturers and distributors through their ads in trade magazines, as well as at trade shows. Alternatively, look through the *Thomas Register* (ThomasNet.com), which lists thousands of companies by product and brand name.

with four shelves and doors that can be padlocked). You can find them at home-improvement stores and even department stores like Target.

If your retail operation consists of a room in your home, your basement or your garage, you also will want to organize your products neatly on shelving units. Just make sure that basement or garage is watertight and otherwise protected from the elements. In addition, there may be restrictions on where you can store your products if you're selling pet food. Check with your local municipality for information.

If you simply don't have room at your home for your merchandise or you need additional space because your inventory is growing, you may find that an off-site self-storage unit can be a life-saver and a business-builder. The smallest unit is usually around 10 feet by 15 square feet, which is about the size of a large bedroom. The next size up is 10 feet by 20 square feet, or approximately the size of a small one-car garage. Install heavy-duty shelving for instant storage and organization and you'll be ready to move in. Again, check to make sure there aren't any restrictions on food storage. You can expect to pay about $100 to $200 a month for self-storage rent.

Another viable option for product storage is to build an addition on your home, as Amanda Miller's partner, Cathy Jackson, did. The 1,000-square-foot room inside her Scottsdale, Arizona, home houses the luxury pet beds the pair sells and also serves as the fulfillment center for shipping out product to wholesale customers and upscale boutiques. The room consists of little more than four walls, electricity, heat, and air conditioning, but that's essentially all they need to ship out those orders.

On Display

Depending on the type of store you plan to sell from, you'll want to buy appropriate displays for your merchandise. That chic retailing operation you're envisioning should have glass display cases that lock (to protect the priciest merchandise), as well as glass shelving attached to the wall and racks for displaying pet clothing. Unusual display pieces, like an antique sideboard or a Victorian dresser with an oval mirror, will give your store an eclectic and distinctive look. Just don't overload the display racks, especially if you're going for a look of exclusivity and luxury. A few well-placed items are always preferable to racks stuffed to the gills.

Some suppliers will even provide you with display racks at no charge—but most of the time you have to ask for them. Use a little psychology and tell them you'd be happy to carry their product if only they would just throw in the display, and you just may find one on your doorstep faster than you can say "kibbles and bits."

Under Control

To keep track of all the products you have in your store or storeroom as they come and go, you need to invest in an inventory-control software program. There are a number of products on the market for this, including Mind Your Own Business, QuickBooks, or Microsoft Excel. You'll find contact information for them in the Appendix. In addition, a scanner for reading barcodes is a useful add-on to your inventory-control software. In the case of pet food, you also must track product by its shelf life to make sure edibles are always fresh and safe to eat. When pet food or dog biscuits approach their "sell by" date, rotate the stock by putting it on sale. Just be sure to let your customers know that the expiration date is near or they could be upset when they get the product home.

Money Matters

To purchase products, you'll need to establish credit with the suppliers. Credit terms of 30 days are common among suppliers, and you should be prepared to produce

Dollar Stretcher

A sales tax ID number not only allows you to buy at wholesale costs, but you also won't have to pay sales tax on the products you purchase for resale, since that would amount to double taxation.

documentation like your financial statements (or income and expenses report, which we'll discuss in Chapter 18) and proof of your creditworthiness. Since you're just starting out, you may find some suppliers won't want to do business with you, but if you seem well-organized and have some money in the bank, more often than not suppliers will bend over backward to secure your business. When that happens, treat that supplier like gold—it can be used as a credit reference for the next supplier you approach.

And finally, don't forget about those pesky sales taxes. As you probably already know, nearly every state requires retailers to collect sales tax on products sold. (The exceptions are Alaska, Delaware, Montana, New Hampshire, and Oregon.) In addition, more and more states are now also beginning to enforce heretofore little-known state regulations that require internet merchants to collect sales tax. You'll also find that some municipalities have their own little tax pecadillos, like Denver with its use tax and many Alaskan cities with their local sales taxes. Since the whole issue of sales tax varies by state and is somewhat complex, you might want to refer to the Business Owner's Toolkit website at toolkit.cch.com, then search for "Your State Tax Obligations" for a state-by-state listing of information related to tax obligations. Alternatively, you can check directly with your state's department of revenue, taxation, or treasury for information and guidance.

Once you know what your tax obligations are, you can apply for a sales tax license (aka resale license) through your state's department of revenue, taxation, or treasury. The good news is some states don't charge for this license, while others collect only a nominal fee (in the neighborhood of $1 to $20). The bad news is you'll have to keep careful records of how much sales tax you collect from customers, then send it in to the state revenue department on a quarterly basis. Your accountant no doubt would be more than happy to handle this extra little task on your behalf.

13

Pick of the Litter

Although you probably started this journey toward pet-business ownership with the intention of being a one-man (or woman) band, you may be coming to the conclusion that there could be more work involved than you can handle yourself. And you'd be right. Depending on how successful your business is, how much you'd like to continue to have a home life and take a vacation, and how much you want to grow the business, you may need to hire staff to help you.

Adding staff is a big step, and it's one that can make your business life much more complicated. You'll have more paperwork. You'll have to deal with personnel management issues. You'll have to hire and fire. And most sobering of all, you'll have other people depending on you for their livelihoods, which can really make you nervous even at the best of times.

Yet the reality is that if you want to operate more efficiently and take your business to the next level, you will one day need employees. This chapter will give you some insight into how to make the process as painless as possible. But of course, if hiring helpers truly is the furthest thing from your mind at the moment, feel free to move on to Chapter 14, where you'll find a discussion of professional development possibilities and opportunities.

Purr-fect Timing

Sometimes new entrepreneurs get so busy they don't even realize they've bitten off more pet business than they can chew. Then one day it dawns on them they have no other life and they're spending time on tasks that keep them from doing the job they started the business to do—namely, training or grooming or pet sitting or selling. Or they're turning down business because they can't fit one more client into their schedule. When that moment arrives, it's time to start thinking about bringing on staff, as Exton, Pennsylvania, products business owner Joyce Reavey did almost from day one.

"It's really important not to get trapped in the day-to-day activities if you want the business to grow," Reavey says. "Since in this business you have to live your life six months before you want anything to happen, you need good help, plus you need people to bounce ideas off on a daily basis."

If you're homebased, there's one thing you need to check before bringing on employees. Many municipalities will not allow homebased business owners to have employees on-site unless they are family members, presumably because neighborhoods are not zoned for commercial businesses. So place a quick call to your city, township, or other local government entity and ask about restrictions, then abide by them if you are told employees are *verboten*. Of course, if the answer is no, you still may have some recourse. Use your best powers of persuasion to make a case that your employees will not disrupt the neighborhood, that

> Tip...
>
> **Smart Tip**
>
> When you call to check whether zoning laws will permit you to employ people in your homebased business, make sure you've already applied for and acquired a legitimate business license to keep all the bureaucrats happy.

Pinch Sitters

If you're contemplating a career as a pet sitter or dog walker, you undoubtedly have already considered that you're likely to be on duty days and nights, weekends and holidays—in short, whenever others want to enjoy their own time off or have other commitments. So what happens when you want to take a vacation yourself, or you or your child wakes up with the flu? You need to call in someone you trust to handle your workload, and in this industry, that someone may very well be another professional pet sitter or dog walker.

Even though you're vying for the same business, these pet professionals can help you out when you have too much business or need a day off. It's important to develop a network of sitters and walkers you can count on before you ever need them. One way to find reliable people is through your membership in the National Association of Professional Pet Sitters. You should look for a couple of people in your general market area but not so close by that you're pursuing the same clients. Then meet them to discuss how the arrangement will be handled and how much you'll pay. You don't have to turn over the entire fee to the fill-in person; it's perfectly legitimate for you to take a commission of, say, 10 percent or more, and it's not necessary to tell your temporary helper the amount of the commission. Just be sure to pay the pet professional promptly so he or she will be willing to help you out again the next time you need assistance.

they'll park on your property rather than on the street, that they'll contribute to the local economy by patronizing nearby shops and restaurants, etc. It could work. Try it.

A Breed Apart

There are three types of employees you may need in your business: skilled, administrative, and sales. Check out the chart on page 158 for a rundown of the various types of employees you might need, either today or in the future. Keep in mind that some of these folks can double up on jobs so you don't have to hire a whole bunch of people. For instance, your receptionist should be able to handle all the general office duties like opening mail and stuffing and sticking labels to envelopes in addition to answering phones and greeting customers.

As you can see, the professional who has the potential to have the most employees is a dog groomer, while the pet sitter/dog walker probably will need the fewest different types of employees (although he or she may need several pet-care assistants to keep the

Types of Pet-Business Employees

Task	Pet Sitter/ Dog Walker	Dog Trainer	Pet Groomer	Retail Pet Food	Retail Pet Products	Internet Food/ Products
Skilled						
Pet-care assistants	x		x			
Training assistants		x				
Pet groomer/trimmer			x			
Pet shampooer			x			
Administrative						
Greeter/receptionist		x	x	x	x	
General clerical assistant (answers phone, opens mail, etc.)		x	x	x	x	
Direct-mail specialist (manages mailing list, stuffs envelopes, writes offers)		x	x	x	x	x
Telemarketer		x	x	x	x	
Salon/office manager		x	x	x	x	x
Employee trainer		x	x			
Sales						
Sales clerk				x	x	
Fulfillment/mail clerk						x
Stock clerk				x	x	x

business growing). Of course, this chart assumes you have all the operating capital and clients you could ever want. Since the reality is that you're probably years away from needing (or being able to afford) everyone suggested on this list, consider it food for thought.

Let the Search Begin

Once you've made the commitment to hire employees, you probably think your toughest job will be overseeing them and inspiring them to work to their best potential.

Dollar Stretcher

Your local state university or community college can be a great source of inexpensive labor. Students' high energy level and willingness to work long hours for pizza or book money can make them valuable additions to your staff. Just be flexible when it comes to their work hours—they'll be fitting the job in around their school schedules.

But pet-business owners will tell you the biggest challenge you'll have is to find qualified help in the first place. Pet care may be a warm-and-fuzzy kind of business that seemingly would attract a lot of people, but the truth is, that warm-and-fuzzy aspect actually narrows your pool of prospects. After all, people in this type of work must have a true love of and affinity for animals, and if they don't, they simply will not work out. (This goes for pet-business owners as well, but we're assuming you fit that profile.)

Many pet-care business owners rely on referrals and word-of-mouth to locate help. Columbia, South Carolina, wholesaler/manufacturer Susan Benesh gets leads from her lawn guy "because he knows everyone," she explains.

David Lipschultz, the Oak Park, Illinois, pet sitter/dog walker, doesn't necessarily look for experience in a potential hire. "I'd like to find people with dog knowledge when I'm hiring, but that's not my top priority," he says. "I'd rather find nice, good people I can train. I'm a pretty good judge of people so I go with my gut reaction."

Start your search for employees by spreading the word among your friends, family, and business acquaintances. People who come recommended by someone you trust often end up being better and more reliable employees—after all, in a sense they were prescreened for you. Veterinarians can be particularly good sources of referrals, so don't hesitate to call them.

Other places to find good help are local pet-grooming or vocational schools, colleges (especially those in veterinarian programs), pet shelters, and web-based job boards like Monster.com. Some pet-business owners also look to their own clientele for help, which isn't a bad idea because they at least know their clients are pet lovers. But do be aware that if the relationship doesn't work out, you could lose not only an employee but also a regular customer, so tread lightly.

Of course, the traditional method for seeking job candidates is through the help-wanted classified section of your local newspaper—which in some U.S. markets is online in addition to being in print. Seeking job applicants this way can be unreliable. If you're lucky, you'll get a lot of responses, but chances are

Smart Tip

When hiring employees—especially those who will be going into clients' homes to care for pets—always be sure to ask for three to five references, then check each one. You might also want to run a criminal and credit check on prospective employees to make sure they are good, upstanding citizens.

> **Bright Idea**
> Make sure to give each employee you hire sufficient training before letting him or her loose to do a job. In particular, training in the safety and security measures that must be taken with the pets in your care must be stressed so you never have a tragic accident due to careless handling of your furry friends.

many of the applicants will not be qualified, and you'll have to sort through all of them to find out. Alternatively, you might advertise and get few to no responses. It's enough to drive a business owner crazy, and it's another reason to compensate and treat your employees well when you do find those gems.

If you still choose to go this route, at least make your employment ad stand out, and spring for a larger ad with a box around it. That type of ad, known as a display ad, will catch the attention of the reader better than a line ad, which is one of those three-to-five-line ads that is listed alphabetically by its first word. A boxed display ad will also give you enough room to state the specific job requirements that are most important to you, so use the space to your best advantage.

Be prepared to run your ad more than once—and maybe indefinitely. "The response you get from an ad can be pretty unpredictable," says Lipschultz. "I pretty much have to advertise continuously to get a steady stream of applicants."

Behind the Scenes

Before you invite any prospective employees for an interview, you need to put all the qualifications and responsibilities related to the job on paper. This job description not only serves as a reference for you and the applicant during the interview, but also it becomes a record of exactly what the job seeker agrees to do while on your payroll. As such, the job description should include the specific job title, the number of hours a week the employee will work, the employee's specific job duties, and any required education, work-related experience, and physical requirements (like being able to lift 100-pound Great Danes). It's also a good idea to have an employee manual that includes everything related to the operation of the business, from what to do on a visit to how to handle keys, alarms, and different types of pets. Both David Lipschultz and Seattle pet sitter/dog walker Dan MacDonald have detailed employee manuals and wouldn't do business any other way.

The best time to weed out the people who are not suitable for the job is before they're sitting in front of you. You might want to conduct a preinterview discussion by phone before inviting prospects to come in for a full-fledged interview. But before you call anyone who looks promising, read through his or her letter of application and resume carefully. Although it's possible you'll receive applications from people with pet-care experience, chances are your applicants will have experience in many other types of fields instead. Look for signs that a person has been successfully employed, which may include a record of continuous employment with the same person or company and no (or few) gaps in the job history. A person who has worked in a customer service capacity for a while (say, more than a year) might also be a good candidate for a pet-care job.

During the phone prescreening, take note of the candidate's enthusiasm for the job. Does he or she sound truly interested in the job, or just the paycheck? Does it sound like he or she sincerely loves animals? You can find out by asking questions like, "Why do you want this job?" or "What would you like best about working with animals (or pet-related products)?" If the answers seem appropriate and the person sounds likable, you should then invite him or her in for an interview. And do keep in mind that while skills can be taught, attitude and personality can't be changed. So if you find an ex-McDonald's French fryer who's enthusiastic, bright and eager, give that person a chance to learn the job. You could end up with a gem of an employee.

Raleigh, North Carolina, pet sitter Jerry Wentz has a surefire method for weeding out undesirable employees: If they ask about being paid under the table, the interview ends. "I'm not interested in hiring someone without integrity and who doesn't want to play by the rules," he says. "This whole business is about trust and selling peace of mind, and if someone is silly enough to ask about being paid illegally, the conversation is over."

Seattle pet sitter Dan MacDonald concurs. "I don't pay anyone off the books because I don't want to get audited," he says. "I have enough in my life working with animals, doing the books, running the business, and making it successful. Why deal with Uncle Sam, too, and possibly be shut down or fined?"

Wentz also recommends doing a background check before bringing someone on board. "These checks are relatively inexpensive," he says, "and you can look at credit history, bankruptcies, criminal history, traffic tickets, computer trespass, assault with deadly weapon, and so on."

Pay Day

Another thing you should decide before you bring anyone in for an interview is how much you'll pay for the job. You don't have to publish this amount in your ad or even discuss it at the first interview, but you still need to have a pretty good idea of what you can afford to pay. Suppose an applicant walks in the door and has five years' grooming experience, is very personable and intelligent, and immediately pets and coos over your shop dog. This is a real dog lover who has excellent credentials, but if all you plan to offer is minimum wage, you may be in for a disappointment when he or she decides to go elsewhere for more money. If you know you can go as high as $8 an hour, you might be able to snag this perfect employee.

The same thing goes for pet sitters. The going rate is about $4 per visit for a beginning pet sitter and up to $6 for someone more experienced. If you can offer a little more to a beginner—say, $4.50 a visit—you may find your employment efforts will be more successful.

Beware!

All new employees must fill out INS Form I-9 (*Employment Eligibility Verification*) within three days of the start of employment, as well as provide acceptable proof of citizenship (like a passport) or legal residency (a so-called "green card"). Independent contractors are not required to do this.

If you need help figuring out how much to pay, you can find some general information in the Animal Care and Service Workers category of the *Occupational Outlook Handbook, 2006–07 Edition* (published by the U.S. Department of Labor). According to OOH, the median hourly earnings for nonfarm-animal caretakers were $8.39 in 2004 while those of animal trainers were $11.03. Cashiers in general merchandise stores (like pet-products or food stores) earned $7.27 per hour. Another useful source of salary info, at least for groomers, is Salary.com, where you can type in your zip code and get the low, median, and high salaries in two categories: animal groomer and animal groomer/bather. If you're in a small town, you might want to plug in the zip code of the nearest medium-to-large community.

As you can see, like most service industries, pet care isn't an especially high-paying field. Many small-business owners can only afford minimum wage or a little better for entry-level employees, up to perhaps $8 to $10 an hour for skilled and experienced pet-care providers. Product-company employees usually don't fare much better, earning minimum wage or a tad more for sales and stock jobs. It's also quite common in the pet-care industry to use independent contractors so owners don't have to do a lot of paperwork. As a result, they are often paid a little more because the contractor takes on all the financial and tax liability.

But if you want to retain good people, Santa Fe, New Mexico, retailer/wholesaler Diane Burchard, contends, "You really have to pay your employees well. I don't expect my people to work without what I have, which includes good pay, a big bonus at the end of the year, and two weeks' paid vacation. That's why both of my employees have been with me for eight years, which is phenomenal in the retail industry."

Although it's not a common practice among homebased pet-care service business startups to offer benefits like health insurance to their employees—at least, not in the beginning—entrepreneurs who start site-based retail operations are more likely to offer benefits like group health insurance, partly because they are somewhat more likely to have full-time employees. But you'll find that offering basic benefits, like a week off with pay after six months or a personal day or two, can really build goodwill among your employees and may actually be a lure for job seekers. Pet organizations like Pet Sitters International offer access to group health insurance that you might like to explore.

Lone Rangers

As we said earlier, some pet-care business owners—especially pet sitters and dog walkers—prefer to hire independent contractors to avoid the financial liability and paperwork requirements that go with having regular employees. Variously known as subcontractors or freelancers, independent contractors usually have their own company and offer their services to other business owners basically with no strings attached. The employer's only responsibility with contractors is to report any income greater than $600 on a 1099 form at the end of the tax year.

> **Tip...**
>
> **Smart Tip**
>
> To help make the process of paying federal employee taxes easier and more manageable, try using EFTPS-OnLine, the government's free electronic payment system. You can pay by check either over the internet or by phone using your employer identification number or Social Security number. For more information or to enroll, call (800) 945-8400, or log onto eftps.gov.

Contractors are attractive to small-business owners because they don't qualify for benefits, and the employer doesn't have to pay employment taxes on their wages or cover them under a workers' compensation policy. But of course, the IRS has a lot to say about the use of contractors. To begin with, a person who works in your place of business, whether it's your home or a shop or store, is automatically considered to be a regular employee. If you pay a contractor by the hour, that makes him or her an employee, too. In fact, the IRS has 20 different measures to determine whether someone is a true contractor or an employee. To make sure you're legal, go to irs.gov and type in "Independent consultants vs. employees" in the search window. You also should download a copy of Publication 15-A, *Employer's Supplemental Tax Guide*, for further guidance, or you can pick one up from an IRS field office.

And by the way, for all you pet sitters and dog walkers who pay your helpers by the job rather than by the hour, you shouldn't run into any trouble with Uncle Sam. But to be sure, discuss your contractor relationships with your accountant.

Now, About Those Taxes

Once you have employees, you need to start anteing up the payroll taxes. Payroll-tax management is a time-consuming task. Many pet-business owners turn the whole complicated job over to their accountants, who will see that the right amount of taxes is filed at the right time. Others, like Lipschultz, handle some or much of the task themselves using a program like QuickBooks. In fact, Lipschultz says, "I stay pretty involved in the financial side of the business and spend a couple of hours a week on the books. That allows me to keep a close eye on the taxes."

But even though he's tuned into his tax situation, Lipschultz prefers to rely on a payroll service to handle that paperwork. "Payroll is a monster of a job, and payroll taxes are incredibly complicated," he says. "A payroll service is indispensable for producing 30 to 40 checks biweekly for my company. It would be a massive project timewise, and it's one that I'd rather pay $80 biweekly to have done for me."

Pet-food business owner John Zambelli of Elmwood Park, New Jersey, concurs. "I'd really rather run the business than do accounting," he says. "Also, when you use a service you don't run the risk of an audit. The last thing you want to do is play games and fiddle with the IRS, especially when the cost for the service is just $30 a month."

14

Learning New Tricks

"You don't understand anything until you learn it more than one way." So says Marvin Minsky, a professor at the Massachusetts Institute of Technology and scientist in the field of artificial intelligence. And that pretty much sums up why pursuing educational opportunities is so important to your development as a pet-care business owner.

Whether you're weeks or decades out of the classroom, there's always something new you can learn about your profession or business in general that can help you run your operation better. Now, we all know that one of your greatest strengths as a business owner is your knowledge of your industry. But you need to keep that knowledge up-to-date by staying abreast of changes and innovations in your field. The best way to do that is to join industry-related organizations, take both professional and business classes, and read publications pertinent to your field.

Industry organizations are a great forum for learning. They often offer a wide range of activities, such as workshops and seminars, as well as valuable networking opportunities. But perhaps more importantly, they bring together professionals with common interests and goals so they can share stories and solutions, commiserate over problematic situations and clients, and trade tips that can help them perform better.

"Serious people interested in business...can significantly shorten their learning curve just by being members [of an association] and participating in the many free resources the association provides," says Jerry Wentz, president of the board of directors of the National Association of Professional Pet Sitters (NAPPS). "Also, becoming involved in furthering the mission of [an association like NAPPS] provides an even greater opportunity to meet and share and learn from other successful entrepreneurs."

While you may find that organizations keyed to your industry will be most useful for your development as a pet-care professional, you'll also find that membership in groups like the local chamber of commerce, Kiwanis Club, Rotary International, and others can be just as valuable. Not only can you glean business insight from other professionals that can be adapted for your own use, you'll also make contacts among people who can be great sources of referrals or might be potential bartering partners, if you're so inclined.

Traditional learning resources like professional and academic courses certainly have plenty to offer business professionals. Many of the organizations discussed in this chapter offer hands-on training and certification coursework that can enhance your skills. In addition, you may find it very helpful to pursue traditional learning through community colleges and adult education classes to fill in any gaps that may exist in your business knowledge. You don't have to enroll to gain such knowledge—many colleges and universities admit guest students. Or you may be able to audit a class, which means you take the class alongside the other students, but you won't get a grade at the end of the semester (how great is that?). Business management, accounting, and marketing are all course areas that you may wish to investigate.

Finally, business publications can really help you keep up with developments in your field. Their chief benefit is that you can pick them up when you have time; you also can file them away as reference material for later use. These publications are great sources of industry intelligence on new products, techniques, and even legislation that could impact your pet-care business.

In the sections below you'll find information pertinent to your area of pet care. Contact information for each of the professional development tools discussed here, as well as several others, appears in the Appendix. (No endorsements are intended; this information is meant as a tool to make your fact-finding missions easier.)

Pet Sitting/Dog Walking

Associations

- *National Association of Professional Pet Sitters (NAPPS).* This nonprofit organization was founded in 1989 to promote excellence among pet sitters while providing tools and resources to help its members become successful. It offers education, certification, insurance, monthly teleconferences, and a virtual library. Membership is $140 annually.
- *Pet Sitters Associates LLC.* This organization's chief claim to fame is that it includes general liability insurance for pet sitters in its annual membership dues. The group also offers quarterly newsletters. An annual membership and basic insurance is $159. It also offers pet day-care and grooming coverage at $135 and $90 extra, respectively.
- *Pet Sitters International (PSI).* PSI has more than 7,000 members and works to promote, support, and recognize excellence in pet sitting. The organization offers group liability insurance; a subscription to *The World of Professional Pet Sitting*, a bimonthly magazine; access to accreditation; an annual conference; and discounts on products and supplies used by pet sitters. Dues are $109 annually, with a $20 one-time application fee.
- *Professional Dog Walkers Association International (PDWAI).* Largely targeted to our friends north of the border, PDWAI is based in Toronto and is the only Canadian national association devoted entirely to the profession. The organization offers a free listing on its website for members (including U.S. members), insurance company referrals, and continuing education. A one-year membership is $50 CAN.

> **Fun Fact**
>
> Professional Pet Sitters Week is held annually in March to educate pet owners about the advantages of in-home pet care. Founded by Pet Sitters International, the observance is also meant to promote pet sitting as a viable career that is personally and professionally rewarding.

Education/Certification

- *NAPPS.* A home-study course in business management, animal care, and health issues, followed by an exam, leads to certification. The course is $230; the certification exam is $125.
- *PSI.* Accreditation is offered for its members after completing coursework and taking a final exam. The fee to become an accredited pet sitter is $279, while accreditation for a pet-sitting service (for an owner who employs pet sitters or independent contractors) is $199.

Software

There is a lot of software available on the market to help you manage your business. Here are the names and prices of a few:

- *Bluewave Professional Pet Sitter (Bluewave)*: priced according to the number of employees; the "Chihuahua" level (for one to three employees) is $49 a month
- *Kennel Connection (Blue Crystal Software)*: $649 for the pet-sitting module; $329 for the "KC Lite" pet-sitting module
- *Petrax (Ten Dog Development)*: $499

Dog Training

Associations

- *Association of Companion Animal Behavior Counselors (ACABC).* This organization offers professional and academic benefits for behaviorists, veterinarians, trainers, and others interested in animal behavior. Membership benefits include a peer-reviewed certification program for certified dog-training instructors; a listing in the ACABC membership directory; a profile of your business on ACABC's website (but only after you're certified); a members-only bulletin board; *The Behavior Counselor*, a quarterly e-newsletter; and access to low-cost dental and prescription insurance. A professional membership is $125 per year, while an individual membership is $65.
- *Association of Pet Dog Trainers (APDT).* Founded in 1993, APDT has more than 5,000 members worldwide. It focuses on education, offering an annual conference as well as seminars, a membership directory and trainer search database, and a newsletter. Membership is open to anyone who provides training services; a full membership is $100.

- *National Association of Dog Obedience Instructors (NADOI).* This organization's mission is to expand knowledge about dog training and to endorse instructors of the highest caliber. It offers a quarterly journal, *Forward*; a code of ethics; and networking opportunities. Membership is $45.

> **Smart Tip**
> Annual industry conventions are great places to network and trade tips with other pet-care industry business owners and vendors who understand your business and concerns. Be sure to attend the social events as well as the business seminars—they give you a great opportunity to make contacts and share industry intelligence.

Publications

OffLead & Natural Pet is a bimonthly for professional trainers, instructors, behavior therapists, groomers, kennel operators, and pet-care professionals published by Barkleigh Productions. Six issues are $24.95, but you can sign up for a free trial issue on the Barkleigh website at barkleigh.com/OL_subscribe.html.

Education

There are a lot of ways you can learn how to be a dog trainer, but not all of them are equally effective. Training experts recommend against relying solely on internet-based or home-study courses, which tend to be expensive and don't give you the hands-on training you need to learn how to train dogs properly.

"There is much more to training dogs than just loving them or knowing how to get them to sit," says APDT president Teoti Anderson. "You need to fully understand the science—learning theory, operant and classical conditioning, reinforcement schedules, and more. You need to understand different breeds. You need to understand canine temperament and behavior. You also need to be an excellent educator of people because if you can't communicate with your human clients, then you won't be able to help their dogs. My recommendation is to choose [a study program] that offers modern, reward-based training that's based on scientific learning theory—not one that shows you how to muscle a dog into submission."

> **Smart Tip**
> While industry-specific education is a good way to learn the skills side of your profession, don't overlook the value of business classes like marketing, accounting, and business management. They, too, will make you a better businessperson and can even reduce the amount of money you have to spend on professional services.

Having said all that, the optimal place to learn how to be a trainer is at a university that offers degrees in applied animal behavior or ethology (the study of animals). But you don't

Out of School

As a business owner, it's important that you never stop learning, especially when it comes to learning new techniques that can help you run your business better. But it can be hard to find time in your schedule for traditional coursework, especially during the startup phase of your business. So here are a few nontraditional learning opportunities you can try instead:

- *Enroll in an adult education class.* They're usually offered in the evening or on weekends, and meet for a finite period of time—say, 10 or 15 weeks. There are no tests, but there is a lot of good instruction from practitioners in the field being studied. The cost to attend is generally pretty reasonable as well.
- *Take an online class.* Many universities now offer distance study programs on the internet that are perfect for busy people or those who are too far away to attend class on campus. Some coursework has to be completed in real time; other work can be done on your own schedule.
- *Apprentice with successful business owners.* Organizations like the chamber of commerce offer educational forums taught by members with experience in various fields. These learning opportunities alone can make the cost of membership worthwhile.
- *Make a friend at SCORE.* The experienced executives who make up this volunteer small-business organization will help you solve business problems and learn new skills, and they can act as a sounding board for ideas as well. There's no charge to use the service, which you'll find at score.org or in your local phone book.

have to get a degree to become successful in the field. Two educational institutions to consider:

- *Animal Behavior College (ABC).* The dog-obedience training program offered here is part home-study correspondence course, part hands-on apprenticeship and can be completed at locations nationwide and in Canada. Successful course completion results in an ABC Certified Dog Trainer designation. Tuition ranges from $2,500 to $3,250, and 100 percent financing is available.
- *Thompson Education Direct.* This school includes in its various offerings a dog obedience/trainer/instructor long-distance learning program with 12 learning modules that can be completed in about six months. Graduates qualify to take

the National Association of Dog Obedience Instructors certification exam. The tuition is $898.

If you do train using a long-distance program, you must get hands-on training by working with a practicing trainer. You can't learn to be a dog trainer out of a book.

Certification

- *ACABC.* This organization offers certification for professionals who wish to teach basic obedience or obedience classes, or work with families to change unwanted behavior. You earn the peer-reviewed Certified Dog Training Instructor (CDTI) credential after completing coursework, practical skills workshops, seminars, and a mentorship with a certified member. You'll need three years and 80 continuing education credits to qualify for CDTI-level certification, although people with less than three years' experience may qualify for the Associate Dog Training Instructor credential. Professional certification is available only to members of ACABC at an initial cost of $495, which includes a one-time mentor honorarium, and is renewable every three years.
- *Certification Council for Pet Dog Trainers (CCPDT).* This program offers certification based on humane training practices and current scientific knowledge. The exam covers learning theory, instruction skills, husbandry, ethology, and equipment. Candidates must have at least 300 hours' experience in dog training in the past five years, a high school diploma, and references. The certification exam is offered twice a year in locations across the United States, as well as at the annual APDT conference; special testing can be arranged if the candidate lives more than 500 miles from a testing center. APDT members pay $300; nonmembers pay $350. Passage of the exam allows you to use the designation "CPDT" (Certified Pet Dog Trainer) after your name.

Software

There are a number of software packages out there that are just for pet trainers that you may find helpful in managing your business:

- *EdogTrainer.com*: online dog-training business management service; $9.95 a month and up
- *Kennel Connection* (Blue Crystal Software): $649 for the training module; $329 for the "KC Lite" training module
- *PetSOFT* (Get Physical Software): $295 for the "lite" version; $495 for the unlimited version

Pet Grooming

Associations

- *International Society of Canine Cosmetologists (ISCC)*. This organization is committed to continuing education and the advancement of professional pet stylists. It provides networking and educational programs at the local, regional, and national levels. Its multilevel certification program is designed to help groomers achieve pet-styling excellence. There are six levels of membership; the basic individual membership is $100 and includes eligibility for certification.
- *National Dog Groomers Association of America (NDGAA)*. Established in 1969, NDGAA offers a professional liability program; continuing education and certification testing; a membership directory; a gold MasterCard; access to a credit system for help with collections; *Groomer's Voice*, published three times a year; and seminars, trade shows, and competitions. Membership is $75.

Publications

Groomer to Groomer is offered free to qualified grooming salon managers and employees. It's published by Barkleigh Productions, which also publishes a free *Mobile Groomer* supplement.

Education

The NDGAA holds continuing education workshops at various locations around the country. According to the NDGAA, these workshops offer all groomers the opportunity to enhance their grooming skills, stay current with industry trends, and enhance ideas, methods, and opinions with colleagues. Among the topics covered are breed demonstrations, stripping, thinning and carding, patterns, and mixed-breed evaluation. The NDGAA recommends that groomers complete these educational workshops before taking its certification exam (discussed in the next section).

For an extensive listing of other grooming schools located around the United States, check out searchgigi.com/grooming. Look for the "Schools for Grooming Instruction" link.

Dollar Stretcher

It's possible to deduct the cost of all the professional publications to which you subscribe on your business income taxes. Just be sure to retain a copy of your canceled check or online receipt as proof of the payment for the IRS.

Perhaps an even more effective way to get a hands-on grooming education is to apprentice with a working groomer. "You have to handle pets a lot to be able to groom them," says Houston pet groomer Barbara Menutes. "Bathing dogs like I did [when I started out] is a good way to learn. A lot of people don't realize what hard work grooming is—for instance, you just want to help a dog, and it just wants to bite you. Hands-on experience teaches you how to deal with all of that."

Certification

The NDGAA offers a National Certified Master Groomer designation earned after demonstrating grooming skills on numerous breeds in controlled testing. It's recommended that you attend at least one accredited NDGAA workshop (held in various places nationwide) before taking the 400-question written exam. Check out its website listed in the Appendix for more information.

Trade Shows/Conferences

- *PetGroomer.com*. The industry's only internet trade show can be found at PetGroomer.com. It has 75 exhibitor booths, contests, reading room, chat room, and an internet radio station—and there's no charge to enter!
- *Groom Expo*. Barkleigh Productions' flagship educational seminar and trade show for pet-care professionals is held annually in Hershey, Pennsylvania, and draws nearly 3,000 attendees. It includes an International Judges Association-sanctioned grooming contest.
- *Groom and Kennel Expo*. Another Barkleigh Productions event, it features a trade show, educational programs, and contests.
- *Intergroom*. This pet-grooming industry conference is attended by more than 2,000 dog and cat groomers from more than 20 countries. The event features a trade show, educational seminars, grooming competitions, and more.

> **Bright Idea**
>
> When exhibiting your products at a trade show, be sure to bring plenty of giveaways—either samples of a product you're selling (like dog biscuits), or what's known as "trinkets and trash," which are those advertising novelties you can have inscribed with your company name and contact information. Pens and refrigerator magnets make great giveaway items.

Software

There is a lot of software on the market to help you manage your grooming business. Here are the names and prices of a few:

- *123Pet* (CMJ Designs): $199 for small shops or mobile groomers, $699 for up to 2.1 billion employees!
- *Groom Manager* (Dog Days Software): $400
- *Kennel Connection* (Blue Crystal Software): $649 for the grooming module; $329 for the "KC Lite" version grooming module
- *KennelSuite* 7 (Plane Software): $275 basic; $749 professional
- *PetSOFT* (Get Physical Software): $295 for the "lite" version; $495 for the unlimited version
- *The Groomer's Write Hand* (The Groomer's Write Hand): $99

Pet Products/Food

Associations

- *American Pet Products Association Inc. (APPA)*. This nonprofit association's mission is to promote and advance pet ownership and the pet-products industry. It offers a number of benefits like insurance, industry and market research, educational seminars, teleconferences, export assistance, and a pet-products trade show called Global Pet Expo. Its annual publication, the *APPA National Pet Owners Survey*, contains a wealth of information about the industry. To qualify for membership, 75 percent of your income must come from the manufacturing or importing of pet products. There is a $1,000 initiation fee, and dues for companies with sales of less than $500,000 are $500 annually.
- *Pet Industry Distributors Association (PIDA)*. This association is for distribution professionals only, but we're listing it here because it's a great place for pet-products retailers to look for product distributors. You don't need to join to peruse its online member directory.
- *World Wide Pet Industry Association (WWPIA)*. America's oldest pet-industry trade association has a membership that includes manufacturers, product distributors, and retail businesses, among others. Its mission is to promote responsible growth and development of the pet products and services industry. It offers an online directory of pet stores, a certified

> Tip...
>
> **Smart Tip**
>
> The petstorecaresheets.com website has printable care sheets for dozens of different types of pets, from dogs and cats to chinchillas and hermit crabs. They can easily be customized with your store or business name and logo and are available at no charge, although donations are accepted.

groomer listing, and benefits like industry publicity, educational programs, and materials. The retail membership is $25 per location.

Publications

- *Pet Age* (H.H. Backer Associates). Considered the pet industry's most popular business-to-business magazine, *Pet Age* is sent monthly at no charge to qualified members of the pet industry, including retail pet-supply business owners. It covers topics like industry trends and legislation and has information for front-line employees and managers.
- *Pet Business* (Macfadden Communications Group). This monthly covers new products, marketing and legal issues, and more. From the same publisher comes the Industry Yellow Pages & Buyers Guide twice a year. Qualifying pet-business professionals, including retailers, can subscribe free.
- *Pet Product News* (Bow Tie). A monthly news magazine with the latest information about the pet-supply industry, including new product reviews, emerging trends, financial reports and merchandising display tips. Free to qualified pet industry retailers.

Trade Shows

Trade shows abound in the pet-products industry. Here are a few you might be interested in:

- *H.H. Backer's Pet Industry Trade Shows*. The number-one destination for pet-industry professionals. Held in the spring and fall, these are massive shows—the 2004 Christmas show had 818 manufacturers and wholesalers exhibiting in 1,309 booths and drew more than 8,500 retail buyers from around the world. These are the shows to go to if you want to see and be seen.
- *SuperZoo*. WWPIA's trade show for consumers can be a great place to exhibit your pet products. There's an east and a west show annually. Exhibitors include manufacturers, product distributors, suppliers, retail stores, and other businesses. WWPIA also hosts the America's Family Pet Expo twice annually. This consumer show is held in Southern California and

Bright Idea

Need a surefire way to get people to stop at your booth when you exhibit at a trade show? Hold a drawing for a pet-related prize. Simply put a "fishbowl" on your table that can be used to collect business cards, and if possible, display the prize for all to see. Then as people stop by to check it out, make your pitch.

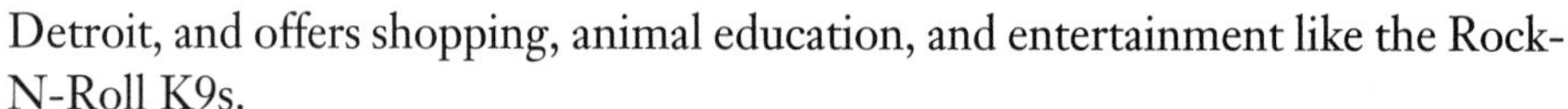
Detroit, and offers shopping, animal education, and entertainment like the Rock-N-Roll K9s.

- *Global Pet Expo*. Co-sponsored by PIDA and APPA, this show is directed at pet retailers and offers new products, seminars to help boost business, and animal-care insight.

Although trade shows tend to be rather expensive, Exton, Pennsylvania, products manufacturer Joyce Reavey recommends going, both as an exhibitor and an attendee. "You might not get sales at the show, but retailers hold onto your materials and call you later," she says. "Plus these shows are good places to network and get insider information. However, the pet industry is becoming very competitive, so you need to be cautious about what you say to the people there."

Wholesaler/manufacturer Amanda Miller adds, "Going to trade shows is all about getting your name out there. It's more beneficial for the company from a marketing perspective than as a place to get orders. But eventually it pays off—you get to see what's new and eventually everyone knows you."

15

Blue-Ribbon Advertising

Want a proven way to land new work, increase profits, and build name recognition that in turn will lead to even more work? Then get your checkbook ready—it's time to enter the wonderful world of advertising.

Advertising in carefully selected media is the quickest way to get the word out about the products or services you provide. This is especially important in the early days of your business startup, when you're still an unknown but eager entrepreneur. In a way, advertising is a lot like dating: If you stay home on Saturday night, no one will know you're available. But if you hit the social circuit, you'll meet new people and possibly forge new relationships.

Now, we know the thought of advertising can be a little frightening. It can be expensive and time-consuming, not to mention unproductive if you don't reach the right audience. That's why it's important to try a number of different advertising tools until you figure out which ones work best for your business. Then you need to keep on advertising to make sure you continue to have a presence in the marketplace. In this chapter, we'll discuss some of the methods that have worked well for successful pet-business owners, including Yellow Pages ads, direct mail, business cards, print advertising, magnetic signs, association directories, word-of-mouth, referrals, and portfolios.

Plan of Attack

As you might suspect, it's not enough to spend a whole bunch of money on random advertising vehicles and hope that at least some of them will snag paying customers. Rather, you need to formulate a tactical plan based on income-generating strategies that have been successful in your line of work that will ultimately help you achieve your goals. This becomes your master marketing plan, which like your business plan is meant to help keep you on track to taking your business where you want it to go.

It also serves as a primer for helping you make strategic decisions. If you haven't completed the exercises discussed in Chapter 7 related to identifying your target market, understanding the demographics of the area, and so on, it's a good idea to do so right now, before you ever spend a buck on advertising. By figuring out upfront who lives in your market area, how many pets they own and how much discretionary income they have available for services or products like yours, you'll be able to reach the pet lovers in your target market in the most efficient and cost-effective way possible.

Check out *Marketing Made Easy* by Kevin A. Epstein (Entrepreneur Press) for in-depth information and step-by-step instructions about how to write a marketing plan. But there's one more thing you can do right now to understand yourself and your market better: Create a SWOT analysis.

Dollar Stretcher

One very affordable place you can advertise your pet-sitting business is on Petsit USA, an online listing of pet sitters, dog walkers, and dog day cares. For \$36 a year, your business is listed by zip code, and both your e-mail and website addresses can be linked to the site. Check it out at petsitusa.com.

SWOT stands for strengths, weaknesses, opportunities, and threats, and it is used to analyze your capabilities as a potential business owner in your given marketplace. Strengths are any personal characteristics that can make you successful, including intangibles like education, experience, and so on. Weaknesses include those traits that may impact your success negatively, including a gap in your knowledge that needs to be addressed. Opportunities are steps you can take to improve or strengthen your business, while threats could be both tangible and intangible factors that might impact your ability to make money.

Honestly analyzing your own capabilities and shortcomings this way helps put your new business on the firmest footing, not only because you will identify where your greatest strengths and opportunities lie, but also because you'll see where you may need business help or professional development.

On page 180, we've provided a sample SWOT analysis for a homebased pet-food business owner who plans to sell from a shop and online. We've also included a SWOT analysis worksheet that you can use. Take a moment now to fill in the boxes—then create a separate SWOT analysis for any competitors you've already identified as well. Analyzing the competition is as important as having a snapshot of your own business.

With your marketing plan and SWOT analysis in hand (or at least in development), your next step should be to establish a preliminary advertising budget. Sales experts recommend setting a budget of 2 to 5 percent of gross sales when you're starting out. If you're a dog trainer, pet groomer, or food/products store owner, part of that budget should fund a grand opening celebration, even if you're homebased. In the meantime, here's a look at the different types of advertising and how they can be used to promote your pet-care business.

Yellow Pages

If you decide to invest in a business telephone land line (definitely recommended), you will automatically receive a one- to two-line listing in the Yellow Pages directory published by your local phone company. Now, it's no secret that this type of line ad, which gives just your business name, address, and phone number, doesn't exactly deliver a whole lot of punch. If you want to stand out (not to mention include a frolicking puppy or kitty in your ad), you'll have to ante up for a display ad, which is one of the larger boxed ads you'll find sprinkled throughout the directory. Display ads definitely command more attention, particularly since it's possible to include more lines of information, website and e-mail addresses, and details like pictures and maps. Plus you can add spot color to make the message really pop. However, all those add-ons can be pretty pricey, and some pet-care business owners don't think they're worth the cost.

SWOT Analysis

Sample SWOT Analysis

Strengths	Weaknesses
• Degree in packaging from major university (helps me understand winning product psychology) • 14 years' retail experience selling appliances at Sears (sales skills) • Animals instantly gravitate to me	• Financial management skills are a little shaky • My ADD sometimes makes it hard to focus on paperwork
Opportunities	**Threats**
• New pet spa just opened in my target market (partnership possibilities?) • Several new upscale subdivisions are under construction (discretionary income!) • Nearest pet-food store is more than ten miles away	• Local population is older and may not be willing/able to buy online • Past experience with local packaging store was poor; concerned they won't be able to handle my internet sales volume efficiently

SWOT Analysis Worksheet

Strengths	Weaknesses
______ ______ ______ ______ ______ ______	______ ______ ______ ______ ______ ______
Opportunities	**Threats**
______ ______ ______ ______ ______ ______	______ ______ ______ ______ ______ ______

“I used to say that every pet sitter needs to be in the Yellow Pages and needs to have more than just a line ad,” says Jerry Wentz, the Raleigh, North Carolina, pet sitter. “But last year they messed up my display ad, and I haven’t had the call volume I had come to expect from previous years. I spend $10,000 a year on my ad, and they didn’t do anything when they messed up, so I’m not quite as enchanted with the Yellow Pages as I once was.”

Neither is Oak Park, Illinois, pet sitter David Lipschultz. “In the past, my Yellow Pages ad was great, but it’s becoming less so as more people search for services on the internet. I actually get a lot more business from my website than my Yellow Pages ad.”

Here’s one last caveat to consider if you’re contemplating taking out a display ad: Once you’ve signed on the dotted line, you’re committed for the full term that the directory is in print. So even if you discover early on that your Yellow Pages ad isn’t generating much business, you can’t pull out until your contract expires. End of story.

To figure out whether a display ad is worth the money, open your local Yellow Pages right now and check the listings for pet-care businesses in your area to find out what your competition is doing. What you’re likely to find is that many pet-care/pet-products businesses—and especially the smaller ones—just have those modest “freebie” line ads. For example, the pet-sitting category in the December 2004 SBC East Area Metropolitan Detroit Smart Yellow Pages has 19 listings, two of which are boxed color ads with puppy photos, and two of which are larger all-type boxed ads. Likewise, the pet-training category, which has 15 listings, has just four boxed ads (all type, no color). Interestingly, one of the humble line ads in the training category is for PetSmart, the pet superstore, which goes to show that even the big players in the market aren’t necessarily sold on the idea of spending a lot of money on Yellow Pages advertising.

There’s one more useful thing your local Yellow Pages can tell you, which is how many businesses of the type you’re starting are operating in your area. (Loosely speaking, of course—businesses that choose not to pay for a business phone line will of course not be listed.) If there aren’t too many listings, that could be beneficial for you, since your company will be one of the few people will find when they open the book or go to yellowpages.com. Our best advice is to go with the basic listing when you start your business, then track how many customers find you through the Yellow Pages. In your second year, you can make the decision to upgrade to a larger ad if you wish.

Bright Idea

There are many special-interest directories that serve very specialized local markets, like ethnic groups, religious organizations, and civic groups. If any of these organizations serve the market you want to be in, you should consider a listing in their directories. Even high school sports or theatrical production programs can be great and affordable places to advertise.

It’s not our intention to talk you out of Yellow Pages advertising—we just want you to

In Grand Style

If you're doing business out of a facility, as in the case of a pet groomer or brick-and-mortar pet-supplies/food company, a grand opening or open house is a great way to spark interest in your new business. Although a grand opening is meant to announce your presence in the local business community, you should hold it a few weeks after you open to make sure everything you need, from equipment to inventory, is in place before the grand debut.

Prior to the actual event, launch a preopening promotional campaign that includes ads in the local paper, direct-mail pieces and fliers, all of which give the hours of the event, your location, and details about any giveaways you're offering (such as a coupon for a free training session or free pet food for six months). Then on the day of the event, offer miniservices like free nail trimming or give away product samples (check with your distributor to see if it will "donate" small sample packs of dog food, for instance). You'll also want to serve refreshments like soft drinks, coffee, and snacks, and possibly give away inexpensive promotional items like key chains and refrigerator magnets that have your name and phone number/website address. You can also hold hourly drawings for door prizes such as a complimentary grooming or a pet bed as a way to entice people to stop by. Finally, make sure you have a large quantity of business cards and maybe even a flier with a discounted coupon on hand, and put a guest book in a conspicuous place near the door. Later you'll be able to build your first mailing list from those names.

think about it carefully. Besides, consider this: The 2005 Yellow Pages Integrated Media Association usage study, which tracks the number of times individuals look up a particular Yellow Pages heading, showed that people looked up the following pet-related categories millions of times:

- *Veterinarians*: 169.8 million
- *Pet Grooming*: 52.8 million
- *Pet Shops*: 33.4 million
- *Pet Supplies & Foods (Retail)*: 21.5 million
- *Kennels*: 15.1 million
- *Animal Shelters*: 7.3 million
- *Animal Hospitals*: 7.1 million

Millions of consumers can't be wrong, right? Of course, there is such a thing as too much success, as dog trainer Jamie Damato of Oak Park, Illinois, can tell you. She received what she considered to be too many calls from her display ad because most were not productive. "The calls were actually annoying—mostly just people asking what you can do for them," she says. "It takes a lot of time to answer the phone and deal with 'shoppers.' I prefer to spend my time with my current customers, who are the revenue generators and whose satisfaction can lead to good word-of-mouth."

Today, Damato has just a line ad, and instead puts her advertising money into community fundraisers since her website and word-of-mouth bring in plenty of business.

Direct Mail

No matter how you may have felt about direct (aka junk) mail in the past, chances are now that you're a new business owner, you've had a change of heart. Can there be any better way to reach prospects than by sending mail directly to their homes or offices? Maybe not, especially when there's a catchy/memorable/provocative teaser offer on the outside of the envelope that induces the recipient to open it.

There are three types of direct mail that are particularly useful for pet-business owners: brochures, postcards, and fliers. An important part of their value is their price—they're all fairly inexpensive to produce and mail. They also can be timed to drop (direct-mail parlance for "go in the mail") at certain times of the year when people might need your service or products most. For example, if you're a pet sitter/walker, you might time your mailing to coincide with the start of spring break (when families with school-aged children often travel), just before the start of summer vacations, and around the holidays (another time for family vacations and college bowl games). A dog groomer might find it beneficial to send out a mailing in the late spring (when shedding begins and the weather starts heating up), while an upscale pet-products purveyor will definitely want to mail advertising materials before the start of the holiday shopping season. Pet-food sellers and dog trainers, whose wares/services are used year-round, may do better on a regular mailing schedule that skips the holiday season (although gift certificates for obedience classes could be a big seller).

Another type of direct mail that can work for you is not traditional mail at all, but what Columbia, South Carolina, product wholesaler/manufacturer Susan Benesh calls an "e-blast." Using an online direct marketer called My

> **Dollar Stretcher**
>
> 
>
> Check with your local newspaper to find out whether it has any special advertising sections scheduled that might be a good place to advertise your particular service or products. Do the same thing with the publications that target your prime audience to get the biggest bang for your advertising buck.

Privacy Pointers

Locating your business in your home has many advantages in terms of the low overhead and short commute to work every day. But inviting people into your home also can be an invasion of privacy unless you take a few steps to protect yourself and your family.

Once you invite clients to your home for training or grooming, you'll want to take care that they (and their children) stay in the business portion of your home and out of the living areas. If your facility is in your garage or basement, always keep your front door securely locked and the key in your pocket. Since inevitably someone will need to use the bathroom while at your business, it is strongly recommended that you install a basic bathroom facility in or near the work area. Otherwise, you'll have to escort the client personally to your home bathroom—which of course encroaches on your living space and takes valuable time.

Finally, because you will have a parade of people through your home business area, you should think seriously about installing a home security system. The cliché might be trite, but it truly is better to be safe than sorry.

Emma (myemma.com), she e-mails catalogs to her boutiques and other wholesale customers on a regular basis. It's a great way to keep direct-mail costs down (it costs her just $50 a month for these e-blasts).

Brochures

When designed well and printed on good paper stock, brochures give you a lot of look for the loot. The simplest type of brochure is the two-panel brochure, which is a single sheet that, when folded lengthwise and trimmed, can be inserted into a No. 10 business envelope. That configuration gives you plenty of space to describe your services or list the products you sell. If you need more space to show products like rhinestone-studded leashes or cashmere dog sweaters, you might want to opt for a three-panel brochure instead so there's plenty of room for text and photographs. It, too, folds down to fit a No. 10 envelope. (You'll find a sample three-panel brochure on the next page.)

Software programs like Publisher (part of the Microsoft Office package) have made it easy to create your own brochures without the assistance of a graphic designer. You simply choose a brochure template, type in the copy, download and paste in photographs, and output the file to a CD-RW that can be taken to a print shop for downloading and printing. However, while this can be a very cost-effective method for designing

Sample Brochure

Inside Flap | **Back Cover** | **Front Cover**

Who needs a kennel? You have Buffy!

No matter whether you're going away on vacation or on business, or if you just want your pet to have company and some fresh air during the day, Buffy's Pet-Sitting and Dog-Walking Service can help. We offer a variety of worry-free services provided by bonded and insured employees to make sure Fido, Fluffy, Nemo or any other pet is happy, healthy and well-cared for when you can't be there.

Call today for a free consultation.

561-555-7563

Buffy's Pet-Sitting
and Dog-Walking Service

Jupiter, Florida, 33458
Phone 561.555.7563
e-mail: buffy@buffyspetsitting.com

BUFFY'S PET-SITTING
AND
DOG-WALKING SERVICE

Loving care
when you can't be there

Inside Spread

Pet Sitting

- Feed pets
- Change water bowls
- Play with pets
- Brush pets
- Scoop cat litter boxes
- Clean up accidents
- Administer medication
- Give injections
- Give subcutaneous intravenous treatments (cats)
- Water plants
- Bring in newspapers and mail
- Alternate lights
- Drop off/pick up at vet/groomer

Overnights

An alternative to boarding your pet! Buffy's will care for your pet when you need to be away overnight. The service includes a p.m. feeding, several walks between 5 and 11 p.m., another a.m. feeding and walk, and enough love to keep your baby happy until you return.

Overnight hours run from 5 p.m. to 7 a.m. Pickup and drop-off at your home is available, and multiple night schedules can be arranged.

Dog Walking

- Feed Pets
- Play with pets
- Bring in newspapers and mail
- No pack walks! Individual attention for your best friend!

Call today for a free consultation • Buffy's Pet-Sitting and Dog-Walking Service • 561-555-7563

Photos Courtesy: Jon Sullivan

Beware!

You may need a permit if you're planning to deliver advertising fliers or brochures door to door. Check with the municipality in which you plan to distribute your materials, then be sure to carry the permit in your pocket while you're working in case someone (i.e., the law) asks to see it. The cost for the permit should be nominal.

a brochure, it's not always the best way. After all, you want to strive for professionalism, and unless you have had graphic arts training, you might not be the best judge of what works well. In addition, the Microsoft templates are widely used, which means your brochure could end up looking a lot like those of your competition.

To find a professional designer, check the Yellow Pages under "Graphic Designers." When you call, don't be afraid to ask exactly how much you can expect to pay. Designers' rates vary widely, so call around until you find someone you can afford. You also might try contacting the Fine Arts department of your local community college or university for a referral to a talented commercial art student whose rates are likely to be far less than those of a professional designer. Finally, quick-print shops like FedEx Kinkos and American Speedy Printing also may have in-house staff who can design your brochure.

You may feel more up to the task of writing the text than designing the overall look, since an introductory paragraph may be all you need before launching into a list of your products and services. When writing that opening paragraph, focus on the reader and what he or she wants and needs to know (a reader-oriented approach) rather than talking about the business itself (a writer-oriented approach). For example, don't say: "Denehen Dog Academy is the area's newest obedience school and already has won rave reviews from home owners interested in humane and effective pet training programs."

Do say: "Your dog will learn clever new tricks and socialization skills that will make him the darling of the neighborhood when you enroll him in the Denehen Dog Academy."

Next, list the services you offer or give a brief description of each. Just be sure to check your spelling, grammar, and punctuation—or better still, have someone else do it for you to make sure everything is correct. Also provide full contact information, including your phone number, website, and e-mail address.

Printing your brochure is a breeze. A small print shop like FedEx Kinkos or American Speedy Printing can handle the job cost-effectively. Just give them a disk with your brochure copy and

Tip...

Smart Tip

A photograph on your business cards and brochure can be a great attention grabber. But don't use your own photograph—rather, use a cuddly puppy, kitty, or other animal that directs the spotlight on your business and its beneficiaries rather than on yourself. The same thing goes for your website—pet photos sell stuff!

they'll do the rest. (As mentioned previously, they also can take your copy and create a layout for you if you're so inclined.) The internet is also a good source of printing companies, many of which can both lay out and print your brochure for you. All you do is type in the specs for the job (including size, number of colors, and so on) and attach a file with the brochure copy or the printer-ready copy, and they'll take it from there. We've listed the names of a few companies you can check out in the Appendix, although if you Google "brochure printing," you'll come up with plenty of companies to choose from—in fact, a recent search turned up 1.6 million hits. You can expect to pay about $350 for 1,000 full-color, 8.5-by-11-inch brochures printed on good-quality paper.

David Lipschultz prefers online printing companies over traditional printers, and in fact uses PrintingForLess.com for all his promotional materials. "They're amazing," he says. "The first time I used a local printer, I paid $1 per brochure, while the online company charges half or one-third of that. Plus the quality is better, and they don't mess up the order."

Postcards

Another type of direct mail that can be effective for new pet-business owners is a small rectangle of paper: the postcard. In addition to being inexpensive to create, print, and mail, you can put a lot of information on it—including a coupon for a few bucks or a percentage off a product or service. Microsoft Office has dozens of postcard templates you can use easily to design your mailing piece, or you can put the design in the hands of an online printer. As with the brochure, you should have the card professionally printed rather than using an office supply store kit. And don't worry if there's a large minimum order like 1,000 cards. You'll use up lots of them mailing to the same list more than once. Postcard printing resources can be found in the Appendix.

> **Bright Idea**
>
> Contact your local Welcome Wagon or Realtor organization to find out if you can include a flier with information about your services or products in any packages they give to new homeowners. (Apartment communities also have similar welcome packages and may be willing to include your flier.) There may be a small charge, but it can be worth it for the opportunity to introduce yourself to every new resident in your market area.

Fliers

Fliers are easy to create on your home computer using a Microsoft Office template and are usually printed on one side of an 8.5-by-11-inch sheet so they can be folded to fit into a standard No. 10 envelope. (For inspiration, look at the sample flier for a dog-training business on page 188.) Fliers often find their way under windshields in mall parking lots, onto bulletin boards in pet stores, and under doormats, but they're really

Sample Flier

Doggoned tired of bad behavior?

Teach your dog some manners at

A Matter of Manners Dog Training Academy!

We can help your pet overcome annoying and dangerous behaviors like:
excessive barking • biting • aggression • hyperactivity
separation anxiety • digging and chewing
and other unwanted behavior

And we love good dogs, too!

Now offering obedience classes (private and group), puppy kindergarten, new pet orientation, competition obedience, Schutzhund and more!

Call now for information about in-home and group classes

(906) 555-5555

A Matter of Manners Dog Training Academy
Menominee, Michigan 49858
www.matterofmanners.com

most effective when you put them right into the hands of homeowners via the U.S. Postal Service. Fliers have a significant cost-saving advantage over brochures: They can be mailed without an envelope. Simply fold the flier in thirds and secure the open edge with a wafer seal (available in office supply stores). Then affix a pressure-sensitive address label and postage on one of the panels, and you're good to go. Just remember that this type of advertising looks homespun, which might not be the image you're going for in a more upscale neighborhood.

You'll recall from Chapter 7 that you can easily and fairly inexpensively rent a mailing list that can be precisely targeted to your market. If you're planning to address the brochure envelopes or postcards yourself, you should request the list on pressure-sensitive labels. You also can ask for the list on disk, but of course you'll then have to feed each envelope or postcard through your printer one at a time. This is fine for a small mailing list and in fact has a more custom look than pressure-sensitive labels do, but it can be a time-consuming process if you're mailing more than a few hundred cards. You'll also have to hand-affix the postage, which is 57 cents each for a brochure in an envelope, 57 cents for a flier, 27 cents for a standard-size postcard (maximum size 6 inches wide by 4.5 inches high), or 39 cents each for an oversized postcard.

Business Cards

When sending out your brochure (or any other mailing for that matter), always be sure to include a business card in the envelope. That hard-working rectangle of paper is more likely to go into an address book or Rolodex for future reference than the actual brochure is. The value of a brochure is for catching the attention of clients who may at that very moment be in the market for a pet-care service or product—or expect to be in the very near future.

And speaking of business cards, make sure you always have a good supply of them in your purse, wallet, or glove box, then hand them out liberally. (Just be sure to protect them by keeping them in a business card case—there's nothing more unprofessional-looking than dog-eared business cards.) Some people see it as shameless self-promotion to whip out a card every time you get into a conversation with someone while in line at the post office or while pumping gas. Smart businesspeople see it as an opportunity.

Business cards are very inexpensive—about $50 for 1,000 cards. That $50 usually includes nice card stock and a logo or a piece of clipart (say, a puppy or kitty). Avoid the impulse to save a few bucks by printing your own business cards using one of those do-it-yourself business card kits you can get at the office supply store. They just won't look as professional, plus the ink can run or smudge if the card gets wet. Since you want to be taken seriously as a business professional, invest in professional tools like custom business cards. It'll be 50 bucks well spent.

Print Advertising

While usually expensive, print advertising is a great way to reach a lot of prospects. Even the smallest community newspapers may be distributed to tens of thousands of readers, which can amount to every household in a community when it comes to free "shopper" newspapers. Whether readers actually pick up the phone depends both on their needs at the moment and the effectiveness of your ad. Frequency is also important. You can't advertise just once and expect an avalanche of calls. You have to advertise regularly—perhaps as often as every issue—both to build name recognition and to be top of mind when readers do happen to need you. At the very least you'll want to time your ad campaign so you have a greater presence at the times of year when your service or product would be in highest demand (around the holidays for a pet-products business, for instance, or in the summer or around spring break for a pet sitter).

Some of the types of print advertising you might like to consider include:

- *Community newspapers and free weekly shoppers.* As mentioned earlier, these papers often are home-delivered at no charge to every household in the community. They're a great advertising buy because the ad insertion rate is usually quite affordable, and they reach people right in the community where you wish to do business. Important tip: Readers of these types of papers respond well to discount offers, so you should consider including a coupon or other discount offer in your ad. Important tip No. 2: This is not the place to advertise if you're after an upscale market, unless of course you're considering the freebie paper delivered in Martha Stewart's neighborhood or South Beach. Do a little due diligence to discover what's out there.

  Newspaper ads are sold in full pages and fractional sizes as small as one-eighth of a page. The more often you run your ad, the less you'll pay per insertion, so make an upfront commitment to buy as many ads as you can afford. You can use a desktop publishing program like Microsoft Publisher to design your own ad, but if the newspaper has its own graphics department, you might want to leave the job to

> Tip...
>
> **Smart Tip**
>
> Always request a media kit from the newspaper or magazine's advertising representative before making any decisions about where you'll spend your hard-earned cash. Media kits contain useful information about the publication's editorial focus and readership demographics that can help you determine whether it's the right buy in your promotion strategy.

them. A graphic designer can also design an ad for you using the newspaper's specs.

- *Weekly and daily papers.* If you're doing business in a larger newspaper market, you'll probably want to advertise in the weekly and/or daily papers. Advertising will cost more in these papers, but the benefit is that they reach a wider market. In addition, the larger papers also may have zoned editions, which means they will allow you to purchase advertising only in the papers that go to the zip codes or even the neighborhoods you specify. This costs more, of course, but can be useful if you're after a very specific market, as in the case of, for instance, a pet groomer who services only a specific geographical area. On the other hand, if you have an internet-based pet-food company, zoning wouldn't be necessary.

  The larger papers almost always have their own design staffs to help small-business owners to create their ads. Be sure to ask how much the service will cost before you agree to use it.
- *City magazines.* Prevalent in larger metropolitan markets, these publications are usually printed on glossy paper and in full color. You'll find that even a very small ad at the back of these publications can be expensive, and multiple insertions are likely to be necessary to land any business. (As with newspapers, always make a multiple insertion buy to get the best rate.) But if you're after a certain type of reader—often more affluent with more disposable income—the cost to advertise can be worth it. Santa Fe, New Mexico, retailer/wholesaler Diane Burchard has found that Santa Fe's specialty tourist magazines are a great place to advertise. Her ongoing ads in them result in continuous business.
- *Special-interest publications.* If your city newspaper or other local publishers happen to print a special issue devoted to pet care or possibly general business services, that's the one to be in. This is one case where you can buy a one-time ad with confidence; after all, readers of such an issue are likely to be interested in what you have to sell because otherwise they won't bother turning the pages. The cost for the ad will probably be higher, but since the issue may have a longer "shelf life" (people tend to keep these special-interest publications), it can be worth the cost.

Dollar Stretcher

Cable TV can be a surprisingly affordable alternative to print advertising, even for a small-business owner. Plus many cable networks serve a fairly small regional area, which means an ad on the community channel's bulletin board can reach exactly the target market you're interested in. Just be sure to check the ad rates before you pay to produce a commercial.

Magnetic Signs

Magnetic signs offer a cost-effective and very visible way to grab what amounts to free publicity every time you hop into your vehicle. They are like mobile billboards and should include your business name, a brief description of what you do if it's not obvious from your business name, your phone number and website address, all in letters large enough to be read when you're stopped at a light or parked in a shopping center lot. At about $60 each, magnetic signs give you a lot of advertising clout and can be removed without damaging the paint on your vehicle when you're not working. (Although, some business owners leave them on all the time, whether they're at the opera or a Little League game.) Call a sign shop for a quote, or try one of the internet sources listed in the Appendix.

The only type of pet-business owner who probably should not have a magnetic sign is a pet sitter—or at least, the sign shouldn't be displayed when you visit a client's home. Chances are you'll often be sitting for vacationing clients, and someone with larceny in mind might take note of your comings and goings and logically conclude that the house is ripe for the picking because no human is at home. You certainly wouldn't want to jeopardize your clients' homes this way, so leave the sign off when you visit.

Association Directories

As you know from Chapter 14, each of the pet-care businesses discussed in this book is supported by at least one association. Many of them, like the National Association of Professional Pet Sitters, have online directories the public can access to find a service or product provider. You have to join the association to be able to advertise in the directory, of course, but the leads can be worth the cost. You'll find contact information for the major pet-care organizations in the Appendix.

Word-of-Mouth

Arguably the best type of advertising of all, both because it costs you nothing and because it tends to have a lot of credibility with new clients, is word-of-mouth (WOM). All you have to do to get good WOM advertising is to do the very best job you can do—and your clients will obligingly tell their friends and family about you. WOM testimonials are worth their weight in gold (or dollars, more accurately) because such a referral comes with an implication that you're trustworthy and worth the price you charge.

Bright Idea

Always check the effectiveness of your advertising by asking customers where they heard about your service or product, then note that information on a tally sheet. Or if you're using coupons to spur sales, include a unique code on it so you can see exactly which publication it was clipped from.

"You want to have the vets, trainers, and customers all raving about you and recommending you," says Houston cat groomer Barbara Menutes. "Unfortunately, bad word-of-mouth gets around a lot quicker than good. I personally witnessed a lady go into hysterics because the hair on her Sheltie's tail was cut too short, and someone like that can ruin 10 or 20 clients for you after she tells them about her experience."

On the other hand, Menutes quietly and without fanfare inspires her own WOM by doing what she calls "mercy groomings" for the pets of owners like the elderly, who no longer have the manual dexterity necessary to keep their pets groomed. You can imagine that word of kindnesses like these will get around just as much as any bad WOM will.

Because WOM is so valuable, some pet-business owners offer referral awards to clients who send business their way—say, a $5 discount on a service for each referral or a percentage off on a product purchase. Tracking referrals and rewarding the person who gives the referral isn't even all that difficult—try printing up referral cards that can be left with your customer after you've provided a service or delivered a product. Have a place on the card where the customer can write his or her name so when the referred client presents you with the card, you know where it came from and you can reward the person who made the referral.

You don't have to wait until the WOM publicity machine cranks up to reap the benefits; you can generate your own positive buzz. For instance, try calling your clients shortly after completing a job to ask for feedback and verify that they're satisfied. It's pretty rare for business owners to follow up like this after the sale and can impress the heck out of your valued clients. If you're a pet sitter, you could leave a thank-you note and a small gift for new clients on the kitchen counter as a token of your appreciation for their business (no chocolate, though—it can be toxic to both dogs and cats). Consider donating your time, services, or products to a pet shelter or other pet charity in your community. Donating gourmet treats to the local no-kill shelter, for instance, can build a lot of goodwill and garner positive publicity.

Beware!

Bad word-of-mouth can be devastating for a small business. Customer service experts say dissatisfied customers may not complain to you but will tell six or seven people about their bad experience. So if you ever suspect a client is unhappy, do whatever you can to fix the situation immediately to head off any bad publicity.

Finally, it's a good idea to develop a relationship with the veterinarians in your community. As trusted sources of information, vets can throw a lot of business your way. So offer to groom the house dog or provide pet treats to animals that are being treated at the vet's clinic and the doctor is likely to return the favor.

"Veterinarians can definitely have an impact on a dog trainer's business," says Lexington, South Carolina, dog trainer Teoti Anderson. "A couple times a year, I drop by their offices with home-baked cookies and logo pens and notepads, along with fliers and business cards, and now many of my referrals come from them."

Referrals

Speaking of referrals, asking clients for referrals is another way to advertise your services and products at low-to-no cost. If you provide a pet service, always ask your satisfied customer whether he or she knows anyone else who might need your services. By the same token, if a client raves that your low-fat gourmet dog food helped his cocker spaniel slim down, ask if he knows anyone else who might like to pare down a pudgy pet. You'll probably find it best to send a note asking for referrals (as well as a self-addressed stamped return envelope) rather that expecting someone to come up with names on the spot. Also always ask whether you can use the client's name when contacting the prospective client. Dropping a name is a very effective way to get someone's attention.

Portfolios

Here's an advertising tool that's useful for pet groomers. Collect photographs of the pets you've primped and pampered and place them in a leather presentation book (preferred), photo album, or three-ring binder that you can show to prospects. For the most effective presentation, you should have both before and after photos. If you have a good camera, you can take the photos yourself. But as any professional photographer will tell you, animal photography is difficult, so you might want to engage a professional to do the job. This can be expensive, but you don't have to have a lot of photos—five or six good ones that demonstrate various techniques should be enough. You can also keep the cost down by hiring a student photographer.

If you have a website, an online portfolio is a must. This gives prospective customers access to your work 24/7 and can give them the confidence to make an online appointment right away. Just be sure to update the portfolio periodically with new photos. People like to see something new when they visit, and they'll stop logging in if nothing changes.

16

Boning Up on Cyberspace

These days it's pretty hard to miss how the internet has infiltrated every aspect of daily life, from banking to ordering pizza. And of course there's a lesson in that when it comes to your pet business: Clearly, you need to be out in cyberspace, too, no matter what type of business you're running. People now expect to be able to find the information they need

24/7 because they're online at all hours of the day and night looking for products and services. So to make sure you don't miss an opportunity to connect electronically with prospective clients who are looking for a pet sitter for an upcoming vacation, people whose dogs need a clip job, or those who are looking for just the right gift for Fluffy, you need to have an internet presence.

In addition to making yourself available on the internet to hordes of prospective clients, you'll also find the web can help you manage your own business better. Need a rhinestone collar in fashionable chartreuse for a client's Maltese? Google all the terms, and 1,720 hits will pop up. Need to know when the next NAPPS certification test date will come to a location nearest to Waukegan? You can find that information quickly with just a few keystrokes.

To help you harness the power of the internet, this chapter will cover designing and launching your site, as well as selecting a name. For the purposes of this chapter, we're assuming you're already somewhat cyber savvy—or that you at least have spent a little time surfing the net and reading e-mail. But if you're not up to speed because of lack of time or interest, get thee to a class anon. No small-business person can afford to be out of the cyber loop these days.

Admittedly, it will take time for your site to catch on. Santa Fe, New Mexico, retailer/wholesaler Diane Burchard says she started with a business card site (which basically gives contact information and nothing else) in 1996. Since she switched to an interactive site in 2002, the number of hits has grown slowly, but sales have increased 8 to 10 percent a year, and she's now shipping to places like Japan, France, and Monaco. The sales curve has been worth the wait.

Oak Park, Illinois, pet sitter/dog walker David Lipschultz also has had great success with his site. He gets about 30 to 40 hits a day and figures close to 50 percent of those hits wind up as new business for Out-U-Go, his pet-sitting company, and about 75 percent for Urban Tailblazers, his dog-walking company.

Beware!

Internet experts say that if it takes longer than 30 seconds for your web page to load, your visitors will lose interest and move on. So if you decide to use graphics or flash on your home page, keep an eye on the clock during testing and reconfigure the site if it takes too long to load.

Bells and Whistles

Ever wonder how mop-topped five-year-olds manage to have their own web pages chock full of photos of their newborn baby brother, their favorite toys and their first day in kindergarten—even though they (presumably) haven't earned their first dollar yet? It's because their parents subscribe to an ISP that gives them a few megabytes of space at no charge.

Test Drive

In the early days of your new business, you're probably going to be watching your expenditures pretty closely, so here's a way to try out the wonderful world of internet commerce absolutely free. If you're already online, check with your local ISP to see if it provides free web space as part of your monthly service fee. Many ISPs offer 10MB to 20MB of space at no extra charge.

Using a reasonably priced program like FrontPage or a professional program like Dreamweaver and your ISP web page wizard and sample pages, it's a breeze to set up your own site. Although that's not a lot of space (and you'll have to forgo the flash animation), it's enough to put up a few pages about your business, as well as some samples of your work. You also can use one of the free pages available on the internet (good ones to try can be found at angelfire.lycos.com or geocities.yahoo.com/ps/info1).

But if you're serious about doing business online and having a professional presence, our best advice is to launch a website designed especially for your business, on which you can customize content, include lots of photos, and generally expound on the products or services you offer.

Some of the features you should consider including on your website are:

- *Flash intro.* Flash is, well, flashy, with spinning logos, blinking lights, swooping graphics, and other eye-catching visuals. The rationale is that such graphics compel the surfer to eagerly click on a link and get started. But some users can be turned off, either because they don't like gimmicky stuff or they're too impatient to wait for the flash intro to load and play. If you use flash always include a "skip intro" link on the page so the reader can buzz right past the frolicking puppies and snorting horses and get to the useful info on the next level. If you're curious about what you can do with flash, check out the cute flash intro on David Lipschultz's pet-sitting website at outugo.com (watch for the saxophone-playing puppy!).
- *Service menu.* This is where you'll give details about the various services you offer. This page can be as simple as a list (i.e., "walk pets, change food and water, administer medications," etc.) or as elaborate as a detailed description of the services you offer with bibliographic references. (OK, maybe this is a little extreme for some businesses. But if you're a pet trainer, for instance, you may wish to refer site visitors to other industry information about your training methods or

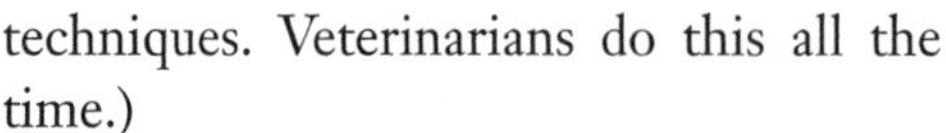

techniques. Veterinarians do this all the time.)

The jury is still out on whether you should disclose the rates for your services on your website. On one hand, posting rates makes it easy for prospects to see at a glance what you charge, and it keeps those who can't afford you or are unwilling to pay what you think you're worth from wasting your time on the phone. On the other hand, not posting rates can turn away the timid or suspicious, as well as those who will simply move on to another site where the rates are published. Our advice is to check out your local competition and see what their practices are. If your competitors are not online, then you can be the trend-setter.

Dollar Stretcher

If you're short on cash for website design, call the IT department of your local university and ask for the name of a talented student website designer. Not only will a student charge you less than a professional, the site he or she creates will probably be very creative and fun to use.

Of course, it goes without saying that if you're selling products, you must publish your prices in your online catalog. And don't forget to state that shipping and handling charges are extra. To help customers estimate their shipping costs, you can include a link to the postage calculator found on the U.S. Postal Service website at ircalc.usps.gov. Make sure you include the item's weight in its description so the customer will be able to determine the shipping cost. Alternatively, you can easily calculate the cost yourself using a program like Desktop Dozen Postage Calculator ($34.95, Spud City Software). You'll find contact information for this company in the Appendix.

- *Portfolio*. As we said in the last chapter, you're a good candidate for a virtual portfolio if you're a pet groomer by trade. Posting photos of the pets you've groomed instills confidence in prospects that you know what you're doing. (Try posting before and after photos for dramatic effect.) It helps to have a knack for photography if you plan to create a portfolio of your work. Pets are notoriously difficult to photograph, both in terms of their wriggle factor and the difficulty lighting them adequately. If you can get good crisp photos of your furry clients, feel free to post them. If not, then forgo this feature.
- *Product catalog*. Give enough information so customers can get a good idea of what they're buying, and provide multiple views (such as front and back) if there are details that should be seen to be appreciated. In addition, always provide dimensions and sizes so there's no guesswork on the part of the customer (and fewer returns later).
- *Biography*. While we don't recommend that you put your photo on your website (your appearance really doesn't matter in the execution of your job), it's a good

idea if you're running a pet-service business to list your credentials, including any prior experience you have caring for animals, in a short biography. People love their pets and want to know they're being handled by a caring, capable person. You might also want to offer references (although never give their contact information on your website) or testimonials If you're running a pet-products business, a biography isn't necessary unless you think that previous sales expertise might sway potential buyers (usually your merchandise speaks for itself).

- *Contact information.* List a variety of means by which a prospective client can reach you, including your phone and fax number, and e-mail address—but we don't recommend giving out your home address on your website. If a client will be bringing his or her pet to your home for a service, you can hand out such personal information over the phone. It is helpful, however, to include a statement like "serving the metropolitan Kansas City area" to clue your readers in to your location.

Once you have all this useful information on your site, don't just put it out of your head while you get to work walking, grooming, training, or selling. You need to revisit the site periodically to make sure everything is updated and current. This is especially important because repeat visitors who don't see any change in the home page will stop dropping in. Doing something as simple as regularly changing the adorable pictures on your ferret-sitting site will freshen it up and make the rest of the information seem new.

Under Construction

One way to achieve the professional look you want for your website is to hire a web-page designer. An experienced designer is invaluable because he or she will be able to advise you about page content, appearance, and optimal word count per page. (News flash: Studies show that cyber readers hate scrolling down to read text—they often impatiently skip to new pages instead.) The designer also is the best judge of where and how many links should be inserted to lead viewers from one screen to the next, and often can either write or farm out the writing of your website for you.

The cost for website design is usually based on the number of pages on the site. Although one pet-business owner we know paid $10,000 to have a website designed, typically you'll pay anywhere from $1,000 to $4,000 for a professional, fully functional website with links, then

Tip...

Smart Tip

According to a recent study by Inktomi and NEC Research, there are more than 2 billion websites—and the number is climbing. With all that online noise, you really should turn the design of your website over to a professional web page designer, who can create the most useful and user-friendly website possible for your business.

you'll usually pay a per-hour fee for future maintenance/updates to the site. In most cases, the update process is simple enough that you should be able to handle it yourself. Be sure to mention to the designer during the design phase that you want to be in control of your web page destiny so the updating steps should be within your capabilities.

If you are fortunate enough to have technical skills in your personal bag of tricks, you could try creating your own website rather than using a designer. There are a number of web page programs available that don't require a master's of science degree to figure out, including Dreamweaver MX by Macromedia (retails for $399, macromedia.com) or Microsoft FrontPage (retails for $199 or less, available from computer superstores).

The Host with the Most

Once your designer has done his or her magic and you have a working website ready to go, you have to find a place to stash it in cyberspace. So your next task is to select an internet host site. (By the way, this is separate from your ISP, which is your electronic gateway to the internet. The host site is the place in cyberspace where your site resides.) There are zillions of internet hosts to choose from—including popular favorites like EarthLink and NetPass—with price being the distinguishing feature among them. But there are other things to consider when selecting a host: namely, how long the company has been in business (hosts sometimes come and go quickly), how often the site goes down, and how quickly it gets back online after experiencing downtime. A site that has a demonstrated track record of success is the best choice because it means your site will be up and running as much as possible.

Web hosting is very competitive, so it pays to shop around for the best deal. It typically runs around $19.95 per month for 20MB of disk space, although you might be able to find a deal if you surf the host sites. To get you started, we've provided a few well-known host names with contact information in the Appendix.

Getting a Handle

Just as you selected a unique business name for legal purposes, you also must select and register a unique website name. This name, known in cyber circles as a domain name or URL (for universal resource locator) enables users anywhere in the world (even that shepherd in New Zealand with the unruly collie) to find you on the internet, no matter which host you have selected.

Bright Idea

If you've ever fantasized about having a website named after yourself (as in billjohnson.com), dream no longer. The site namesecure.com will allow you to register your name using one of the common commercial suffixes (including .com, .net, .org, .biz, or .info) for as little as $7.49 a year. Bad news for all you Bill Johnsons, though—that one's already taken.

Many pet-business owners use their business name as their cyber handle, as in BarkysCanine Coiffures.com. That's usually a good idea, especially if you've given your business name serious consideration. Keep in mind, however, that as with a DBA, it's possible that someone has already snagged your chosen name. You should have a couple of stand-by names at the ready when you try to register. (For example, you could use barkys.com or caninecoif fures.com instead and get the same basic message across. And FYI, the latter has already been taken by a groomer in California.) Selecting an ending on the address other than .com (like .net) might also be a way to land your preferred name.

Tip...

Smart Tip

Registering your website on as many search engines as possible will increase the chances that people will be able to find it. To make your presence known on Google, Lycos, Yahoo!, and thousands of other worldwide search engines, try using a service like Add Me (addme.com), which charges a modest fee to hook you up.

Domain names are registered for a minimum of two years for about $70 and are renewable ad infinitum. Among the companies that can register your name is Domain.com, which offers five- and ten-year registrations at a cost of $23 and $18 per year, respectively.

Keyed In

One final thing you should consider investigating is search engine keywords. These are clickable advertising links that appear on search engine pages whenever someone calls up information on a particular topic. (For instance, on Google, the keywords appear on the right side of the screen under "sponsored links.") When you click on one of these links, you're taken directly to an advertiser's website, and the advertiser pays for that hit. The hope is that these click-throughs will result in business for your company, although the reality is that the conversion rate of "click to order" is very low—about 1.5 percent.

Nevertheless, Elmwood Park, New Jersey, pet-food business owner John Zambelli is a big believer in keywords and spends the lion's share of his advertising dollars bidding on them. (Type "Flint River Ranch" into your browser right now and you'll see his sponsored link pop up at the top of the list.) He has 30 to 50 keywords at a time, for which he pays around $3,000 a month.

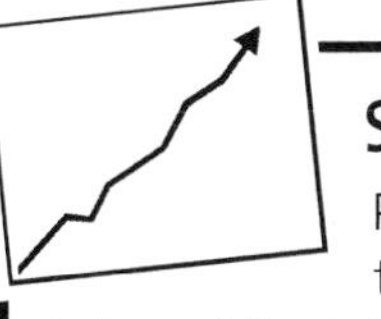

Stat Fact

Pet owners routinely surf the internet for information. A recent study by the American Pet Products Association determined that 14 percent of dog owners, 19 percent of cat owners, 18 percent of fish owners, 23 percent of bird owners, 28 percent of small-animal owners, and 34 percent of reptile owners get their pet information online.

"Keywords are a way to catch people who want to buy now," he says. "Our conversion rate is higher than average because our product is niche-y—when people find us, they tend to buy. But the key is to be one of the top three bidders—that gives you the best visibility."

David Lipschultz also uses keywords, although he sets it up so his ad appears only until he has reached a certain number of hits in a month, say equal to $10, to keep costs under control.

Keywords are purchased through various companies, but you don't automatically get them just by handing over your credit card number. Rather, you have to bid on them, and whoever pays the most gets the top keyword on the sponsored links list. Remember that "Flint River Ranch" keyword used by Zambelli? It was at the top of the list when this book was written because Zambelli bid more than anyone else for the privilege. Depending on the category, you might pay a few cents for a keyword or several dollars per hit, which is billed monthly and payable by credit card. A few keyword providers you can check out are adsense.com (serviced by Google), searchmarketing.yahoo.com, and keyword.com.

17

Pedigreed Publicity Ploys

A couple of chapters ago, we talked about the paid promotional efforts you can launch to attract new business. Now let's discuss some low-to-no-cost publicity tools that can positively pump up your presence in the community and as a result drive even more business to your door. We are talking, of course, about public relations.

The online encyclopedia Wikipedia defines public relations as a "means...of influencing public opinion of an organization. It is distinct from advertising as it is generally not aimed at selling a particular product from a particular business." In other words, it's a way to give the public a positive opinion of you and your business, which in turn can make them want to do business with you. But why on earth does this work? Because: a) people like to do business with people and companies they like; and b) the power of suggestion is often more persuasive than in-your-face advertising.

So in this chapter, we'll talk about the various publicity techniques that have proved successful for pet-care business owners, including news releases, newsletters, writing feature stories, special events, networking, public speaking, teaching, and gift certificates. Most require a very low investment of cash and time yet can yield big benefits.

News Releases

Have you ever wondered how some business owners are lucky enough to be featured in a newspaper story or even on the evening news? Well, luck probably had little to do with it. Rather, your competition probably landed that coveted spot in response to a news release (aka press release) he or she sent to the organization that was interesting, endearing, amazing, or cute enough to catch someone's attention.

News releases are kind of like free ads for your business, but with a gentler touch. They should focus on positive things you've done in your business, such as grooming a dog who won a ribbon at a local dog show, winning a neighborhood beautification award for your newly remodeled building, or donating pet treats to the local animal shelter. By getting the word out about your good deeds and your business in this way, you are subtly telling customers that yours is a good business to visit.

And news releases do work. Exton, Pennsylvania, products manufacturer Joyce Reavey says she sees a surge in hits on her website every time she sends out a news release. "A lot of magazines get excited for you when you launch a new product and give you more space," she says. "When I launched the Fab Imperial Bed, which looks like a Fabergé egg, *Giftware News* put it on the cover because it was new and exciting, and it sold really well."

There's no guarantee that your news release will be printed, but we can tell you that editors of local and community newspapers in particular love receiving well-written news releases about interesting subjects. That's because as they're

Bright Idea

When e-mailing a news release to a large number of people, address the message to yourself and send a blind copy (bcc) to the recipients. That way you won't have to send a lot of separate e-mails, plus the recipients won't know who else is getting the same information.

laying out their issues, they'll invariably have holes to fill, and if your news release comes along at just the right time, bingo—you're in. If you're lucky, the editor will drop the news release into the paper in its entirety. Other times, editors will chop off the bottom of a release to fit a space, which means you want to make sure your full company name and address appears early in the release so it has the best chance of seeing print. And sometimes, if you're really lucky and all the planets are lined up auspiciously in the heavens, the editor will call you and interview you for a feature story—all on the strength of your news release.

Up for Promotion

A good promotion strategy is all about the mix—you need to get your message into as many publicity channels as possible to get the best results. Here's how to collar some valuable publicity at low or no cost:

- *Position yourself as an expert.* The media are always looking for local or national experts who can talk about their products or comment on issues. Make yourself available by sending out a news release about anything newsworthy that comes your way. Here's an example: Tell *Good Morning America* about that clever new pet bed you designed that has cup holders, air conditioning, and a rear windshield defogger for the doggie on the go. (That will get their attention!) Or follow up a news report about a dangerous, vicious dog in your community with a news release that shows how proper training can rehabilitate most dogs. Or have your public relations firm get those coveted media placements for you—they're experts at it.
- *Donate goods or services.* Organizations are always looking for goods and services to auction off at fund-raising events. Just make sure what you donate is substantial enough to create some interest. For instance, a pet sitter/walker could donate a week of daily visits, a groomer could buff and fluff an average-sized pet, a trainer could offer private lessons, and product sellers could donate a month's supply of horse chow or one of those dog palaces mentioned above.
- *Support your community.* Offer your time or a financial contribution to a pet rescue league, humane society, or other animal welfare organization. Pet lovers will be happy to patronize a business with such a caring owner.
- *Become an activist.* Support local animal organizations by seeking a seat on their boards and becoming a spokesperson for animal rights.

Bright Idea

Sending a photograph of whatever you're selling or pets you've worked with along with a news release increases the chances that it will be published. Prints should be 5 x 7 or larger and printed on high-quality photographic paper, while e-mailed photos should be either in .tif or .jpg format and at least 300 dpi.

There are many types of things you do that are suitable for news release treatment. First, you can write a "backgrounder" when you first open your doors that gives details about the business, yourself, and why you opened. You also can send out releases about accomplishments such as how you trained that annoying dog on Northline and Eureka to stop barking at falling leaves, cracks in the sidewalk, and fire hydrants. You can write releases about new services you're offering, awards you've won for your professional work or community service, interesting products you're selling (like those mink dog blankets you just received, for instance), or the donations you make to charity auctions (say, a one-hour dog-training session for the local cancer charity auction). It doesn't have to be breaking news *The New York Times* would be clamoring to have—just something interesting to a general audience.

News releases should be only about one page long with enough information to catch an editor's interest, as well as contact information so he or she can reach you if there are questions. To make sure you get all the pertinent details into the release, answer journalists' basic questions of who, what, where, when, why, and how in the first couple of paragraphs. You also should follow standard news release formatting conventions when preparing the release so editors will know what it is when they open it. See the sample news release on the next page to see what the standard format looks like. Need some professional assistance? Contact local professional advertising organizations, the chamber of commerce, or university public relations programs for leads to a freelance public relations writer, or look in the Yellow Pages under "freelance writers."

Bright Idea

If you need help building a media list, try the free resources at mondo times.com and usnpl.com. For a list with more teeth, check out the resources at bacons info.com. Its list is $425, but it contains all the information you need to build a national mailing list. For a fee, Bacon's also will distribute and track your releases.

If you have a bit more promotion money to spend, you might want to consider hiring a public relations firm as your professional media handler. PR firms have the contacts to get your product or service in front of the public eye and know how to package the details in a way that editors and producers will notice.

"PR carries an implied endorsement with it," says Julia Hutton, CEO of Orca Communications Unlimited, a Phoenix public relations firm that specializes in pet marketing. "When you pay for

Sample News Release

Molly's Snips and Clips

Lic. #123456

123 Oceanview Rd., Galveston, TX 05402

(000) 555-5555 • www.mollyssandc.com

News Release

For Immediate Release

Media Contact: Molly Bear
Telephone: (000) 555-5555

Date: September 15, 200x

GALVESTON, TX— It may look like your average pet-grooming salon, but exciting things are going on behind the doors of 123 Oceanview.

Owner Molly Bear, an award-winning pet groomer with five years' experience, trimmed, fluffed and styled three local dogs who all went on to win ribbons in the recent All-State Dog Show. The dogs—a sheltie and two poodles—took first- and second-place honors.

But canines aren't the only ones to benefit from Bear's award-winning touch. Last fall, Trixie, the darling "daughter" of Lorna Jones of Galveston, was named Top Cat in the house cat (long-hair) division at the Southern States Cat Show in Houston.

How does she do it, especially when her clients wriggle, snarl, scratch, drool and bark as she works?

"It does take a steady hand," Bear said, her scissors flashing as she worked on a Pomeranian. "But I've always had a way with both cats and dogs, and I find that whispering sweet nothings in their ears gets their confidence and settles them down."

She also has a way with clippers and scissors. But the real secret to her success is her novel style. She models many of the cuts she gives on hairstyles worn by celebrities and fashion models—and the results are so unusual that competition judges can't help but be impressed.

"I've always preferred working from life rather than just copying standard grooming styles," Bear said. "I'm delighted that so many people have found my work so fresh and appealing."

In fact, the Kelly Ripa clip she gave to Darla, an Australian silky terrier, recently came to the attention of the talk-show host, who has invited Bear, Darla, and Darla's "mom," Ruth Wilder of Houston, to appear on her show next month.

Molly's Snip and Clip is open Monday through Saturday, 10 a.m. to 6 p.m. For an appointment before Bear goes off to fame and fortune in New York, call (000) 555-5555.

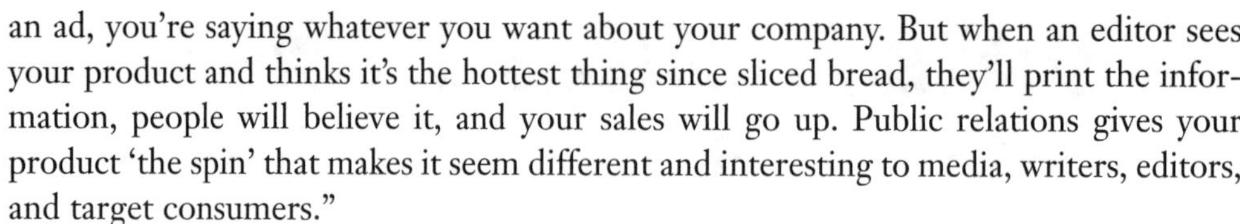

an ad, you're saying whatever you want about your company. But when an editor sees your product and thinks it's the hottest thing since sliced bread, they'll print the information, people will believe it, and your sales will go up. Public relations gives your product 'the spin' that makes it seem different and interesting to media, writers, editors, and target consumers."

Newsletters

Have you noticed how everyone from your state senator to your local lawn-service company is sending out newsletters these days? The reasons are simple: Newsletters provide a great medium for spreading the word about the services and products you offer, they're easy and inexpensive to produce, and they can be mailed right to your customers' homes or offices. These, of course, are exactly the same reasons why you should consider sending out a newsletter that promotes your pet-care business. All it takes is a computer, software like Microsoft Office (which has a number of newsletter templates to choose from), and a little imagination.

Informational newsletters tend to work best for pet-care business owners. Include pet-care ideas, feeding tips, information about new products or services, bios of new staff members or employees, and anything else that might be interesting to a pet owner. Features like checklists ("Six ways to protect your pet from summer heat") and quizzes ("How well do you know your Pomeranian?") are also interesting and fun for readers. Finally, include full contact information, including your phone number and business hours, to make it easy for readers to pick up the phone and make an appointment or stop by your store.

Your newsletter doesn't have to be long. A single 8.5-by-11-inch sheet printed on the front and back (or designed as a two-page .pdf file for an e-newsletter) will give you plenty of room for your news and views. (Or feel free to do just a one-sided newsletter if that's all the news you have.) In addition, this size works great because it's inexpensive to produce—you can print it yourself on a photocopier at the local copy shop—and it can be mailed in a No. 10 business envelope for just 42 cents. Alternatively, save the envelope cost by designing the newsletter with a blank mailing panel at the bottom of side two so the sheet can be folded in half, closed with a self-stick wafer tab, and mailed for 42 cents.

You'll want to use your newsletter both to prospect for new business and to keep in touch with your existing client base. And you don't have to publish it very frequently. A newsletter sent out twice a year—for instance, timed to coincide with summer vacations for service businesses and the holidays for product businesses—should be enough. Including a coupon for a few dollars off one of your products or services is a sure way to catch readers' attention.

If your basic writing skills aren't too rusty, you should be able to write your own newsletter, especially if you keep articles short and to the point (always a good idea in a newsletter). However, if you need help, you can hire a freelance writer to produce the text for you. As mentioned earlier, you can find a freelancer through local professional advertising organizations, as well as through the chamber of commerce, university journalism programs, and the Yellow Pages. Depending on the writer's experience, expect to pay $150 to $300 for a two-page newsletter.

Once you have the text in hand, you can try designing the newsletter yourself using one of the Microsoft Office templates or one of the many affordable desktop software packages that come with newsletter templates. You just type in the headlines (story titles), paste in the copy, and the program will do the copy fitting and formatting for you. Of course, for an even more professional and custom look, you should use a freelance graphic designer. Have him or her create a simple newsletter template that you can fill in yourself each time you produce another newsletter. A designer will charge $30 to $60 per hour, or about $300 for a two-page newsletter. Check the Yellow Pages under "Graphic Designers" or contact an art school to find a designer.

One important thing you should include in your newsletter is artwork so it's not a sea of type. If you're doing an e-newsletter, include pet photos that relate to the stories. But if you're photocopying the newsletter, forgo the photos because the reproduction quality may not be very good and your newsletter won't look professional. In addition, clip art will give your newsletter some visual interest. Microsoft Office comes with a variety of business clip art (plus you can access more online), but if you want clip art of pets, you'll have to buy a separate graphic package like ClickArt 950,000 from Broderbund, which retails for $49.99.

Feature Stories

If you consider yourself to be a pretty good writer, you might want to try writing feature stories as a way to gain more visibility for your business. Newspapers and magazines are always in the market for well-written feature stories of around 500 to 1,000 words, and it's likely they'd be interested in articles with pet-related themes. In fact, the same type of articles you'll be writing for your newsletter would be appropriate for other print media—they just need to be longer. Informational articles (like why a raw pet-food diet is superior to processed canned food) and how-tos (such as how to train a rambunctious puppy) have the best chance of being picked up by editors. And don't worry that you're giving

> Tip...
>
> **Smart Tip**
>
> If you want to increase your chances of getting your feature article published, write a query letter to the editor before you write the article. Describe what you'll cover and your qualifications as an expert on the topic. Include your phone number and e-mail address so the editor can contact you if he or she is interested in the story.

away trade secrets by sharing your knowledge and insight with readers. Think of it as positioning yourself as an authority in your field, which will make readers want to use your services or shop at your online or bricks-and-mortar store because you're so knowledgeable.

Editors these days generally prefer to have manuscripts submitted on a CD or e-mailed with the document attached. (You might also want to paste the text into the body of the e-mail in case the editor doesn't open attachments.) The manuscript should be formatted on the screen as a double-spaced document with 1-inch margins all around. If you're saving the document to CD, save it as a text file as well as a Word file so the editor won't have any trouble opening it. Then send the CD or e-mail with a brief pitch letter that describes what the article is about and why it would appeal to the readers of the publication. (Never write a generic "Dear Editor" letter—always call the publication and ask for the editor's name and/or e-mail address so you can personalize your cover letter.) Don't forget to include your full contact information so the editor can reach you, and feel free to call a few days after you send the article to find out whether the editor thought it was appropriate for her audience, as well as what you can do in the future to increase your chances of being published. And good news—most publications will pay you at least a token amount for your work, although frankly, the byline you receive on the article is worth much more in terms of publicity than the pocket change you're paid.

Special Events

You'll remember back in Chapter 15 that we discussed holding a grand-opening celebration for your business. Special events like that are almost always newsworthy if you're doing business in a small community. In a larger city, you'll find they create some excitement both among your current customers and prospective clients to whom you mail an invitation. Use your imagination when dreaming up a special event. Celebrate your shop cat's birthday. Have an open house and give away samples of the new dog food you're carrying. Invite a local celebrity and dog owner in to model your new designer dog duds. The sky's the limit!

Tip...

Smart Tip

Calendars and pens make great giveaway items, both for current clients and for prospective customers you meet at trade shows, business meetings, and so on. Not only do they remind the recipient that you're available, but they give you free publicity every time they're pulled out of a pocket or purse. You can buy promotional items from advertising specialty companies.

Networking

Petworking—er, networking—is an outstanding and usually low-cost way to get to know other business owners in the community and spread the word about your business.

Organizations like the chamber of commerce and Rotary Club hold meet-and-greets for members to exchange tips and contacts. Join one of these groups and get involved. You'll meet some people that might be useful later and possibly land some new business. In fact, it's common to be asked to barter services at these types of gatherings. Whether you want to trade services is entirely up to you, but keep in mind that bartering can lead to referrals, which definitely is something that can benefit your business in the long run.

The cost to join these types of civic organizations is usually quite nominal, plus the membership cost is deductible as a business expense.

Public Speaking

Still interested in more ways to position yourself as an expert in your field? Then try landing a few public speaking engagements. Service organizations like the Lions Club, as well as libraries, garden clubs, alumni associations, parent associations, ladies' auxiliaries, and various other groups are always in the market for speakers to address their meetings. You may receive only an honorarium or a warm handshake for your time, but the pay really isn't the issue—the exposure for your business is what you're after. So if you feel comfortable standing in front of a group of people and sharing your knowledge, keep an eye out for public speaking opportunities. They're valuable platforms for promoting your business.

Teaching

Another publicity ploy with benefits similar to public speaking is teaching. Dog trainers and pet groomers in particular will find that the public will happily pay to attend a workshop or seminar on topics like how to groom poodles or paper-train a puppy. Then you'll discover that some of the people in the audience will either come up to you afterward or call you to set up an appointment because they haven't had any luck trying to accomplish these feats themselves or they simply don't have the time to make it happen. Be sure to bring a lot of business cards and brochures to your workshop. Put a supply on the table where the sign-up sheet is posted for maximum impact. Also, don't forget to let the media know about the course by sending out a news release. If you're lucky, the information will be published in the paper's community calendar and your attendance will increase.

Among the places you can schedule a seminar and workshop are adult and community education programs and pet stores that don't offer the same services themselves. Call around your community to see if there's any interest.

Gift Cards

Considering that money changes hands when you sell a gift card, it may seem odd to include them in a chapter about publicity. But think of them this way: Gift cards and gift certificates do indeed generate positive interest in your services among the people who receive them as gifts. If nothing else, the recipient will come in once to use your grooming or training services, or to purchase products. Once he or she walks in the door, it's up to you to dazzle so he or she will want to return for additional products or services.

It's actually quite easy to run a gift-card program. There are a number of companies that can supply you with either plastic gift cards similar to the ones used by the big retailers or paper gift certificates. Promote them like you would any other service, and you may be pleasantly surprised by how much extra income they can generate. You'll find the names of a few gift-card providers in the Appendix.

18

Corralling the Cash

While there's no denying that most of the pet-care businesses discussed in this book have very low startup costs (particularly those of the homebased variety), you can certainly see from reading this far that plenty of inescapable expenses will crop up every month as you run your new business. You'll be spending your precious capital on everything from inventory and pet-care supplies to advertising and telecommunication services—and a considerable number of things in between. Your challenge, of course, is to earn enough money each month to cover those expenses and have enough left over to cover your personal living expenses, save for the future (which—who knows?—could include a global chain of pet-care businesses one day!), and maybe finance a couple of weekend getaways each year. So sit back and let's get the dog-and-pony show on the road.

Tracking Income and Expenses

As we've discussed in previous chapters, it's important to keep good records when you're in business, both to satisfy your inquisitive Uncle Sam and to keep yourself up to speed so you always know how the business is doing. A simple income and expense statement (also known as an I&E) that you've customized for your business will do the trick. Your accountant can set up this I&E for you, or you can use QuickBooks to do the job. But for now, you may wish to use the I&E worksheet you'll find on page 228 to jot down your estimated expenses as you work through this chapter. In addition, you'll find a sample I&E statement on page 227 that shows the typical operating expenses for a hypothetical pet-grooming business called Molly's Snip and Clip, which is an S corporation operating out of a small shop with two part-time assistants. Read on for more details about some of the ongoing expenses you can expect in your business.

Mortgage/Rent

If you're operating out of a facility, insert your monthly rent or mortgage payment on this line. If you're working from home and are planning to deduct the cost of your home office, plug in a figure, a percentage of your house payment or rent, that represents the percentage of your home you actually use for business. If you're renting a storage facility for your products, you should include that monthly payment as well.

Utilities

Depending on your rental/lease/purchase situation, you may have various utility costs that should be included on this line, including gas, electricity, and/or water. To get the most accurate figures, call your utility company and ask for an estimate for a facility of your size. If you're using your home for business, include the appropriate percentage of the known utility costs on this line. Look at the previous year's bills to figure out the amount. For our sample I&E, we've estimated a water-only cost of $100 per month.

Dollar Stretcher

A new technology called Voice over Internet Protocol (VoIP) can save you big bucks on your phone bill. You simply use a special adapter to hook your existing phone line to a high-speed internet connection like a DSL line or cable modem. One VoIP provider, Vonage (vonage.com), offers unlimited calls anywhere in the United States and Canada for about $25 per month.

Phones

If you're working from home, having a dedicated business phone is important for your new business. First, it makes you seem more professional, which is very important for a homebased business owner. Second, you'll be entitled to a business listing in the Yellow Pages the next time the directory is printed (plus you'll be immediately accessible to customers through directory assistance). And third, the cost of the line can be written off as a business expense. But we'll admit, at $150 to $400 a month for a business line, the cost can be a little hard to take. So you might instead install a second residential line in your home office at a cost of about $30 to $40 a month, then make sure it's strictly off limits to everyone else in the house. (And don't forget, you may need yet another line for your fax machine.) Another option is a cellular phone used strictly as your business line, which is actually advantageous if you work out of clients' homes since you can carry it with you when you're on the road. No matter which option you choose, make sure you have voice mail (or an answering machine for a landline) so you never miss a call—and of course be sure to pick up your messages regularly.

The $90 on our sample I&E includes monthly landline and cell-phone service. Other add-ons that can be particularly helpful for homebased pet-business owners are voice mail ($12 to $18 per month), call waiting ($5 per month), and caller ID (about $7.50 for number identification and $2 extra for name display). Many telecom companies offer bundled service packages that include these and other premium services. For instance, Sage Telecom has a service plan that includes local service, one hour of long-distance calling, and free call forwarding, caller ID, call waiting, and repeat dialing for about $40 a month.

Office Supplies

If you budgeted $150 for office supplies in your startup budget as recommended in Chapter 10, it's reasonable to assume you'll need only about $50 to $75 a month for future purchases, which may include toner cartridges ($25 to $80; possibly more for laser printer cartridges), copier paper ($25 to $50 per case), and little stuff like pens, legal pads, and file folders. If $50 seems a little high for your needs, track your expenditures for a few months and adjust your monthly I&E figure downward later.

Postage

You'll need to have postage on hand for direct-mail efforts, invoices, payment reminders, and the payments you make to suppliers like product wholesalers and the office supply store. As you know, first-class postage is 42 cents per ounce for letters, while postcards less than 6 inches wide by 4.5 inches high require 27 cents postage each. If you're sending out a big mailing and want to keep mailing costs low, you can mail bulk instead and save a few pennies on each piece. However, a lot of people will automatically file your letter or postcard in the circular file when they see a bulk-mail permit instead of a stamp. Ditto a "stamp" from a postage meter. To circumvent the trashing of your special offer, you could affix postage stamps to the mailing piece if you have the time and manpower to devote to the job. It should be safe to earmark $100 a month for postage, which will cover 238 pieces at 42 cents each. Estimate higher if you think you'll mail out more than that (possible when you launch the business) or lower if you're planning to send out postcards. We've taken the high road on our I&E and used a figure of $100.

Licenses

Since you would have included the cost of your municipal license in your startup costs, you may not have anything to insert here. However, we've included the line in the event that you may need additional licenses in the future (including the renewal of that municipal license in your second year).

Wages

There are two lines for wages on the I&E—one for the owner's salary and one for employee wages. It's very important to include a salary for yourself in the monthly expenses, even if you're fortunate enough to have a spouse or significant other who is paying the main household bills. Being able to prove you have an income is important if you ever want to buy a house, finance a vehicle, apply for credit, lease a building for your growing business, etc.

Oak Park, Illinois, dog walker/pet sitter David Lipschultz offers another important reason why a business owner should take a salary. "As an employee of my company, I am an actual expense, too, and taking a consistent salary helps me to know exactly how much my monthly expenses are and how much the company is worth," he says. "I don't take a big salary—basically, I take what my accountant says I can afford to take—but taking that salary makes me look like a legitimate businessperson to everyone who matters."

To emulate Lipschultz's example, set up a separate payroll account and pay yourself a regular salary even if the amount is small because you're trying to plow as much back into the business as possible. On our sample I&E, we've used a figure of $1,800 per month for the owner, or $21,600 per year, because, like Lipschultz, this hypothetical owner chooses to work for less until the business is up and running. The amount you plug into the employee wages line will depend on the type of employee(s) you hire. As discussed previously, skilled workers like pet groomers and assistant dog trainers generally earn more money than the folks you hire to walk dogs or sit at the reception desk. Shop assistants often start at the federal minimum wage, which will be $7.25 in 2009. Since some states (including Alaska, California, Connecticut, Delaware, Hawaii, Illinois, Kansas, Maine, Massachusetts, Ohio, Oregon, Rhode Island, Vermont, Washington, and the District of Columbia) have their own minimum wage laws, check with your state's department of labor for the correct amount. But you might want to offer them a little more—say, $9—so you don't end up having a lot of turnover among people who will decamp for another job down the street at a clothing store that pays $9.25. On our sample, we've figured in a $9-per-hour wage for each of the part-time assistants, or $1,440 a month.

Benefits and Taxes

In Chapter 13, we discussed how offering benefits can be a good way to attract and retain good help. But the fact is, many small-business owners simply cannot afford to extend company-sponsored health insurance and other traditional benefits to their employees. So instead, consider rewarding good employees and make them feel valued by offering a benefit like a one-week paid vacation, a paid sick day when needed (within reason), or even a holiday bonus.

Beware!

The IRS strictly regulates which home office expenses are deductible. You can usually deduct the percentage of mortgage payment and interest, real estate taxes, utilities, and insurance related to the business. But while painting and repair costs generally are deductible, services like lawn care are not. See IRS Publication 587, *Business Use of Your Home*, for more information.

As you might expect, employment taxes will take a big bite out of your business proceeds. Employers pay a lot of taxes for the privilege of hiring people to assist with the running of their business. Among the taxes are FICA (at 6.2 percent), the matching portion of Medicare taxes (1.45 percent), federal taxes (aka FUTA, at 6.2 percent, although you may qualify for a 5.4 percent credit), state unemployment taxes (variable), and workers' compensation insurance (also variable). Because you're an employee of the company, too, you have to pay all those taxes on your own earnings, as well as a self-employment tax if you're a sole proprietor. The only tax you're exempt from is workers' comp, which covers only employees—not the boss. It can be difficult to come up with an estimate of the employee taxes you can expect to pay, but your accountant should be able to lend a hand so you can get a reasonably accurate figure for your worksheet.

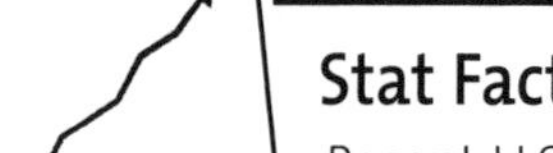

Stat Fact

Recent U.S. Department of Labor statistics indicate that benefits typically comprise 29.6 percent of total employee compensation. However, pet retailers and services are nowhere near that league—8 to 10 percent is a much more typical benefit cost for these types of small businesses.

We've used a figure of 10 percent on the $1,120 wages paid to the two hypothetical employees, or $112, which would cover the taxes mentioned above (a total of 8.45 percent) plus a little more for workers' comp and state unemployment taxes. As the business owner, your personal income taxes are not included in the monthly expenses—rather, you will subtract them from your monthly income and send them in as quarterly estimated tax payments. Check with your accountant to figure out how much to remit. In addition, we're not including any benefits costs on this line because, as we've mentioned, it is usually too costly for a startup business to offer benefits at first.

If you're using subcontractors rather than employees, your tax situation will be a little less dire because you don't have to collect or pay any income taxes on their wages—rather, they're responsible for paying their own taxes. Your sole responsibility is to issue a Form 1099-MISC at the end of the year to any subcontractor who earns more than $600 that year. Don't forget, the IRS has very specific criteria regarding what constitutes an independent contractor vs. an employee. Before you bring any independent contractors on board, make sure you know the rules. Pick up a copy of IRS Publication 15-A, *Employer's Supplemental Tax Guide* (available at IRS field offices or at irs.gov) for additional information about the employee/independent contractor distinction.

To offset your taxes, you can of course take legitimate business deductions, beginning with the mileage deduction of 50.5 cents per mile (as of January 2008). Although it's possible to charge your customer for mileage costs (especially these days when gas prices are so high), it's usually a better idea to keep track of your mileage costs to job sites and write them off on Schedule C of your 1040 income taxes (if you're a sole proprietor), or on your business tax return. Handling mileage that way will certainly build goodwill with your customers. However, if a client lives far outside your normal service area, charging for mileage becomes much more appropriate—as long as you discuss it with your client so there is no misunderstanding later.

You'll also want to keep detailed records about all other business expenses, including those office supplies we mentioned earlier, dog biscuits, grooming products, and so on, since they're all deductible.

It should be fairly obvious by now that tax matters can be complicated and time consuming, especially for a business novice. Since you probably will have other important things to do, we strongly recommend that you hire an accountant who will work with you to maximize your deductions, handle business and personal taxes, and do all the other things necessary to keep you on Uncle Sam's good side.

Insurance

If you filled out the insurance worksheet in Chapter 9, you already have a good idea of what your insurance premiums will be. One-twelfth of the estimated figure should be inserted into your I&E.

Online Service and Web Hosting

If you need speedy internet service, be prepared to pay a lot. Here are the going rates for the five different types of internet connectors currently available:

- *Standard ISP*: $20 to $25 per month
- *ISDN*: $50 a month, plus $20 to $25 a month for an ISP connection
- *DSL*: $30 to $40 a month
- *Cable modem*: $40 a month, plus basic cable TV service at the very least
- *Broadband high-speed satellite internet*: $99 a month

Web hosting to maintain your website will add another $20 to your monthly expenses.

Bright Idea

When choosing an ISP, select one that gives you multiple e-mail boxes so you can keep your business and personal e-mail separate. Just keep in mind that you can't deduct the entire amount as a business expense. You'll have to make a rough estimate of what percentage of your computer usage is business-related and deduct only that amount.

Merchant Account

You'll need a merchant account if you're planning to accept credit and debit cards (pretty much a foregone conclusion for site-based and internet companies, as well as many pet-service businesses these days). A merchant account is basically an electronic clearinghouse that's used to verify that a customer's credit is good. You'll need a telephone line to transmit data, as well as a point-of-sale (POS) terminal and a credit card receipt printer or specialized computer software (all discussed in detail in Chapter 10) to be able to clear payments. As you probably know from charging purchases yourself in the past, purchase authorization is obtained by swiping a credit or debit card through the POS terminal, which transmits the data to the clearinghouse. If all is well, the transaction is approved and the funds are transferred to the business's account.

The cost for a merchant account can vary widely. You'll usually pay a discount rate on each transaction, which is a fixed percentage deducted from the purchase price by the merchant account provider. This can amount to anywhere from 1.5 percent to 4 percent per transaction. Most merchant account providers also charge a statement fee of about $10 a month, plus a small fee for each transaction processed (usually around 20 cents each). Other typical charges include an initial programming charge, a monthly minimum fee, a "gateway" fee for secure payments, and a chargeback processing fee. All this can add up, but because the merchant account industry is pretty competitive these days, it pays to shop around for the best rate. You'll find contact information for several merchant account providers in the Appendix, but there are many more to choose from. The easiest way to find them is to Google the words "merchant account." In the meantime, we're using an estimated amount of $30 per month for merchant account fees on the sample I&E statement.

Dollar Stretcher

Although you don't absolutely have to use a thermal receipt printer when processing credit card payments, being able to give a printed receipt to your customers will certainly look more professional. Alternatively, you could invest in software that allows you to print receipts from your computer.

Check List

If you're planning to accept personal checks, you should sign up with a check-verification service to help reduce your risk of accepting a bad one. Verification service databases contain the recent transaction history for more than 76 million checking accounts, and they will warn you about checks written on accounts with unpaid returned checks, as well as about high check-writing volumes that may signal a suspicious or fraudulent use of an account. If you accept a bad check, the information is automatically forwarded to a collections department and you'll receive 100 percent of the funds from the bad check writer once he or she pays up. All this can be accomplished online using a check reader or offline using the phone. Verification service fees are similar to those of merchant accounts. You'll usually pay a set monthly fee of around $20, plus a per-item fee of around 20 cents and a setup fee (often around $100). There may also be a discount rate in each check processed. Rates vary, so it pays to shop around for the best deal.

Legal Services

This monthly charge is a little tricky to compute unless you plan to have an attorney on retainer (which frankly is unlikely for a sole proprietor who's just starting up). If you have a retainer situation, simply insert the monthly charge into the I&E. If you don't anticipate using an attorney for much more than your startup services package (i.e., incorporation filings, basic letter writing, etc.), you can simply include that charge on your startup work sheet and leave the legal services line blank on the I&E. However, if you encounter a situation later for which you'll need ongoing legal consultation or representation, you can either figure that monthly amount into subsequent I&Es or add the amount into the "miscellaneous" category. In our sample we've figured in $900 annually, or $75 a month, which should cover any situation that might crop up (other than litigation, of course).

Accounting Services

This charge is easier to calculate because accountants usually work on an hourly basis. Simply multiply your accountant's rate by the number of hours you plan to use him or her each month to arrive at a realistic figure. So how many hours might that be? Of course, it depends on the complexity of your business, but it's reasonable to assume you'll need three to five hours of the accountant's time when you launch your business to keep up with tax filings, receivables/payables, business taxes, and any other financial tasks you'd like to turn over. You can call around to find out how much accountants are charging in your community, or if you prefer, you can go with the median salary given in the *Occupational Outlook Handbook, 2004–05 Edition* (published by the U.S. Department of Labor), which is $49,500, or $23.80 an hour. For the sake of simplicity, we've rounded that figure up to $25 an hour and plugged $75 into our sample I&E for three hours of accounting work per month.

Tip...

Smart Tip

To keep your accounting costs under control, don't use the shoebox method of accounting—meaning don't just dump all your receipts and paperwork into a box or file and hand it to your accountant. Sort these documents into logical categories yourself so your accountant can spend less time on organizing and more on number crunching.

Payroll Service

This isn't a necessity by any means, but you'll find that it is a great time saver. David Lipschultz pays $80 biweekly to a service that takes care of issuing checks and figuring out payroll taxes—freeing him up to focus on other aspects of his business. "It's absolutely worth it," he says.

Advertising/Promotion

Experts generally recommend setting aside an advertising budget of 2 to 5 percent of revenues for small businesses. Thus if you expect first-year revenues of $30,000, you should set aside a minimum of $600 (2 percent) for advertising for your pet business, which works out to $50 a month. Doesn't sound like much, does it? Of course you can spend more, but frankly, you can print and mail a lot of fliers or postcards for that amount. If you feel more comfortable with a bigger budget, you could earmark 5 percent instead, which would be $1,500 annually, or $125 a month. That will get your business a lot of exposure in the market. Based on the projected monthly income for Molly's Snip and Clip, we're using a moderate figure of $100 per month.

Transportation/Maintenance

Depending on which type of pet-care business you're starting, travel costs may eat up a significant amount of your monthly budget. Pet sitters and dog walkers are likely to have the greatest out-of-pocket travel expenses because all their business is conducted at the pet owner's home. Likewise, dog trainers and pet groomers who are mobile will incur significant costs in this category. But even a homebased pet-food or pet-products business owner will have transportation costs incurred for trips to the post office to send out products, trips to the wholesaler/supplier to check out merchandise, visits to pet stores that are carrying your items, etc. Other costs for products like windshield wiper fluid, regular maintenance like tune-ups and oil changes, and bridge and tunnel tolls should all be added up and included on your I&E.

If you'll be relying on public transportation like taxis, buses, or the subway to get you to and from a job site, you need to figure in those costs, too. Mass-transit tickets and transfers are legitimate business expenses that should be tallied up. For the sake of simplicity, we're using a nice round figure of $100 on our I&E with the caveat that it may be too low for new business owners in major metropolitan areas.

Magazine Subscriptions/ Membership Dues

Did you see any publications in your business-specific chapter that you might be interested in subscribing to? If so, you need to include the cost on your I&E, or to make matters even simpler, plug in a cost on your business startup sheet instead and use the I&E line to estimate the cost of instructional and/or business books you might like to pick up throughout the year.

As you'll recall from the professional development chapter, there are a number of pet-care industry organizations that can be valuable sources of information and networking opportunities, so you should seriously consider joining any you think may be helpful to you as a small-business owner. In addition, don't forget about adding in dues for general business organizations like the chamber of commerce. We've allotted $20 a month in our sample to cover subscriptions and dues.

Loan Repayment

If you have to take out a loan to purchase a vehicle or the tools or equipment needed to outfit your business (say, grooming equipment, or shelves and storage units for your retail establishment), you need to include the dollar amount of that capital expenditure on your I&E. If you're planning to use your personal or family vehicle in the business, it's perfectly legitimate to include a dollar amount representing the percentage of use related to the business on the repayment line.

Other Miscellaneous Expenses

Unexpected expenses will always crop up in the course of doing business, so to cover them adequately, include a figure equal to 10 percent of your estimated monthly costs in your I&E. And, yes, the cost of dog biscuits and cat treats can go on this line!

Tally It Up

If you've been penciling in your own costs on the I&E worksheet on page 228, you now should have a fairly good idea of what your monthly expenditures might be. On our sample I&E for Molly's Snip and Clip, you'll notice that the company has a little more than 10 percent profit after expenses. This is considered a healthy amount for a startup business.

Receivables

Keeping close tabs on your receivables is just as important as monitoring your expenses. Your accountant will happily track your receivables for you, but to save money and keep a close eye on the state of your finances at the same time you may prefer to track those payments yourself using an accounting software package. The most popular business accounting software package is QuickBooks, which can handle everything from invoicing to check-writing and expense and sales tax tracking. In addition, it interfaces seamlessly with TurboTax, which makes filing your personal

Beware!

If you have clients who write checks that bounce or don't pay their bills, you may need to contact a collection agency. You can expect to pay 35 percent to 40 percent of the nonpayment amount to the agency, although this may vary depending on the volume of work you send their way.

or business taxes easier. It also meshes perfectly with Microsoft Word and Excel if you prefer to keep records in one of those programs. QuickBooks Pro retails for $199.95 and is sold at office supply and computer stores everywhere. Another accounting package to check out is Peachtree Accounting. It retails for $199.95 and is available from computer stores and directly from Peachtree (peachtree.com).

Financing

Unless you will be starting your business life in a retail storefront or other facility, or you need to buy a vehicle for the business, you can pretty much expect your startup costs to be fairly low. If you're a pet sitter, dog walker, or dog trainer who makes house calls, for instance, you may find all you need are some business cards, basic office equipment, dog yummies, a business phone line and a cell phone, and gas to get to and from your jobs. You may find it's possible (and preferable) to finance your startup using personal savings and your plastic (just keep an eye on those scary finance charges!). Since it takes time to establish a new business, the best-case scenario is to have enough working capital available in an accessible account that can be used to keep your business running for about six months. (The I&E statement you just worked on will tell you how much cash you'll probably need.) That way you should be able to keep the business running even when times are slow and give it the best chance at survival.

This is exactly how Amanda Miller, the Scottsdale, Arizona, wholesaler/manufacturer, started her business with her mother and partner, Cathy Jackson. Over a period of three years, they located their designers, investigated manufacturing, and prepared their startup, and they paid for everything piece by piece as the business came together. "My mother and I both had jobs, so we put money in as we went along," Miller says. "We didn't have a business plan and didn't get a loan. It wasn't the conventional way to get started, but it worked."

> Tip...
>
> **Smart Tip**
>
> The SBA has a number of free online business calculators to help you calculate startup costs, analyze cash flow, and perform a break-even analysis, among other things. You'll find the calculators at bplans.com/contentkit/index.cfm?s=tools&affiliate=sba.

Other sources of capital you may already have on hand include stocks and bonds, certificates of deposit, savings bonds, and income-tax refunds, or you could sell assets like real estate, vehicles, and jewelry to come up with some cash. Finally, you might be able to borrow from retirement funds like pension plans, IRAs, 401(k) plans, SEPs, and Keoghs. If you do put the bite on your retirement savings, you'll need to include the cost of the monthly repayment amount on your I&E statement.

Angel in Your Wallet

Need a quick infusion of cash for your business? Then look for an angel investor. Angels are private individuals who provide cash to young companies in exchange for equity in the business. They are similar to venture capitalists, but their pockets aren't as deep. Even so, a study by the University of New Hampshire's Center for Venture Research said that in a recent year, 42,000 angels invested $18.1 billion in early-stage companies, while venture capitalists invested a paltry $304 million. And because they do typically invest fewer dollars in the companies they support, angels are often good choices for small-business owners who just need a helping wing—uh, hand.

When looking for angels, seek out people who understand your business. For instance, if you're starting a pet-products business that will manufacture what you sell, look for an angel who has been there, done that for other products.

An angel can also act as an advisor and mentor. Not only will they bring cash to the table, but they can also provide heavenly assistance in the form of knowledge and networking opportunities to help your business grow.

If you don't know an angel personally, you can find them flying around on the internet. In fact, there are organized groups, such as the Angel Capital Association (angelcapitalassociation.org), that are just waiting to hear from you. Try Googling "angel investor groups" and see who lands on your desktop.

Of course, if your startup needs will be greater—if you must pony up for inventory, hydraulic grooming tables, or manufacturing costs for your pet-food line, for example—you may have to seek traditional financing from a bank or other lending institution. Depending on where you bank, you may be able to get a small unsecured personal loan on the basis of your signature alone—no collateral required. Credit unions are particularly amenable to offering this type of loan.

If you're planning to seek financing from a traditional lending institution, first make sure you have a well-conceived and well-written business plan, then set your sites on your local community bank. As you might guess, such banks generally are small-business-friendly because they're committed to supporting the community in which they do business. For a list of small-business-friendly banks, check out *Entrepreneur* magazine's "Best Banks" at entrepreneur.com/bestbanks, or visit the SBA's small-business-friendly lender page at sba.gov/financing/basics/lenders.html for leads.

Yet another source of funds you may wish to consider is the largesse of your friends and family. Just remember, though, that friendships and families are easily broken over money disputes, so if you do turn to loved ones, make sure you structure the loan in a professional, businesslike way. Always sign a promissory note that lists the amount borrowed, the interest rate, and the monthly repayment terms. Then live by those terms, even if the money is borrowed from the Bank of Dad.

Beware!

Although some banks will allow you to take a home equity loan to fund your startup, it's usually not advisable. If the unthinkable happens and you can't make a go of the business, you will lose not only your livelihood, but also your home. Think carefully before going this route.

Last, but not least, there is one more source of readily available funds that may surprise you. The Fed has numerous resources available to assist citizens who wish to make the leap to small-business ownership. (Not surprising, really, when you consider that 80 percent of America's businesses fall into the small-business category.) The most well-known of these sources is the SBA, which offers loan programs, free counseling, and training seminars on topics like business plan or marketing plan development. Interested? Check the SBA's website at sba.com, or call the SBA answer desk at (800) 8-ASK-SBA.

Sample Income and Expense Statement

Here is a sample income and expense statement for a hypothetical pet-grooming company that reflects typical operating costs for this industry. Molly's Snip and Clip is an S corporation with one full-time employee (the owner) and two part-time assistants.

Molly's Snip and Clip Projected Monthly Income		**$6,500**
Projected Monthly Expenses		
Mortgage/rent	$650	
Utilities (water only)	$100	
Phone (office and cell)	$90	
Office supplies	$50	
Postage	$100	
Licenses	$0	
Owner salary	$1,800	
Employee wages	$1,440	
Benefits/employment taxes (10 percent of wages)	$144	
Insurance	$45	
Online service	$20	
Web hosting	$20	
Merchant account	$30	
Legal services	$75	
Accounting services	$75	
Payroll service	$0	
Advertising/promotion	$100	
Transportation/maintenance	$100	
Subscriptions/dues	$20	
Loan repayment	$500	
Subtotal	$5,359	
Other miscellaneous expenses (10 percent of subtotal)	$500	
Total Expenses	**$5,859**	
Projected Net Income		**$641**

Income and Expense Worksheet

Projected Monthly Income		**$**
Projected Monthly Expenses		
Mortgage/rent	$	
Utilities (water only)	$	
Phone (office and cell)	$	
Office supplies	$	
Postage	$	
Licenses	$	
Owner salary	$	
Employee wages	$	
Benefits/employment taxes (10 percent of wages)	$	
Insurance	$	
Online service	$	
Web hosting	$	
Merchant account	$	
Legal services	$	
Accounting services	$	
Payroll service	$	
Advertising/promotion	$	
Transportation/maintenance	$	
Subscriptions/dues	$	
Loan repayment	$	
Subtotal	$	
Other miscellaneous expenses (10 percent of subtotal)	$	
Total Expenses	**$**	
Projected Net Income		**$**

19

Groomed for Success

Congratulations! By reading through to the end of this business guide and completing the various startup tasks mentioned along the way, you've taken an important step toward achieving your dream of business ownership. It's a journey that will take you on one of the most exhilarating, rewarding and satisfying head-out-the-window-wind-up-your-snout rides of your life. Just think—everything you build in this profession you love will be all yours. You won't have a grumpy boss peering over your shoulder anymore. Plus you can manage your time however you want—for instance, you can do paperwork at 3 A.M. if that's when you do your best thinking, or you can take off every other Monday simply because you always hated going back to the office after a weekend off.

But we don't have to tell you that along with self-employment comes a lot of responsibility. You can take off those Mondays, but if you want your income to stay consistent you'll have to put in more hours during the week or work on Saturday to make up for it. In fact, it probably won't come as a surprise that when you own a small business you're likely to work longer hours overall and more days without a break than you would if you had a nine-to-five job in corporate America. But you probably won't care—after all, you're in charge of the best business in the whole world, right?

Well, yes. But even though your enthusiasm level may be high and your commitment rock solid, know this: Not all small businesses succeed. The reasons for small-business failure are many, including the following reasons:

- Bad planning or no planning
- Inadequate capital and inattention to business and seasonal cycles
- Lack of focus and commitment
- Lack of experience
- Poor records and useless financial reports
- Revenue problems—failure to identify a narrow customer base; inadequate marketing to the target customers
- Too much capital tied up in equipment and inventory
- Too rigid or too lax an organization; failure to delegate or ignoring need for leadership and direction
- Location, location, location
- Failure to communicate with accountant, banker, or mentors

Staying Out of the Doghouse

So what can you do to make sure your business has the best chance at success? Plenty, as it happens. To begin with, make sure you have a cushion of at least six months of working capital available to get you through the lean months that invariably occur when you are building a client base. (A 12-month nest egg is even better and will give you more peace of mind.) These can be funds you've borrowed from your 401(k) plan or another personal resource, or they can be set aside out of your startup loan. In any event, make sure these funds are fully liquid—in other words, don't tie them up in long-term investments because you may need to put your hands on them immediately when you need to meet payroll or pay your home mortgage. A home equity line of credit

Staying Connected

While launching a business is exhilarating, it can also be lonely at the top of your own little empire. Here are some tips for avoiding loneliness and staying connected from home-office gurus Paul and Sarah Edwards, authors of numerous self-employment books, including *Home-Based Business for Dummies* (IDG Books):

- *Get involved with community, professional, and business organizations.* This gives you an outlet to share experiences that are common to all new business owners.
- *Stay in touch with people you've worked with professionally.* Pick up the phone and share news or discuss projects with former colleagues, or call other people whose work you admire and ask how you can become involved with their work. The Edwardses say they've met many valued new colleagues this way.
- *Log on.* Surf the internet to find pet-related or self-employment bulletin boards where you can share knowledge and discuss business issues.
- *Create your own networking group.* Invite people with similar business interests to join an informal group that convenes regularly—say, once a month over breakfast—to trade referrals, commiserate, and otherwise connect over business issues.
- *Form business relationships.* This is a natural for a pet-care business. If you groom pets, form an alliance with a pet photographer to swap leads. If you sell pet food online, seek out local pet-food store owners who might be interested in carrying your all-natural brands. The possibilities are endless.

(LOC) could also serve as your safety net, but as we mentioned in the last chapter, this should be a funding source of last resort.

When deciding how to use those startup funds, you absolutely should use some of them to hire the professionals we spoke about in Chapter 9. In particular, an accountant and an attorney can help you with those business management tasks that you: a) are not proficient in, and b) don't have the time to do anyway. Remember, lack of professional assistance is a common failure factor for new businesses.

Yet another wise thing you can do to improve your chances of success is to learn as much as you can about the business of business management. As we mentioned in the professional development chapter, you can take courses in entrepreneurship, accounting, finance, marketing, and other crucial business disciplines at your local community college, or even through the adult education department of your local school district. You don't need a degree—often just one class in each of these areas is enough to give you a solid working knowledge of the discipline. (On the other hand, one class may be all you need to realize that you'd better hire a professional—pronto.)

> **Bright Idea**
>
> Using your 401(k) money to provide a financial stake for your business startup may be even smarter than you realize. Since the money was salted away on a tax-deferred basis, you actually have more money to work with than if the money had gone through Uncle Sam's hands and into your regular savings.

Participating in the activities of a professional organization can also be a good way to learn more about the business paradigm, since members gather to exchange war stories, trade tips, and commiserate about business challenges. And it doesn't even have to be a pet-care-related organization—any place where professionals gather can be a great source of business intelligence, as well as a great place to "petwork" and spread the word about your business. As mentioned previously, professional organization members often barter services, which can be a great way for you to get business services you need for just the cost of a shampoo and clip or a month's supply of bird seed.

Finally, think positively. That may sound trite, but studies have shown that people who are positive, optimistic and confident are more successful in business and even live longer. And just think: You're going into a pet-care business because you love animals, you're thrilled at the prospect of being an independent operator, and/or because you see a lot of opportunity to provide a needed service—one that can pay you a good salary. What more can you ask?

In Hind Sight

Not that you won't encounter bumps along the way to business success. Every pet-care-business owner interviewed for this book admitted there were things he or she could have done better in the early days of the business. For example, pet-food business owner John Zambelli of Elmwood Park, New Jersey, says he would have focused more on backend food products, or those that are ordered over and over by customers. Instead, he stocked nonedible products like flea collars and shampoo, and while they did (and still do) well, they diluted his focus.

Amanda Miller, the Scottsdale, Arizona, pet-products business co-owner, would have liked to have had more professional help when she launched her online business. "It's better not to try to do everything yourself because you're not good in every area," she says. "When we started, we couldn't afford to hand those things over, but it would have been better to contract out what we didn't do well."

Tip...

Smart Tip

Entrepreneurs who think they can do everything themselves often fail in business. When you get to the point that you are turning away work because you personally cannot handle one more thing, give serious thought to hiring someone—or a bunch of someones—to assist you. Bringing employees on board can complicate your life, but they also can open the door to opportunities you otherwise might have missed.

Joyce Reavey, the Exton, Pennsylvania, pet-products business owner, says she wishes she had spoken to more small-business owners when she started out, since they would have been good role models. "You need that perspective because you have to be careful not to think like and try to do as much as a large business," she says. "It's not possible when you're starting out, especially from a financial standpoint."

Oak Park, Illinois, pet sitter and dog walker David Lipschultz believes he should have set more limits when it came to customer care in the early days of his business. "I put myself in difficult situations and ran myself completely ragged trying to bend over backward for clients," he says. "You really need to have stronger rules and control over what you'll do right from the beginning, because clients ask for a million things and will call you at the last minute, like at 7 P.M. on a Saturday night. Everyone likes to be helpful and flexible, but you need to set limits or the demands will never end."

Jerry Wentz, the Raleigh, North Carolina, pet sitter/dog walker, says he would have researched employee status options more carefully. "In the beginning I had difficulty with the whole independent contractor vs. employee situation," he says. "I switched back and forth, then eventually decided to go with regular employees. But it would have saved a lot of time if I had done it just once."

Columbia, South Carolina, pet-products business owner Susan Benesh would have used her advertising dollars more wisely. "I wouldn't have taken out so many space ads in trade publications," she says. "It was very expensive, and I received just a little bit of business—maybe four or five orders. My website is a much better source of new business."

Barbara Menutes, the Houston groomer, would have been more persistent when trying to drum up new business. "I should have done more networking, like visiting more vets to ask them to refer to me," she says. "I also should have contacted more of the dog-only groomers and asked them to send the cats my way. Although there's a lot of joy and money doing cats, they're the stepchildren of grooming because they take longer to groom and are more difficult to handle. A lot of groomers don't do them, and I should have asked for more of that business."

Diane Burchard in Santa Fe, New Mexico, would have tried to round up more cash so she could launch her wholesale/retail business the way she really wanted to. "Not having a lot of cash didn't hinder me—I scraped along," she says. "But I had to do a lot of tasks like accounting that took me away from the everyday business of running the shop."

Tails from the Trenches

Although each of the entrepreneurs interviewed for this book admits there was something he or she could have done better in the early days of the business, not one of them has a single regret about his or her choice of career. One reason is simply because they enjoy knowing that what they do truly benefits both pets and people. But another reason is that this industry is just so darned interesting. These entrepreneurs will tell you that you never know what you'll encounter from one day to the next—and that makes a career in pet care both stimulating and rewarding.

Take David Lipschultz, for instance. He discovered early on that sometimes satisfying the customer can be quite challenging. "I once had a client who wanted his turtle taken for a walk," he says. "It's a ridiculous idea—turtles don't do anything. So you just take them out to where they're supposed to be and they just sit there. Eventually you realize how completely ridiculous the whole thing is and put them back."

People who deal with animals must always be prepared for the unexpected. One pet-business owner says an employee once was attacked by a cat that lunged three feet through the air and inflicted three rapid bites that left five puncture wounds. The employee was treated and was fine, but the cat was taken away by animal control and isolated for ten days as required by state law. The incident could have been prevented if the pet owner had simply admitted that the cat had previously bitten someone, and the business owner could have decided whether it was safe to allow the employee to be near the animal.

Sometimes the unexpected is a stroke of good luck. Joyce Reavey was pleasantly surprised in the early days of her business when she suddenly started getting a lot of orders for one particular pink dog bed she designed that's shaped like a daisy. Although she does a lot of advertising, the spike in sales was still mystifying, so she finally asked one boutique owner why she was buying so many of that particular bed. "Didn't you hear?" the boutique owner said. "Jessica Simpson has one for her dog on the 'Newlyweds: Nick & Jessica' show, and ever since reruns of the show started airing everyone wants one."

No matter how much you love your business, not everyone will get it. In fact, Jerry Wentz admits there is something of a stigma attached to his line of work that can lead to uncomfortable situations. "People don't understand what we do," he says. "You can be a successful pet sitter for three years, and people will still ask you if you have a job yet. In fact, I once went on a trip with my wife, and when her professional colleagues found out what I do, they brushed me off completely. I know pet sitters who earn six-figure incomes, and this is the type of treatment many of them get!"

On the other hand, Amanda Miller has had the opposite reaction from people. "Once when I went to Tahoe, the girl sitting on the plane next to me knew my company," she

Beware!

Too many business owners in financial trouble suffer in silence and don't look for help until it's too late to save the company. If you need help, contact the SBA or the volunteer executive corps at SCORE, both of which dispense sage advice at no charge.

says. "When we get recognized like that we really feel like we've accomplished something and that we're becoming successful."

As might be expected, pet-care professionals who deal directly with animals often become attached to their small charges. Seattle pet sitter/dog walker Dan MacDonald became particularly fond of a 12-year-old peek-a-poo he took for walks twice a day for 13 months. Benjy's owner was an 83-year-old nursing home resident who was unable to care properly for the dog, so MacDonald provided a lot of care, including taking him to the vet and worrying when he didn't eat. "When Benjy stopped eating, I asked the vet what to do and was told to put him on special dog food," MacDonald says. "So I tried that, and when that didn't work, the vet suggested human food. So I shopped for food for him and me, and he ate salmon, spaghetti, whatever I ate."

Then one day the dog's owner called and said it was to be Benjy's last day and asked him to take him for one final walk. "I was so attached to him that I cried as I was walking him for the last time," MacDonald says. "I always tried to make him as happy as possible so that last time was hard."

Groomers also will tell you that a lot of the satisfaction they get from their job comes from knowing how much they're helping their furry charges. Houston groomer Barbara Menutes once did what she calls a "mercy grooming" for ten Persians that belonged to a breeder who had been ill. It was obvious that some of the younger cats had never been groomed because their coats were so matted they looked more like pelts. "[The cats] knew we were helping them because they'd purr even when we were cleaning the [feces] matted up in the fur on their butts," she says. "We didn't even charge for the grooming—we were just happy to help them."

Of course, pets can't speak for themselves, but even when you're working with humans important details can be lost in translation, as Susan Benesh discovered. She once designed an orange Halloween dog sweater that was festooned with black bats. It took two months to get the sweater perfect and involved a lot of conversations and the shipping of samples back and forth between South Carolina and her manufacturer in China. So when she received the order by air express, she was shocked to discover the sweaters were red with black bats, not orange.

Benesh says, "When I called, I said, 'Mr. Wang, we received red sweaters. I thought we decided on orange.' And he said, 'Yes, we think you are a good friend and red is lucky, so we thought it is lucky for dogs, too.' " At the time, I thought, 'I'll be lucky if I sell these!' but you just can't get mad at people like that. Of course, I still do have those red sweaters in my warehouse!"

It's easy to see that there are many challenges and rewards in running a pet-care business—both financial and personal. Here's to hoping all your business efforts litter-ally lead you down the right path, and may all your pet dreams come true!

Appendix
Pet-Business Resources

They say you can never be rich enough or young enough. While these could be argued, we believe you can never have enough resources. Therefore, we're giving you a wealth of sources to check into, check out, and harness for your own personal information blitz.

These sources are tidbits—ideas to get you started on your research. They are by no means the only sources out there, and they should not be taken as the ultimate answer. We have done our research, but businesses do tend to move, change, fold, and expand. As we have repeatedly stressed, do your homework. Get out there and start investigating!

Background Checks

First Advantage Corp.
(800) 321-4473, ext. 8
fadv.com/EmploymentScreening/index.html

Business Apparel

Amsterdam Printing
amsterdamprinting.com

LogoDogz
(888) 827-8866
logodogz.com

PetEdge
(800) 738-3343
petedge.com

Stylist Wear
(800) 288-9327
stylistwear.com

Superior Logowear
(800) 208-1662
superiorlogowear.com

Business Software

Adobe Creative Suite 2
Adobe Systems
(800) 833-6687
adobe.com

Clickart 950,000
Broderbund
(800) 395-0277
broderbund.com

Dreamweaver 8
Macromedia
(800) 457-1774
macromedia.com/software/dreamweaver

Microsoft Office 2003
office.microsoft.com/en-us/default.aspx

Mind Your Own Business
MYOB US
(800) 322-MYOB
myob.com

Sage Software
(877) 495-9904
peachtree.com

QuickBooks Pro
Intuit Inc.
(888) 859-4093
quickbooks.com

Certification

Animal Behavior College
(800) 795-3294
animalbehaviorcollege.com
e-mail: info@animalbehaviorcollege.com

Association of Companion Animal Behavior Counselors
animalbehaviorcounselors.org

Certification Council for Pet Dog Trainers
(212) 356-0682
ccpdt.org

National Dog Groomers Association of America Inc.
(724) 962-2711
nationaldoggroomers.com
e-mail: ndga@nationaldoggroomers.com

Check Verification Services

Electronic Clearing House Inc.
(800) 262-3246, ext. 1
echo-inc.com

TeleCheck Services Inc.
(800) TELECHECK
telecheck.com
e-mail: customerservice@telecheck.com

Conferences

Intergroom Inc.
(781) 326-3376
intergroom.com
e-mail: intergroom@msn.com

Demographic Information

American Demographics
Crain Communications Inc.
adage.com

U.S. Census Bureau
census.gov

Dog-Training Education

Animal Behavior College
(800) 795-3294
animalbehaviorcollege.com
e-mail: info@animalbehaviorcollege.com

Penn Foster Career School
(800) 275-4410
pennfoster.edu
e-mail: info@pennfoster.com

Dog-Training Franchises

Bark Busters Home Dog Training Franchise
franchiseworks.com

Employees

U.S. Department of Labor
(866) 4-USA-DOL
dol.gov

E-zines

Pet Industry Weekly
weeklypets.blogspot.com

Gift Cards

Artemis Solutions Group
(866) 53-SMART
smartcardsupply.com

Zebra Card Printer Solutions
(800) 452-4056
zebracard.com

Government Resources

Minority Business Development Agency
(888) 324-1551
mbda.gov
e-mail: help@mbda.gov

Occupational Outlook Handbook
bls.gov/oco

SBA
(800) U-ASK-SBA
sba.gov

SCORE
(800) 634-0245
score.org

Graphic Design Services

Andy Markison Graphic Design
andymarkison.com
e-mail: andy@andymarkison.com

Groomer Insurance

Gibson Governor Agency Inc.
(800) 843-5522
gibsongovernor.com
e-mail: info@gibsongovernor.com

Grooming Equipment/Products

Dog.com
dog.com

Double K Industries
(800) 821-9449
doublekindustries.com

Groomer's Choice Pet Products
(888) 364-6242
groomerschoice.com

Grooming Supplies

American Pet Pro
(800) 543-9480
americanpetpro.com

Groomer's Choice Pet Products
(888) 364-6242
groomerschoice.com

J-B Wholesale Pet Supplies Inc.
(800) 872-6027
jbpet.com
e-mail: customerservice@jbpet.com

PetEdge
(800) 738-3343
petedge.com
e-mail: order@PetEdge.com

Stazko Associates Inc.
(941) 322-0226
stazko.com
e-mail: john@stazko.com

Incorporation Kits

Inc. Plan (USA)
(800) 462-4633
incplan.net

Quality Books
(786) 552-5042
qualitybooks.com
e-mail: admin@contact-qualitybooks.com

Magnetic Signs

Igoodz Inc.—Mark Gering Magnetics
(800) 966-0915
magneticsigns.com
e-mail: sales@MagneticSigns.com

Lettering Specialist Inc.
(847) 674-3414
amagneticsign.com
e-mail: Sales@aSignCompany.com

The Graphic Guy
(760) 885-8603
thegraphicguy.com

Media Directories

Bacon's Information
(866) 639-5087
bacons.com

Mondo Times
mondotimes.com

US Newspaper List
usnpl.com

Merchant Account Services

Merchant Accounts Express
(888) 845-9457
merchantexpress.com

Monster Merchant Account Inc.
(800) 838-9699
monstermerchantaccount.com
e-mail: Julie@monstercommerce.com

Total Merchant Services
(888) 871-4558
merchant-account-4U.com

Mobile Grooming Franchises

Aussie Pet Mobile
(949) 234-0680
aussiepetmobile.com

Hydro-Groom Mobile Pet Wash
(336) 361-0706
mobilepetwash.com

Wag'n Tails
(800) 513-0304
wagntails.com

Zoomin Groomin
(866) 504-7666
zoomingroomin.com

Mobile Grooming Vans

Custom Vehicles Inc.
(866) 848-1775
customvehicles.com

Hanvey Specialty Engineering
(866) 281-9593
groomingvans.com

Odyssey Mobile Grooming Conversions
(800) 535-9441
odysseyauto.com

Ultimate Groomobiles Inc.
(888) 826-5845
ultimategroomobiles.com

Wag'n Tails
(800) 513-0304
wagntails.com

Office Equipment (Phones and Accessories)

Hello Direct
(800) HELLO34
HelloDirect.com
e-mail: xpressit@hellodirect.com

TeleZapper
Privacy Technologies Inc.
(800) 373-6290
telezapper.com

Office Supplies (Forms and Stationery)

Amsterdam Printing
(800) 833-6231
amsterdamprinting.com
e-mail: customerservice@amsterdam printing.com

Office Depot
(800) GO-DEPOT
officedepot.com

OfficeMax
(800) 283-7674
officemax.com

PaperDirect
(800) A-PAPERS
paperdirect.com
e-mail: customerservice@paperdirect.com

RapidForms
(800) 257-8354
rapidforms.com
e-mail: service@rapidforms.com

Staples
(800) 3-STAPLE
staples.com

Pet-Business Software

123Pet
CMJ Designs
(888) 803-4747
123petsoftware.com
e-mail: sales@cmjdesigns.com

Bluewave Professional Pet Sitter
Bluewave
professionalpetsitter.com

EdogTrainer.com
edogtrainer.com
e-mail: info@edogtrainer.com

Groom Manager
Dog Days Software
groommanager.com
e-mail: sales@dogdayssoftware.com

Groomer's Write Hand
groomerswritehand.com
e-mail: Dennis@groomerswritehand.com

KenlPro
Metro Computing Solutions LLC
(877) KENLPRO
kenlpro.com

Kennel Connection
Blue Crystal Software
(888) 486-4343
bluecrystalsoftware.com
e-mail: sales@bluecrystalsoftware.com

KennelSuite 7
Plane Software Inc.
(800) 662-1835
planesoftware.com
e-mail: support@planesoftware.com

Petrax
Ten Dog Development Inc.
petraxsoftware.com
e-mail: customerservice@
tendogdevelopment.com

PetSOFT
Get Physical! Software LLC
(800) 622-0025
getphysicalsoftware.com
e-mail: info@getphysicalsoftware.com

Pet-Sitter Insurance

Business Insurers of the Carolinas
(800) 962-4611, ext. 1
petsitterinsurance.com
e-mail: Information@PetSitter
Insurance.com

Gibson Governor Agency Inc.
(800) 843-5522
gibsongovernor.com
e-mail: info@gibsongovernor.com

Pet-Trainer Insurance

Gibson Governor Agency Inc.
(800) 843-5522
gibsongovernor.com
e-mail: info@gibsongovernor.com

Point-of-Sale Equipment and Software

Capital Merchant Solutions Inc.
(877) 495-2419
chargem.com
e-mail: info@capital-merchant.com

Credit Card Processing Services
(215) 489-7878
mcvisa.com
e-mail: Kevin@mcvisa.com

InfoMerchant
(971) 223-5632
infomerchant.net

Merchant Accounts Express
(888) 845-9457
merchantexpress.com

MerchantSeek
merchantseek.com

Monster Merchant Account Inc.
(800) 838-9699
monstermerchantaccount.com
e-mail: Julie@monstercommerce.com

Postage Calculators

Desktop Dozen Postage Calculator
Spud City Software
spudcity.com
e-mail: desktopdozen@spudcity.com

U.S. Postal Service
ircalc.usps.gov

Printing Resources

ColorPrintingCentral
(800) 309-3291
colorprintingcentral.com

PrintingForLess.com
(800) 930-6040
printingforless.com
e-mail: info@printingforless.com

Printing Industry Exchange LLC
(703) 631-4533
printindustry.com
e-mail: info@printindustry.com

Print Quote USA
(561) 451-2654
printquoteusa.com

Promotion Xpress
(888) 310-7769
proxprint.com
e-mail: support@proxprint.com

PSPrint
(800) 511-2009
psprint.com

Professional Organizations

ABKA
(For all pet-care service businesses)
(877) 570-7788
abka.com
e-mail: info@abka.com

American Humane Association
(303) 792-9900
americanhumane.org

American Kennel Club
(212) 696-8200
akc.org

American Pet Products Association
(203) 532-0000
appa.org

Association of Companion Animal Behavior Counselors
animalbehaviorcounselors.org

Association of Pet Dog Trainers
(800) PET-DOGS
apdt.com
e-mail: information@apdt.com

Association of Professional Animal Waste Specialists
(800) 787-7667
apaws.org

The Canadian Association of Professional Pet Dog Trainers
cappdt.ca
e-mail: info@cappdt.ca

The Cat Fanciers' Association Inc.
(732) 528-9797
cfa.org
e-mail: cfa@cfa.org

Dog Trainers' Connection
(212) 787-8522
dogtrainersconnection.com
e-mail: info@dogtrainersconnection.com

The Humane Society of the United States
(202) 452-1100
hsus.org

The International Society of Canine Cosmetologists
petstylist.com
e-mail: iscc@petstylist.com

National Association of Dog Obedience Instructors
nadoi.org
e-mail: corrsec@nadoi.org

The National Association of Professional Pet Sitters
(856) 439-0324
petsitters.org
e-mail: napps@ahint.com

National Dog Groomers Association of America
(724) 962-2711
nationaldoggroomers.com
e-mail: ndga@nationaldoggroomers.com

Pet Food Association of Canada
(416) 447-9970
pfac.com

Pet Industry Distributors Association
(443) 640-1060
pida.org
e-mail: pida@ksgroup.org

Pet Sitters Associates LLC
(800) 872-2941, access code 25
petsitllc.com
e-mail: petsitllc@aol.com

Pet Sitters International
(336) 983-9222
petsit.com
e-mail: info@petsit.com

Pigs As Pets Association Inc.
(239) 694-8128
pigsaspets.org
e-mail: PAPA@pigsaspets.org

The Professional Dog Walkers Association International
prodogwalker.com

World Wide Pet Industry Association Inc.
(800) 999-7295
wwpia.com
e-mail: info@wwpia.com

Promotional Items

ePromos Inc.
(800) 564-6216
epromos.com
e-mail: customerservice@epromos.com

Publications

Animal Fair
Animal Fair Media Inc.
(212) 629-0392, ext. 202
animalfair.com
e-mail: subs@animalfair.com

Animal Wellness Magazine
Redstone Media Group Inc.
(866) 764-1212
animalwellnessmagazine.com

Aquarium Fish Magazine
BowTie Inc.
(800) 833-7000
aquariumfish.com

Bird Talk Magazine
BowTie Inc.
(800) 695-6088
birdtalkmagazine.com

Cat Fancy
BowTie Inc.
(800) 468-1618
catfancy.com

Dog Fancy
BowTie Inc.

(800) 896-4939
dogfancy.com

Ferrets Magazine
BowTie Inc.
(800) 937-9467
ferretsmagazine.com

Groomer to Groomer/ Mobile Groomer
Barkleigh Productions Inc.
(717) 691-3388
barkleigh.com
e-mail: info@barkleigh.com

Horse Illustrated
BowTie Inc.
(800) 538-3000
horseillustrated.com

Off-Lead & Natural Pet
Barkleigh Productions Inc.
(717) 691-3388
barkleigh.com
e-mail: info@barkleigh.com

Pet Age
H.H. Backer Associates Inc.
(312) 663-4040
petage.com
e-mail: petage@hhbacker.com

Pet Business
Macfadden Communications Group
(212) 979-4800
petbusiness.com
e-mail: request@petbusiness.com

Pet Product News
BowTie Inc.
(818) 286-3107
petproductnews.com
e-mail: ppncs@magserv.com

Reptiles Magazine
BowTie Inc.
(800) 876-9112
reptilesmagazine.com

The Whole Cat Journal
DNA Publications
(540) 763-2925
wholecatjournal.com

Whole Dog Journal
Belvoir Publications Inc.
(800) 829-9165
whole-dog-journal.com

Shipping Services

DHL Express
(800) CALL-DHL
dhl-usa.com

FedEx
(800) GO FEDEX
fedex.com

U.S. Postal Service
(800) ASK-USPS
usps.gov

UPS
(800) PICK-UPS
ups.com

Small-Business Help Organizations

SBA
(800) U-ASK-SBA
sba.gov

SBA Answer Desk
(800) U-ASK-SBA
sba.gov/SBDC
e-mail: answerdesk@sba.gov

SCORE
(800) 634-0245
score.org

Successful Pet-Business Owners

Teoti Anderson
Pawsitive Results LLC
(803) 356-9170
getpawsitiveresults.com
e-mail: PawsitiveRslts@aol.com

Susan Benesh
VIPoochy
(877) 4POOCHY
vipoochy.com
e-mail: info@vipoochy.com

Jennifer Boniface
Aunt Jeni's Home Made
(301) 702-0123
auntjeni.com
e-mail: jeni@auntjeni.com

Diane Burchard
Teca Tu
(888) TECA TU2
tecatu.com
e-mail: diburchard@cableone.net

Jamie Damato
AnimalSense—Canine Training and Behavior Inc.
(773) 275-3647
animalsense.com
e-mail: info@animalsense.com

Leonard Green
The Blue Buffalo Co.
(800) 919-2833
bluebuff.com
e-mail: lgreen@greenco.com

David Lipschultz
Out-U-Go
(708) 383-7905
outugo.com
e-mail: info@outugo.com

Dan MacDonald
Fantastic Dog and Cat Sitting Service
(206) 547-5947
fantasticdogandcatsitting.com
e-mail: fantasticdog@worldnet.att.net

Barbara Menutes
Barbara's Cat Grooming
(713) 787-0540
e-mail: bmenutes@sbcglobal.net

Amanda Miller
Poochie of Beverly Hills
(888) 867-0400
poochieofbeverlyhills.com
e-mail: Amanda@poochieofbeverlyhills

Joyce Reavey
Pawsitively Posh
(610) 518-1296
pawsitivelyposh.com
e-mail: info@pawsitivelyposh.com

Jerry Wentz
Homesitters of Raleigh
(919) 870-1550
homesittersofraleigh.com
e-mail: jwentz@homesittersofraleigh.com

John Zambelli
NaturesPet.com
(201) 796-0627
naturespet.com
e-mail: topdog@naturespet.com

Taxes

Electronic Federal Tax Payment System
Department of the Treasury
(800) 555-8778
eftps.gov

IRS
(800) 829-4933
irs.gov

TurboTax Business
Intuit
(800) 4-INTUIT
turbotax.com

Telecom Companies

AT&T Small and Medium Business
(800) 222-0400
att.com/business

Carolinanet
(888) 400-5557
https://carolinanet.nuvio.com/index02.php

Sage Telecom
(888) 972-7243
sagetelecom.net

Vonage
(800) 986-4VON
vonage.com

Trade Shows

America's Family Pet Expo
World Wide Pet Industry Association Inc.
(800) 999-7295
wwpia.com
e-mail: info@wwpia.com

Global Pet Expo
Pet Industry Distributors Association
(443) 640-1060
pida.org
e-mail: pida@ksgroup.org

Groom & Kennel Expo
Barkleigh Productions Inc.
(717) 691-3388
barkleigh.com
e-mail: info@barkleigh.com

Groom Expo
Barkleigh Productions Inc.
(717) 691-3388
barkleigh.com
e-mail: info@barkleigh.com

Christmas Show/Spring Show
H.H. Backer Associates Inc.
(312) 663-4040
hhbacker.com
e-mail: hhbacker@hhbacker.com

Intergroom
Intergroom Inc.
(781) 326-3376
intergroom.com
e-mail: intergroom@msn.com

SuperZoo
World Wide Pet Industry Association
(800) 999-7295
wwpia.com
e-mail: info@wwpia.com

Trademark Filings

U.S. Patent and Trademark Office
(800) 786-9199
uspto.gov
e-mail: TrademarkAssistanceCenter@uspto.gov

Web Hosting/Domain Names

Apollo Hosting
(877) 525-HOST
apollohosting.com

Domain.com
domain.com

EarthLink
(800) 327-8454
earthlink.net

iPowerWeb
(888) 511-HOST
ipowerweb.com
e-mail: sales@ipowerweb.com

NetPass
(407) 843-7277
netpass.com
e-mail: support@netpass.com

SBC Webhosting.com
(888) WEBHOST
webhosting.com

Yahoo!
smallbusiness.yahoo.com

Glossary

Backgrounder: a type of news release that gives background information about a business, the business owner, or the company's basic products and services.

Bricks-and-mortar: a physical location in a building, storefront, or strip mall, as opposed to an internet store, which has no physical location.

Broadband: type of high-speed internet connection via cable modem.

Cage dryer: type of dryer that clips to the front of a cage.

Carding: grooming term for untangling and removing excess undercoat.

Clicker training: a type of dog training that uses a tool called a clicker to reinforce positive behavior.

COBRA: a health insurance plan that allows an ex-employee to be covered under his former employer's health plan for a short period of time.

Competition obedience: dog-training term referring to handling techniques for obedience trials at competitions.

Corporation: a form of business ownership that protects the owner's personal assets from lawsuits.

DBA: doing business as; refers to a fictitious name chosen as a business name.

Demographics: characteristics that influence your potential customers' buying habits, which include age, income, education, location, and other factors.

Domain name: the internet address locator of a website (for example, entrepreneur.com); *see URL.*

Drop-shipping: process in which a mail order or online merchant accepts orders for merchandise, then pays a wholesaler or other source to ship the product to the customer.

DSL line: digital subscriber line, a type of high-speed internet access.

Ethology: the study of animal behavior.

Fear biting: a dog's response to fearful situations that cause it to bite to protect itself.

Flash: computer animation technology; also known as shockwave flash.

Fulfillment: the process of shipping orders to customers.

Full-charge pet groomer: a stylist who clips and scissors pets from start to finish.

Full-owner participation training: dog-training term referring to teaching a pet owner how to handle his or her animal.

Hand-stripping: grooming term for removing loose hair from a dog's coat.

High-velocity force dyer: type of salon dryer used to sweep excess moisture from a pet's coat.

Key words: search terms found on browsers that are purchased by advertisers to take those who click on them directly to a sponsored website.

Kong: a hard, heavy-duty rubber toy shaped like a three-tier snowman with a small hole on the top and a larger one at the bottom that can be filled with kibble or other treats.

Lead: the opening line of an article or news release.

LLC: limited liability company, a type of legal business entity.

Lion cut: grooming term for a type of cut in which the hindquarters, muzzle, and base of the tail are sheared, while the rest of the fur is left long.

Martingale collar: dog collar with an extra loop of nylon on the main collar and an attached ring to which the leash is hooked.

News release: a short promotional article that is sent to the media to generate positive buzz; also known as a press release.

Partnership: a business owned by two or more people.

Pitch letter: a brief letter (usually one page) that accompanies a manuscript sent to a newspaper or magazine editor that describes what the article is about.

Prong collar: dog collar with a series of linking prongs that replicates the way a mother dog reprimands her pups; used to teach dogs to walk on a loose leash and to give motivational reinforcement.

Resolution: the sharpness and clarity of a computer printer or monitor, expressed as dpi (dots per inch).

Schutzhund: a sport that develops and trains German Shepherds to become useful and happy companions (from the German word for "protection dog").

Sole proprietorship: a business with a single owner.

Tough strip: grooming term for shaving a pet with an extremely matted coat.

Unsecured personal loan: a loan that doesn't require collateral.

URL: uniform resource locator, or the internet address locator of a website.

Wafer tab: small round sticker used to keep the open edges of a newsletter or other mailing piece closed for mailing.

Index